T0330202

Creating Competitiveness

Creating Competitiveness

Entrepreneurship and Innovation Policies for Growth

Edited by

David B. Audretsch

Distinguished Professor and Ameritech Chair of Economic Development, Indiana University, Bloomington, USA and Honorary Professor of Entrepreneurship and Industrial Economics, WHU – Otto Beisheim School of Management, Vallendar, Germany

Mary Lindenstein Walshok

Associate Vice Chancellor, Public Programs, Dean, University Extension and Adjunct Professor of Sociology, University of California, San Diego, USA

Edward Elgar
Cheltenham, UK • Northampton, MA, USA

Published by
Edward Elgar Publishing Limited
The Lypiatts
15 Lansdown Road
Cheltenham
Glos GL50 2JA
UK

Edward Elgar Publishing, Inc.
William Pratt House
9 Dewey Court
Northampton
Massachusetts 01060
USA

A catalogue record for this book
is available from the British Library

Library of Congress Control Number: 2012943750

MIX
Paper from
responsible sources
FSC
www.fsc.org
FSC® C018575

ISBN 978 1 78195 404 1

Typeset by Servis Filmsetting Ltd, Stockport, Cheshire
Printed and bound by MPG Books Group, UK

Contents

v

Contributors

Thomas Andersson is Professor of Economics and Senior Advisor on Science, Technology and Innovation Policy at the Research Council, Sultanate of Oman. Prior to his current position, Thomas Andersson was President of Jonkoping University in Sweden. Among other assignments, he is President of the Board for the International Organization for Knowledge Economy and Enterprise Development (IKED) and Chairman of the International Entrepreneurship Academy (intentac). He previously served as Deputy Director of Science, Technology and Industry at the OECD and was Assistant Under-Secretary and Head of the Structural Policies Secretariat of the Ministry of Industry and Commerce in Sweden.

Robert D. Atkinson is Founder and President of the Information Technology and Innovation Foundation, Washington, DC, USA. Before coming to ITIF, Dr Atkinson was Vice President of the Progressive Policy Institute and Director of PPI's Technology and New Economy Project, where he wrote numerous research reports on technology and innovation policy, including on issues such as broadband telecommunications, e-commerce and e-government, and privacy. Previously he served as the first Executive Director of the Rhode Island Economic Policy Council, where he drafted a comprehensive economic strategic development plan for the state, and worked successfully through the legislative and administrative branches to implement it. He is also author of the book *Innovation Economics: The Race for Global Advantage* (Yale University Press, 2012).

David B. Audretsch is Distinguished Professor and Ameritech Chair of Economic Development, Director, Institute for Development Strategies and Director, SPEA Overseas Education Program, School of Public and Environmental Affairs, Indiana University, Bloomington, Indiana, USA. Professor Audretsch is also an Honorary Professor of Entrepreneurship and Industrial Economics at the WHU – Otto Beisheim School of Management in Vallendar, Germany. In addition, he serves as a Visiting Professor at the King Saud University in Saudi Arabia and as a Research Professor at Durham University, an External Director of Research at the Kiel Institute for the World Economics, and Honorary Professor at the Friedrich Schiller University of Jena in Germany, and is a Research

Fellow of the Centre for Economic Policy Research in London. Professor Audretsch's research has focused on the links between entrepreneurship, government policy, innovation, economic development and global competitiveness. His research has been published in over one hundred scholarly articles in the leading academic journals. He is co-founder and co-editor of *Small Business Economics: An Entrepreneurship Journal*.

Shiri M. Breznitz is Assistant Professor in the School of Public Policy at Georgia Institute of Technology, Atlanta, Georgia, USA. Professor Breznitz is an economic geographer by training and has two main research streams. The first focuses on the role of the university as a regional and national actor. The second stream involves industrial clusters; in particular, biotechnology industrial clusters and their local economic impacts. Dr Breznitz sat on national committees in both Israel (2008) and France (2005) to review industrial and economic development policy. She is affiliated with the MIT's Industrial Performance Center, and a founding member of the Industry Studies Association.

Dennis P. Leyden is Associate Professor of Economics in the Bryan School of Business and Economics at the University of North Carolina at Greensboro, North Carolina, USA. He received his BA with High Honors in Economics from the University of Virginia and his MS and PhD from Carnegie Mellon University. His current research focuses on the role and behavior of universities in furthering entrepreneurial activity, innovation, and economic development. In addition to prior work on R&D policy, he has a background in bureaucracy, legislative and court behavior, and the public funding of education. His books include *Adequacy, Accountability, and the Future of Public Education Funding* (2005) and *Government's Role in Innovation* (1992, with Albert N. Link). Recent conferences at which he has presented include 'Universities, Innovation, and Territory' (University of Barcelona), 'Science and Technology Research in a Knowledge-based Economy' (University of Turin), and 'Academic Policy and the Knowledge Theory of Entrepreneurship' (University of Augsburg). In the classroom, he is currently involved in a project to revise the structure and content of principles of economics courses to include explicit instruction in the mechanics of critical thinking using his text *Critical Thinking in Economics* (second edition, 2012) and to emphasize the role of knowledge creation in microeconomic and macroeconomic behavior.

Albert N. Link is Professor of Economics at the University of North Carolina, Greensboro, North Carolina, USA. Professor Link is an internationally recognized scholar in the field of economics of research and development. A long-time member of the UNC Greensboro faculty, he previously directed the university's MBA program and headed the Economics department. He also directed both the Industrial Technology and Computer Technology Education programs at UNC Greensboro. He has taught at Auburn University and was Visiting Scholar at the Maxwell School, Syracuse University, New York, USA.

Gerald A. McDermott is Associate Professor in the Sonoco International Business Department in the Moore School of Business at the University of South Carolina, USA and Senior Research Fellow at the IAE Business School of the Universidad Austral in Buenos Aires, Argentina. Professor McDermott specializes in international business and political economy. His first research stream focused on the impact of industrial networks on the creation of economic governance institutions in post-communist countries. His current research in South America uses both comparative and statistical survey methods to examine the socio-political conditions under which societies build new innovative capacities to achieve sustained upgrading in their industries. He has also recently launched a project about the impact of international integration regimes on local institutional development via a comparison of the EU accession, NAFTA, and Mercosur.

Neela Ram received her BS degree in Biology from Emory University and earned an MS in Public Policy and a Master's in City and Regional Planning from Georgia Tech, Atlanta, Georgia, USA, with specializations in urban development and policy and environmental planning. She has several years' experience in both the environmental and economic development fields. She currently works on water supply and water conservation planning issues for the Atlanta Region.

Sujai Shivakumar serves as a Senior Policy Advisor at the National Academies' Board on Science, Technology, and Economic Policy. Since joining the NAS in 2001, he has been a lead researcher in the Academies' evaluation of public–private technology partnerships and its multi-part analysis of the drivers of the information technology-led productivity growth. He was also a leading member of a research team assembled by the National Academies to study the US Small Business Innovation Research program. Currently, he is helping to lead the Academies' comparative review of national innovation policies around the world as well as its review of best practices in innovation policies among US states, and is leading the National Academies' study of best practices in national innovation programs to support flexible electronics. Dr Shivakumar's analysis highlights the important role of institutions in fostering successful cooperation among small and large technology firms, universities, venture capital companies and other actors needed to commercialize new technologies

within complex innovation ecosystems. Dr Shivakumar received his doc-
torate in Economics at George Mason University and pursued further
post-doctoral research in political science at Indiana University, USA.
He is the author of *The Constitution of Development: Crafting Capabilities
for Self-Governance* (Macmillan Press, 2005) and co-author with Nobel
economist Elinor Ostrom of *The Samaritan's Dilemma: The Political
Economy of Aid* (Oxford University Press, 2005). He is also co-editor with
Charles Wessner of a National Research Council report, *India's Changing
Innovation System* (National Academies Press, 2007).

Abraham J. Shragge received his PhD in Modern United States History
from the University of California, San Diego (UCSD), USA in 1998. His
dissertation, 'Boosters and Bluejackets: The Civic Culture of Militarism in
San Diego, California, 1900–1945', has been cited by numerous urban and
naval historians. Dr Shragge has taught History and Urban Studies and
Planning at UCSD as well as at Korea University's International Summer
Campus. He directed the Dimensions of Culture Program at UCSD's
Thurgood Marshall College, where he also created courses in Civil Society
and Public Service. He is curator of the Veterans Museum and Memorial
Center in Balboa Park, and coordinator of the San Diego Ex-Prisoners of
War Oral History Project. He is currently a Visiting Professor at the Korea
Development Institute School of Public Policy and Management.

Donald S. Siegel is Dean of the School of Business and Professor of
Management at the University of Albany, SUNY, USA. Professor
Siegel's research has focused on university technology transfer and
academic entrepreneurship, the economic and strategic implications
of entrepreneurship and technological change; productivity analysis,
private equity and corporate governance; and corporate social responsibility. He is editor of the *Journal of Technology Transfer*, co-editor of
Academy of Management Perspectives, an associate editor of the *Journal
of Productivity Analysis*, and serves on the editorial boards of *Academy
of Management Learning & Education, Journal of Management Studies,
Journal of Business Venturing, Corporate Governance: An International
Review*, and *Strategic Management Journal*. He has also co-edited 32
special issues of leading journals in economics, management and finance.
Dr Siegel has taught at SUNY-Stony Brook, Arizona State University,
the University of Nottingham, Rensselaer Polytechnic Institute, and the
University of California – Riverside, where he served as Associate Dean
for Graduate Studies.

Mary Lindenstein Walshok is Associate Vice Chancellor, Public Programs,
Dean, University Extension and Adjunct Professor, Sociology at the

University of California, San Diego, California, USA. Professor Walshok is a thought leader on aligning workforce development with regional economic growth and innovation. As an industrial sociologist, she has been researching various American regions for the US Department of Labor, NSF, and Lilly Foundation. One of her current research projects is an NSF-funded study of the role of boundary-spanning organizations in shaping the social and cultural dynamics of the highly innovative regions. She is the author of *Blue Collar Women*, *Knowledge Without Boundaries*, *Closing America's Job Gap* and forthcoming at Stanford University Press *Invention and Reinvention: The Evolution of San Diego's Entrepreneurial Economy*. Professor Walshok is also a co-founder of CONNECT, one of the most admired innovation cluster development organizations in the world.

Charles W. Wessner is Director of the Program on Technology, Innovation and Entrepreneurship at the National Academy of Sciences, Washington, DC, USA. He is recognized nationally and internationally for his expertise on innovation policy, including public–private partnerships, entrepreneurship, early-stage financing for new firms, and the special needs and benefits of high-technology industry. He testifies to the US Congress and major national commissions, advises agencies of the US government and international organizations, and lectures at major universities in the US and abroad. Reflecting the strong global interest in innovation, he frequently addresses issues of shared policy interest with foreign governments, universities, and research institutes. He has a strong commitment to international cooperation, reflected in his work with a wide variety of countries around the world.

David A. Wolfe is Royal Bank Chair in Public and Economic Policy and Professor of Political Science at the University of Toronto and Director of the Program on Globalization and Regional Innovation Systems (PROGRIS) at the Munk School of Global Affairs, Toronto, Ontario, Canada. Professor Wolfe's research interests include the political economy of technological change and the role of local and regional economic development, with special reference to Canada and Ontario. At PROGRIS, he is National Coordinator of the Innovation Systems Research Network (ISRN), funded by the Social Sciences and Humanities Research Council of Canada. There he has served as principal investigator on two major collaborative research initiatives, including 'Innovation Systems and Economic Development: The Role of Local and Regional Clusters in Canada', and currently on the 'Social Dynamics of Economic Performance: Innovation and Creativity in City Regions'. He is the editor or co-editor of nine books and numerous scholarly articles.

1. Creating competitiveness: introduction and overview

David B. Audretsch and
Mary Lindenstein Walshok

Competitiveness is a concept that is most readily identified with firms and organizations. A competitive firm can enjoy sustained levels of high profitability. By contrast, a paucity of competitiveness may doom a firm to eroding rates of return and, ultimately, bankruptcy or insolvency. It is not surprising that an entire scholarly discipline within the field of management has devoted itself to understanding what firms and organizations can do to improve their competitiveness, and ultimately their performance.

However, firms are not the only organizational body whose performance is dependent upon being competitive. The varied economic performance of cities and regions, both within a single nation, as well as across nations, during the era of the Great Recession also highlights the need for competitiveness. Those cities and regions that are more competitive enjoy a superior economic performance, while their less competitive counterparts suffer from lower rates of economic growth and increasing levels of unemployment.

During the massive economic expansion of the 1990s, there was a sense that 'all boats are lifted by a rising tide.' As long as the overall economy grew so impressively, most cities, states and regions were also able to enjoy an improving economic performance. However, with the stagnant macroeconomic environment that emerged at the beginning of this century, the disparities in economic performance across regions and cities have increased. This is true not only in the North American context but also in Europe and the rest of the developed world.

In particular, the current crisis in Europe is essentially a competitiveness crisis for many cities and regions, particularly in southern and Mediterranean Europe. Prior to the introduction of the single currency, the Euro, those places could maintain their competitiveness and employment levels through a devaluating currency. But with the disappearance of currency devaluation as an instrument to enhance competitiveness, these places have been unable to find alternative instruments that promote local competitiveness.

In order to provide a systematic analysis for creating local competitiveness, we brought leading scholars, policymakers and business executives from around the world together at a conference in La Jolla, California, December 12–13, 2011. The chapters contained in this volume are edited versions of the most poignant insightful new ideas presented at that conference.

In the following chapter, David A. Wolfe of the University of Toronto explores the way in which the intersection between path dependent trajectories of development and the strategic choices to generate competitiveness made by civic actors in urban settings affects their capacity to deal with external shocks. Efforts to sustain the economic performance of city-regions through periods of disruptive change need to commence with the institutional capacity of those cities to manage their transition. The successful adoption of a 'strategic management approach' at the regional and urban level requires not just a new category of policy approach, but a new style of policy development. Among the important factors to analyze are: the ability of regional and local governments to build on specialized regional assets, including public and private research infrastructure, as well as unique concentrations of occupational and labor market skills; the presence or absence of 'civic capital' at the regional and local level; and the ability of regional networks to work within and across associational boundaries to support the formulation and refinement of strategic management policies in response to changing economic conditions.

Robert D. Atkinson, in Chapter 3, focuses on 'Innovation in cities and innovation by cities.' Atkinson points out that the success of companies and places depends more on innovation than ever before. Despite its luster, many public and private sector leaders cannot really define innovation and therefore stumble when trying to encourage or harness it. In particular, his chapter suggests four challenges sub-national places face when it comes to innovation. The first challenge consists of understanding the integral link between private sector innovation and public innovation policy in economic development. The second challenge involves understanding that innovation comes in many forms and phases of production and development. The third challenge is that of focusing on not just innovation in places, but innovation by places, i.e. states and localities must themselves try new policy approaches. The final challenge involves creating partnerships between places, especially local places and the national government.

In Chapter 4, 'The strategic recombination of regional innovative capacities: public–private institutions as knowledge bridges,' Gerald A.

McDermott argues that generating locational competitiveness is fundamentally a problem of organizational diversity and recombination. McDermott analyzes a unique data set and cases from South America, where societies suffer from long-term low-equilibrium traps. His chapter shows how new types of institutions facilitate new forms of firm learning and also how public and private actors can construct such institutions. The chapter first shows how, contrary to conventional wisdom, knowledge is not 'in the air,' but rather is diffused through particular types of inter-organizational relationships. According to McDermott, the problem then is that these relationships are not distributed evenly in a region or industry and some may insulate a firm from accessing new knowledge. However, McDermott shows how government can help reshape knowledge networks. In particular, his chapter provides empirical evidence showing that firms can improve their access to diverse knowledge resources by improving their learning capabilities, by having multiple strong ties to, in particular, organizations that act as social and knowledge bridges between previously isolated producer communities. Finally, McDermott's chapter demonstrates how government can collaborate with relevant stakeholder groups to construct these bridging institutions, which are based on such principles as rules of inclusion and participatory governance.

In Chapter 5, 'Enhancing economic growth? University technology commercialization,' Shiri M. Breznitz and Neela Ram examine the role of technology transfer and commercialization by universities in promoting locational economic growth. In particular, this chapter suggests that there is no silver-bullet method suitable for university technology transfer everywhere and, therefore, notes the importance of history and environment through a critical case study of commercialization at one university, the Georgia Institute of Technology. Breznitz and Ram conclude that, as a public university serving its state, this successful newcomer to technology commercialization fundamentally designed and organized its technology transfer activities around its local environment and historical strengths, unlike other universities that tried to follow a general trend in technology commercialization.

Donald S. Siegel, in Chapter 6, 'Academic entrepreneurship: lessons learned for university administrators and policymakers,' focuses on the locational impact of university generated entrepreneurship. Siegel points out that, in recent years, there has been substantial growth in academic entrepreneurship. A concomitant trend is that many cities and regions are increasingly viewing the research university as an engine of new firm creation and economic growth. These trends have important implications for university administrators and policymakers. In his chapter, Siegel examines the antecedents and consequences of academic entrepreneurship and draws some lessons learned for those who govern and manage universities. He concludes that universities and regions must formulate a rational and coherent technology commercialization strategy, which includes consideration of faculty incentives, organizational design, administrative policies to promote academic entrepreneurship, and entrepreneurship education.

Chapter 7, by Charles W. Wessner and Sujai Shivakumar, is concerned with 'Driving regional growth: the growing role of policies to promote clusters.' In this chapter, Wessner analyzes specific public policy approaches to creating clusters. As Wessner emphasizes, ever since Silicon Valley and Boston's Route 128 gained global attention as fountains of dynamic new high-technology companies, state and local governments across the United States have tried to create innovation clusters of their own. These innovation clusters are regional concentrations of large and small companies that develop creative products and services, along with specialized suppliers, service providers, universities, and associated institutions. To this end, state and local governments have sought to attract a critical mass of skills and talent. Seeking to promote a high level of interaction among entrepreneurs, researchers, and innovators, they have invested in science parks, business incubators to nurture start-ups, and an array of research collaborations between universities and private industry. Wessner's chapter identifies a rich array of policy instruments that have been effectively implemented to generate local competitiveness through fostering a cluster.

Thomas Andersson focuses on 'Evolving technologies and emerging regions: governance for growth and prosperity' in the eighth chapter. Andersson provides an analysis of how technical progress and its diffusion offer access to new tools that bring radical change around the world. Centuries of economic dominance by the West are broken. The Far East and the Middle East present some of the rivaling models. As Andersson points out, these models of technical change and economic development are not without their problems. In particular, Andersson's chapter addresses the wider context of natural resource-based economies entering the knowledge-based era. Natural resource wealth has been viewed as a curse rather than a blessing for some time, but that is now changing. The natural resource rich economies, notably in the GCC, have made headway in some respects. Yet there remain excessive rigidity embedded in prevailing culture and institutional context, rent-seeking and distortions favoring incumbents, and bias towards tangible rather than intangible investment, quantity rather than quality.

In Chapter 9, 'Collective entrepreneurship: the strategic management of Research Triangle Park,' Dennis P. Leyden and Albert N. Link analyze how local competitiveness was created in one particular place, Research

Triangle Park in central North Carolina. Leyden and Link propose a new and unique theory of 'collective entrepreneurship,' where the creation of Research Triangle Park was the result of many individuals each exhibiting their own entrepreneurial ability along the way. Thus, this chapter proposes the new and compelling concept of collective entrepreneurship. Leyden and Link suggest that collective entrepreneurship might be a critical ingredient to a recipe for generating local competitiveness.

In Chapter 10, Mary Lindenstein Walshok and Abraham J. Shragge provide an analysis of how policy generated the 'Invention of San Diego's innovation economy.' In particular Walshok links key policy decisions as fostering the shift of San Diego from having a competitive advantage based on natural resources to an innovation driven economy.

The Conference held at La Jolla in 2011 and chapters contained in this volume were supported by Indiana University's School of Public and Environmental Affairs (SPEA) and by the University of California at San Diego. We would like to express our thanks to Dean John Graham of SPEA, Chemain Slater and Betty Fiscus of the Institute of Development Strategies at Indiana University, and Alla Resiner of the University of California at San Diego for their capable assistance with the Conference. We are particularly grateful to Adam Lederer for his editorial contributions in helping to bring the manuscripts from initial drafts to the final edited versions appearing in this volume. Finally, we thank Fran O'Sullivan of Edward Elgar for her encouragement and support of this book.

2. Civic governance, social learning and the strategic management of city-regions

David A. Wolfe

INTRODUCTION

Recent theoretical and empirical research on innovation systems describes city-regions as the drivers of economic growth and prosperity. This literature underlines the importance of agglomeration economies and proximity as key factors that facilitate the transmission of knowledge among the leading edge sectors that are increasingly concentrated in urban regions (Wolfe and Bramwell 2008). Complex systems of technology, production processes, industrial organization, and their supporting infrastructures of social and political institutions exhibit distinctive spatial characteristics. In the context of rapid technological change and concerns over the globalization of competition and production, this focus on the importance of the urban scale of economic development underlines how the key elements of innovative sectors are locally rooted. Innovation in a technologically complex and knowledge-driven or 'learning' economy is a *social process* that builds new competencies and skills, a process that requires proximity or face-to-face interaction and thus occurs most effectively at the regional and local scale. However, those interactions also occur in an institutional context that strongly conditions the pattern of knowledge flows and interactions required for effective innovation. The importance of this dimension stems from the fact that,

> ... the making of a regional economy involves not just the development of a productive apparatus on the basis of the atomised decisions of firms and workers, but also a 'politics of place', or in other words, the social construction of those institutional-regulatory structures that must be present in order to secure economic order and continuity. Some of these structures are within the domain of the nation state. Others belong more properly to the level of the region as such. (Scott and Storper 1992, 19)

This chapter explores the way in which the intersection between path dependent trajectories of development and the strategic choices made by civic actors in urban settings affects their capacity to deal with external shocks. Efforts to sustain the economic performance of city-regions through periods of disruptive change need to commence with the institutional capacity of those cities to manage their transition. The successful adoption of a 'strategic management approach' at the regional and urban level requires not just a new category of policy approach, but a new style of policy development (Audretsch 2002). Among the important factors to analyze are: the ability of regional and local governments to build on specialized regional assets, including public and private research infrastructure, as well as unique concentrations of occupational and labour market skills; the presence or absence of 'civic capital' at the regional and local level; and the ability of regional networks to work within and across associational boundaries to support the formulation and refinement of strategic management policies in response to changing economic conditions.

THE GOVERNANCE OF URBAN AND REGIONAL ECONOMIES

Analyzing the contribution that a strategic management approach can make to urban and regional development requires a better understanding of the role of 'governance' at the urban and regional level – one that involves civic actors and integrates across existing levels of government. The ability to create better linkages among relevant institutions and associated actors at the local and regional level is a key factor in the development of effective policy and its implementation. Collaboration by local governments with a wide range of community-based actors supports the effective coordination of economic policy in knowledge-based and innovation-intensive economies. Yet, recognizing the importance of collaboration and coordination for effective policy development is only part of the challenge; better coordination requires an understanding of the conditions that contribute to its emergence and development. Of necessity, it involves a more decentralized, open and consultative form of governing.

This emphasis on the role of governance, as opposed to government, stems from the recognition that policy outcomes depend on the interaction among a wide range of social and economic actors, including provincial or state and local governments, the private sector, voluntary, business and not-for-profit organizations. Central to this approach is the development of styles of governing in which the boundaries between public and private actors and even across different levels of government become blurred. The novelty of the approach lies in the accent placed on the processes of consultation and deliberation, rather than the exercise of formal authority through organizational and administrative structures. It focuses on 'the process through which public and private actions and resources are coordinated and given a common meaning and direction' (Peters and Pierre 2004, 78).

The governance perspective builds on insights derived from the policy literature that there is often a critical gap between the formulation of policy and its implementation. Policy outcomes are not merely the result of legislative or administrative actions, but the product of a complex pattern of interaction between several levels of government and an array of social and economic actors in the community. Federal and provincial or state governments may legislate in any one of a number of areas within their jurisdictional authority, but the effectiveness of that policy is determined 'on the ground' in a specific geographic locality. The extent to which it achieves the desired goal depends on the pattern of interaction between governmental authorities operating a variety of arms-length agencies, private sector firms and a wide range of industry and other voluntary associations. For instance, the impact of national and regional research policies is a product of the responses by private firms, public and private laboratories, post-secondary educational institutions and intermediary associations to the initiatives adopted. As a consequence, the pattern of governance cannot be reduced to the actions of any one actor in either the public or private spheres, but results from their combined interaction across a wide range of socio-political-administrative interventions (Rhodes 1996, 657).

At the heart of this perspective on governance is the belief that the effective implementation of policy has evolved away from the state-centred, bureaucratic and hierarchical systems that prevailed through most of the late 20th century towards a more distributed pattern of authority that is dispersed over the core elements of the economy, society and polity. This distributed pattern of governance invests new degrees of power and influence in communities because the capacity for learning can best be realized through patterns of decentralized and reciprocal relations built on evolving partnerships (Paquet 1997, 26). In the same vein, Scott et al. suggest that governance is now widely deployed to describe the multi-faceted aspects of social and economic coordination in an increasingly interdependent world where various tiers of government must collaborate with each other, as well as with a range of non-governmental organizations, to achieve their goals. The governance of city-regions in particular must be viewed as part of a larger issue of coordination across multiple geographic scales and levels of jurisdiction. This 'sense of the term sees governance as involving a set of complex institutional reactions to the broader problems of economic and social adjustment in the emerging global-local system' (Scott et al. 2001, 22).

Governance and Social Learning

This focus on governance, as opposed to government, leads to a related emphasis on the importance of *social learning*. The emerging knowledge economy places a premium on the ability to acquire, absorb and diffuse relevant knowledge and information throughout the various institutions that affect the process of economic development and change. Organizations need to become more reflexive and adaptive, by tapping into the knowledge and capabilities of their respective members. The challenge for both public and private organizations is how to structure knowledge and intelligence in social ways, through social learning, rather than to access them on an individual basis (Paquet 1999). Learning is defined as the capacity to improve present performance as a result of experience through a redefinition of the organization's objectives, and the modification of behaviour and structures as a result of new circumstances (Paquet 1997, 31). It is a social cognitive process that depends upon the interaction of geographically proximate actors to develop new systems of understanding as the bases for action and adaptation.

The construction of a dynamic local or regional economy depends in part on the past history of the region, its industrial culture and its endowment of infrastructural supports. Yet examples abound of localities and regions that have altered their development trajectory through collective efforts to improve their endowment of institutional and cultural factors, in other words through a process of social learning. They may differ in terms of the industrial structure that characterizes the region, the relative mix of industries on which their success is based, the underlying infrastructure of research and other institutions that supports the local firms and the social or civic culture that creates cohesion in the region or locality, but they share in common a capability for social learning (Wolfe and Gertler 2002).

In his study of successful cities and communities, Neil Bradford identifies three dynamics that contribute to successful cases of social learning processes. The first is a civic learning process that results in recognition among the local organizations, be they private or public sector, of the importance of equity, diversity and interdependence and the need to accommodate these realities in their collaborations. Equally important is the second dynamic of administrative learning, whereby administrators learn new skills for building relationships, seeking consensus, assessing risk and measuring performance. Such skills help foster a form of government that is effectively engaged in its essential roles of ensuring balanced representation of social interests, addressing systemic differences in the capacity to participate, convening and organizing meetings, establishing protocols for monitoring progress and maintaining the focus and commitment of social partners. Finally the culmination of successful civic and administrative learning leads to the third dynamic, that of policy learning or reflexivity. Here, feedback from the various actors within the multilevel governance process refocuses the policy agenda with community-based insights and experiences, as well as new goals (Bradford 2003).

Civic Engagement and Regional Governance

Due to the benefits of proximity, the region is often the site within which better coordination develops. A key question concerns what mechanisms foster the emergence of more effective means of coordination among civic actors at the regional and local level. Among the relevant factors often considered to contribute to more effective coordination is the character of the relationships between actors in a region – described as social capital. Social capital refers to various features of the social organization of a region, such as the presence of shared norms and values that facilitate coordination and cooperation among individuals, firms, and sectors for their mutual advantage. It is defined as the 'social relations among agents, resting upon social institutions that allow for cooperation and communication' (Lorenzen 2007, 801; Maskell 2000). The use of the term capital indicates that it involves an asset, while the term social connotes that the particular asset is attained through involvement with a community. The existence of social capital depends upon the ability of people to associate with each other and the extent to which their shared norms and values allow them to subordinate their individual interests to the larger interests of the community. It secures the conditions that enhance the benefits derived from more tangible investments in physical and human capital. Without its supportive functioning, high levels of these more tangible forms of investment may fail to produce the benefits that should potentially flow from them (Maskell 2000).

The concept of social capital also helps explain why certain kinds of economic activity tend to cluster despite the opposing trend towards dispersal brought on by the spread of globalization. Peter Maskell suggests that it may also explain why some regions continue to be 'sticky' in attracting strong concentrations of firms in related activities. Social capital becomes ever more valuable as the process of globalization unfolds; it is not equally available in all communities; it cannot be purchased or transferred; and it is difficult to imitate or replicate (2000). Lorenzen draws a critical distinction between the business realm and the civic realm of social relations. Business relations include technological learning within the firm and inter-firm trade and knowledge exchanges. Civic relations include those that exist between people in a community who interact with each other through their involvement with schools, various cultural and leisure activities and other civic associations. Lorenzen argues that the civic dimension of social capital is particularly sensitive to geographic distance because many of the activities that enhance the strength of civic relations are based on the specific catchment area of a civic association or membership in a cultural organization. These relations frequently entail face to face meetings that are constrained by distance (2007).

In previous work, the concept of 'civic capital' has been elaborated to identify the institutional dimensions necessary for effective strategic management exercises at the local level. The literature on social capital acknowledges the importance of social networks and collective values, but its broad application makes it difficult to isolate the specific aspects that contribute to the formulation of regional and local development strategies. Building on the distinction between the business and the civic dimensions of social capital, the concept of 'civic capital' is used to analyze the role that cooperative forms of behaviour play in the success of local and regional economies (Wolfe and Nelles 2008). Civic capital is defined as a set of relations that emerges from interpersonal networks tied to a specific region or locality and contributes to the development of a common sense of community based on a shared identity, set of goals and expectations. It comprises formal or informal networks among individual actors or associations at the community level and between members of the community and regional or local governments (Nelles 2009).

Civic capital provides insight into the processes and dynamics that contribute to more successful regional governance. In regions characterized by higher degrees of civic capital, the coordination required to sustain regional cooperation tends to result in more effective governance. Collaborative institutions often embody values and attitudes that are intrinsic to the region and further build civic capital. Successful regional economies benefit from the presence of collaborative institutions, which help communicate the respective needs of different community actors to each other, establish local and regional priorities for economic development, and build effective bridges across different segments of the economic community that might not otherwise be linked. Above all, they contribute to the articulation of a shared vision for the economic community and the local economy and build a consensus among key civic actors and associations around that vision (Porter, Monitor Group et al. 2001, 75).

A growing number of studies that have examined the factors that contribute to the success of cities and regions in improving their economic performance identify the presence of civic capital in the form of strong civic leadership as central to that success. Civic leaders, or civic entrepreneurs, are critical in articulating a regional orientation and intensifying and formalizing collaborative networks within and between communities. Civic entrepreneurs are bridge builders and help to connect localized networks and different communities of actors with one another. These leaders understand the importance of collaboration and through their leadership bring various groups of actors together to negotiate and agree on regional goals. In doing so, they build civic capital by creating the fora and the initiatives for different segments of the local community to collaborate in pursuing these agreed upon goals (Henton et al. 1997, 31).

These cities and regions enjoy a strong degree of civic mobilization where business leaders, local politicians and other key actors, including post-secondary institutions, social and cultural organizations, come together to create a strong local organization to develop a coordinated approach to tackling local economic challenges. However, not every city or region that attempts this approach succeeds. What differentiates the success stories from the rest is an understanding of the critical dimensions of leadership that are required to build an engaged coalition of civic leaders in support of a plan of action (Centre for Knowledge 2007). The source of that leadership may vary. In some cities and regions, it comes from political institutions or industry associations; in others, it originates with an inspirational figure in a university setting or anchor firm that attracts or spins off like-minded individuals in other firms. Increasingly, however, that leadership has come directly from the business sector. In a growing number of cases, business leaders have recognized that the economic prospects for their own firms depend on a number of key factors that are common to the broader community in which they reside. As recognition of this fact has spread, a growing number of business leaders across North America have acknowledged the need to work together to support the economic fortunes of their respective metropolitan regions.

The essential criterion for success in building these new collaborative relationships is finding the right mechanisms to engage members of the community in a sustained effort to advance its economic opportunities. The recruitment of a committed, creative and collaborative leadership is the most essential element for the success of these efforts. These kinds of collaborative leaders invariably share certain characteristics:

- They can see the opportunities opened by the emergence of the knowledge-based economy;
- They exhibit an entrepreneurial personality, in both a business and a 'civic' sense;
- They are willing to cross functional, political and geographic boundaries in pursuit of their strategic goals;

- They demand a sharing of both responsibility and results, and consequently are trusted as credible intermediaries; and
- They are committed to and comfortable working in teams (Montana et al. 2001).

However, not all forms of civic interaction contribute to institutional thickness to the same degree. Safford draws an important distinction between the differences in the structure of those networks that can dramatically influence their effect on levels of civic capital in a community. His case studies suggest that civic relations that tie actors together who are not otherwise connected economically produce far more beneficial results for their communities than civic ties that merely reinforce prevailing economic ties among actors in a community who are already well connected (Safford 2009).

STRATEGIC MANAGEMENT OF URBAN AND REGIONAL ECONOMIES

The presence of civic capital and engaged civic leadership at the regional and local level are critical for helping cities respond to the cascading series of shocks currently buffeting the global economy. Taking city-regions seriously as the focus for economic development initiatives has a number of key consequences for the design and implementation of these strategies: '(g)reater emphasis is placed on territorial rather than sectoral approaches; on the need for policy coordination and improvements in governance; and on bottom-up participatory approaches' (Rodríguez-Pose 2008, 1033). Rather than concentrating on the zero-sum competition for inward investment, the most successful places focus on searching for and generating new economic knowledge that drives innovation and export success. As Feldman and Martin perceptively note, most jurisdictions pursue a strategy, whether it is coordinated or not and articulated or not, which is defined by the collective decisions that actors within that jurisdiction make over time. Jurisdictions can benefit from creating an economic base with unique and valuable assets that provides a differentiated advantage over other jurisdictions. But they emphasize that 'constructing jurisdictional advantage takes the will of all the actors – a consensus vision and vision of uniqueness' (2005, 1245).

An urban-centred focus on the issue of adaptation and response to changing global and technological conditions that affect economic prosperity shifts attention to cities' capacities to formulate responses to their own particular set of challenges. In this sense, there is growing interest in the abilities of cities to alter their own economic fortunes, and a belief that 'communities can affect the tenor and trajectory of regional economies through a concerted, organized, *organizing* approach' (Safford 2004a, 39). While path dependent trajectories of economic development resulting from local factor endowments strongly shape the trajectory of economic change within regions, cities do have a significant measure of control over the direction of economic and social change (Simmie and Wood 2002; Clarke and Gaile 1998). The response taken to assert a greater degree of control over the direction of economic and social change has assumed the form of 'strategic management policy' at the regional and urban level. At the heart of this approach is 'the development and enhancement of factors of production that cannot be transferred across geographic space at low cost' (Audretsch 2002, 174). The successful adoption of a strategic management policy at the urban level requires a new style of policy development, deploying what Gertler and Wolfe have labelled 'local social knowledge management' exercises (2004).

Ultimately, for the strategic management approach to succeed, 'policy prescriptions need to be tailored to the circumstances and strengths of individual urban regions' (Simmie 2002, 214). Much depends on the ability of cities to develop the 'organizational and institutional infrastructure within which collective action [can] be taken' (Safford 2004b, 4). The foundation for this rests on the governance theories discussed above which emphasize the benefits of collaboration across different levels of government, and between public and private actors at the local scale, as the most effective way for achieving better policy alignment and sustaining urban economic growth. This is particularly true with respect to strategies focused on emerging industries and new technologies: '... what matters for place-specific industrial development is not necessarily scientific resources and know-how but the social dynamics that occur within a place and define a community of common interest around a nascent technology or emerging industry' (Lowe and Feldman 2008, 265).

Successful urban economies benefit from the presence of collaborative institutions, which help communicate the respective needs of different community actors to each other, establish local and regional priorities for economic development, and build effective bridges across different segments of the economic community that might not otherwise be linked. 'Collaboration is most effective when it draws new people together, not just the "usual suspects"' (Potapchuk and Crocker Jr. 1999, 179). Collaborative institutions can also provide the critical building blocks for local development coalitions. Above all, they contribute to the articulation of a shared vision for the economic community and the local economy and build a consensus among key civic actors and associations around that vision. In doing so, they build civic capital by creating relationships and developing collective institutions that benefit the community, identifying common strengths or mutual needs and contributing to the development of a common economic agenda.

Among the conditions that contribute to the formation of effective governance arrangements at the urban level is the emergence of strong, dynamic civic leaders with the ability to forge broad and inclusive local development coalitions. A development coalition is a place-based coalition of a diverse cross-section of social and economic groups committed to the economic development of a specific city-region (Keating 2001). Business leaders across North America have increasingly recognized the need to work together to support the economic fortunes of their respective metropolitan regions. These collective efforts have emerged out of a growing recognition that coordinated efforts at a region-wide scale are necessary to promote the economic prospects of both their region and their individual businesses. Such civic-minded business leaders have come together in a large number of cities to forge new organizations (or revitalize existing ones) dedicated to working collaboratively with economic development organizations (EDOs) or creating them where necessary to promote their regional economies. The principal hallmark of these new civic organizations is that they are both collaborative in nature and regionally focused in their scope. They tend to display a number of common features: they are shifting priorities from traditional business climate issues to a broader concern with regional competitiveness; they are often funded through a variety of different mechanisms; and they have resulted in many older organizations restructuring their approach to regional cooperation in order to be able to tackle complex economic development issues at a truly regional scale. This last factor can involve formalizing partnerships with complementary business organizations to operate more effectively at a regional level, as well as creating new public-private partnerships to oversee responsibility for regional economic development (Futureworks 2004).

A key question is how to generate the right conditions for implementing a strategic management approach at the regional and local level. Successful regions must be able to identify and cultivate their assets, undertake collaborative processes to plan and implement change and encourage a regional mindset that fosters growth. For such approaches to succeed, they must build upon available endowments of civic capital and fulfill the requirement for dynamic civic leaders with the vision and commitment to carry these exercises through to their successful conclusion. Effective strategic planning exercises are concerned with identifying a city-region's unique jurisdictional assets that can support the development of its economy. These can include its knowledge economy assets (such as workforce skills, knowledge and research development institutions, creativity, advanced telecommunications infrastructure, quality of place, and financial capital), the strength of its collaborative institutions and organizations (such as regional development organizations, professional networks, research consortia, and entrepreneurial support networks), and the civic culture (values, attitudes and regional mindset governing its approach to urban economic development).

The successful adoption of a strategic planning approach requires a new style of policy development at the urban level that involves the kind of socially organized learning processes discussed above. Successful city-regions are able to draw upon the presence of networks of key actors and associations to launch exercises that identify and cultivate their assets, undertake collaborative planning processes to implement change, and encourage a regional mindset that fosters growth. These exercises can only succeed if the prevailing structures of urban governance provide the support needed to allow them to be effective. Variations in the capacity of individual city-regions to engage in these processes are linked as much to the 'collaboration between agents and their ability to mobilize assets', as the ability to create and diffuse new knowledge (Simmie and Wood 2002, 149).

This approach to regional economic development is characterized by both 'how' it is done, and 'what' it focuses on. Experience indicates that successful strategic management exercises are demand and opportunity driven; promote innovative ideas in all aspects of regional economic activity; facilitate relationship-building and create buy-in; and are ongoing, iterative and non-linear. Successful strategies are reflexive in that they use their past experience to create a more effective process – in other words, they involve social learning processes. An essential criterion for success is finding the appropriate mechanisms to engage key members of the community in a sustained effort to advance its opportunities. The recruitment of a committed, creative and collaborative leadership is an essential element for success. The leadership for these exercises need to create a broad buy-in from the relevant elements of its regional and local community. Based on their experience with launching community-based economic development initiatives, Henton and his colleagues argue that what we have termed 'civic' capital is critical for the success of the most dynamic strategic management exercises. Civic capital can be created, and the basis for doing so is the establishment of collaborative networks between various elements of the business and civic communities.

The presence of *collaborative institutions and organizations*, such as cluster organizations, professional networks, research-industry consortia and entrepreneurial support networks, greatly facilitates this environment. These alliances, networks and other relationship-building mechanisms create connections and linkages vital to economic development in a technology-driven world . . . many regions fortunate enough to have university research assets underuse these knowledge economy resources, precisely because relationships have not been established to connect the university and local industry . . . Relationships matter. (Montana et al. 2001, 10)

A number of additional obstacles lie in the path of the successful implementation of bottom-up associative governance development strategies. One of the limitations faced by a governance-based approach is the lack of financial resources to fully support the desired initiatives. This problem can be compounded by the absence of a formal tier of government institutions corresponding to the actual economic territory encompassed by the city-region. Smaller and less dynamic urban regions may also face a greater challenge in accessing regional and national government resources or even gaining a significant place on their respective policy agendas. An additional danger lies in zero-sum, competitive development strategies through the use of financial incentives and subsidies to attract investment away from more established centres. Engagement in these kinds of bidding wars can reduce the economic benefit to the larger region or nation as a whole (Rodríguez-Pose 2008, 1037–9). However, commencing in the mid-1980s, successful strategic management efforts at the urban level have proved effective at identifying available programs and budgetary allocations at senior levels of government to fund their strategic initiatives. More recently, national programs introduced in the U.S. provide direct funding to support these kinds of focused initiatives at the local level (Wolfe 2010).

The scope for individual agents and local politics to influence local and regional outcomes would seem to be considerable, since these relationships are mediated by key people and organizations that play a leadership role in bringing the economic, social and civic interests in the community together to collaborate. One virtue of a strategic management approach to the process of economic development is the emphasis placed on involving key actors at the local level in thinking about how to design effective innovation strategies. Collaborative organizations and institutions often embody values and attitudes that are intrinsic to the region. This element of the regional culture is an important, but overlooked, component in the design of regional development strategies. The essential criterion for success is finding the appropriate mechanisms to engage key members of the community in a sustained effort to advance its opportunities. The recruitment of a committed, creative and collaborative leadership is an essential element for the success of a strategic planning process in regional foresight and regional economic development.

CIVIC CAPITAL AND STRATEGIC MANAGEMENT IN WATERLOO, ONTARIO

A leading example of a region where this approach has been adopted with great success over the past three decades is the technology cluster in the Kitchener-Waterloo-Cambridge (Waterloo) region, located an hour west of Toronto. Although the present contours of the cluster can be traced back to the formation of the first software and computing firms in the 1970s, the Waterloo region has long been an important location for manufacturing in the Southern Ontario industrial landscape. Kitchener-Waterloo has been the home to major national and international corporations for more than a century, from Dominion Electrohome Ltd to present day success Research in Motion – manufacturer of the iconic 'Blackberry'. The region has had a pioneering presence in some of the major technological advances in North America, including automobiles, radio, processed foods, financial services, biotechnology and computing. Although the region is only about half the size of Ottawa, its more diverse industrial base, as well as the historical capacity of some of its leading firms, such as Electrohome (now part of Christie Digital), to transition from older technologies to new ones, has been a continuing source of regional resilience. A hallmark of the innovation process within the region has been the application of digital technology to advanced manufacturing processes, evidence of a relatively uncommon, but critical, dimension of knowledge transfer across two of the core areas of specialization within the regional economy (Krashinsky 2011).

The high technology cluster in the Waterloo region grew out of its strong industrial base in advanced manufacturing, combined with the early focus of the new university in engineering, math and computer science. Waterloo's first ICT firms were created in the early 1970s when a number of firms began developing software and hardware to support networking and communications applications. Two of the early firms, WATCOM and Dantec Electronic, were spun-off from the University of Waterloo in 1974. A subsequent generation of firms followed in the 1980s, including Dalsa (1980), Virtek Vision (1986) and Open Text (1989). RIM, although not technically a spin-off from university research, was founded by University of Waterloo students in the early 1980s and has since grown to become the leading high technology company not only in the region, but in the national economy as well. Although the university remains central to the continuing development of the regional economy, its primary contribution is no longer through the process of new firm formation, as relatively fewer firms have spun out directly since the late 1980s and its role in feeding the growth of the local talent pool has become a mainstay in contributing to the adaptability of the regional economy (Bramwell and Wolfe 2008; Kenney and Patton 2011).

The Waterloo region is marked by both relatively strong regional governance and dense civic capital, which has grown and intensified over time. From the founding of the University of Waterloo to the establishment of Canada's Technology Triangle Inc. (CTT), Communitech and the recent initiation of the Prosperity Forum, the private sector has played an instrumental role in the economic development of the region. CTT is the regional marketing association of the Waterloo region and is widely regarded as one of the keystone organizations of the region. Communitech was established in 1997, though its roots stretch back to the early 1990s and an informal group of twelve CEOs, whose goal was to facilitate the exchange of ideas and improve networking relations between high technology companies. The partnership was formed as the CEOs discovered that they were facing similar challenges stemming from the weak state of the regional ICT infrastructure. An oft-cited benefit of Communitech membership is access to a pool of shared experiences and support provided by a variety of services to its members. The association currently supports the tech community with a number of services such as Peer2Peer networking events developed to provide a forum to discuss best practices for industry leaders (CEOs, CIOs and CTOs), management and technical professionals. In addition to providing these direct services targeted at its members, Communitech also plays a much larger role in supporting non-members in the tech community as well as in local economic governance (Bramwell et al. 2008).

Both CTT Inc. and Communitech are associations that have transcended their narrowly economic initial mandates to become leaders in regional governance. Both associations have been described as catalysts of regional initiatives with the critical mass and political weight to bring people to the table in a wide variety of areas beyond economic development. While the associations themselves cannot be described as overly inclusive – despite the increasing diversity of their memberships and partners – the scope of their activities shows increasing commitment to diversity, cultural vibrancy, and regional health. In fact, there are few genuinely regional partnerships in the region that don't include representation of some sort from either organization. Despite this expansion of their mandates, at their core, they remain economic development associations and their involvement in cultural and social spheres is consistently in the name of regional prosperity.

A key feature of Waterloo's adaptability and resilience has been the foresight of local firms to recognize emerging technology trends and to mobilize key segments of the local business community, civic associations, and the post-secondary research infrastructure in support of new initiatives to capitalize on those trends. A key initiative in which CTT played a central role was the establishment and marketing of the Research and Technology Park in partnership with the University of Waterloo, the Government of Canada, Province of Ontario, the Region of Waterloo, the City of Waterloo, and Communitech. The Research Park is located on the northern boundary of the University of Waterloo and is the site of several new buildings, one of which houses the Accelerator Centre, legal offices and other support functions directed towards the promotion of local firms in the cluster. Other buildings in the Research Park house some of the leading firms in the region or provide space for growing firms to expand into, as well as a number of amenities deemed to be attractive to employees in high technology firms. The cooperative role played by all major levels of government plus the key regional actors in designing, financing and developing the new Research and Technology Park is strong testament to the collaborative form of governance that has contributed to the resilience of the region.

Somewhat ironically, the cultural centre of Stratford, Ontario is located just half an hour west of Waterloo, but until recently has not been considered an integral part of the region. This gap between the cultural and scientific sectors of the regional economy has been narrowed with a move by the University of Waterloo to establish a satellite campus in Stratford, followed closely by the creation of a new centre in digital media, linking Stratford directly into the Waterloo economy. The new branch of the University of Waterloo – the Stratford Institute, with a strong focus on the creation of content for digital media – is the centre of a national network to promote the growth of digital media across the country. The Corridor for Advancing Canadian Digital Media (CACDM) is a collaborative initiative on the part of partners across the region and Southwestern Ontario to develop a Centre of Excellence in digital media. This project combines the creation of the Stratford campus with a second initiative to establish the Communitech Hub as a digital media convergence centre in downtown Kitchener to combine the region's expertise in digital media and mobile technology. CACDM is supported by the University of Waterloo, Conestoga College and a broader network of universities. Other stakeholders include the municipal governments of Kitchener and Stratford, as well as economic development associations from other centres in Southwestern Ontario. In addition to the support provided by local firms, such as Open Text and Christie Digital, CTT

Inc. and Communitech are also playing a leading role in the strategy and direction of the initiative.

The goal of the Centre of Excellence is to create Canada's largest concentration of digital media R&D and commercialization expertise, and to develop internationally competitive and sustainable capacity in digital innovation. The vision of the Centre of Excellence is that arts and cultural content creation expertise can be combined with digital media in order to produce innovative ways to present and manipulate data and visualize processes. What is most innovative about the initiative is the inspiration to marry the well-established capabilities of the Waterloo region in digital technologies with the cultural and creative capabilities that the city of Stratford has long been recognized for. It represents a significant effort to shift the regional economy onto the path of becoming a preeminent site in the emerging cognitive-cultural economy. CACDM is also significant from a collaborative governance perspective as it is one of the first times that the civic leadership in the Waterloo region has engaged with municipalities beyond its regional boundaries (such as Stratford) and reached out to assume national leadership of an innovative research network.

The success of the region's civic and business leadership in attracting federal funding to support the CACDM was followed quickly by its success in winning a grant from the provincial government to further support the establishment of the Hub. In November 2009 the Ontario government announced plans to invest up to $26.4m (24 per cent of the $107m project) in Kitchener to create the Communitech Hub: Digital Media and Mobile Accelerator, bringing the combined federal and provincial total to $31.4 million. The Hub, which opened in October 2010, provides an attractive location in the heart of the region for entrepreneurs, companies and academic institutions to interact in a 30,000 square foot state-of-the-art facility. Among the many features of the Hub are the immersive 3D H.I.V.E (Hub Interactive Virtual Reality Environment) provided by Christie Digital, one of the key private sector partners, 3D-capable event space, and virtual conferencing facilities. In addition to Christie, the Hub also has representatives from some of the larger firms in the region, including RIM, Open Text and Agfa. Through a wide range of programs administered by Communitech, the Hub's mission is to build global digital media by mentoring tenant start-ups, creating linkages with more established companies in the region, and helping secure financing for digital media ideas. The facility has space to accommodate more than 100 digital media start-ups, and Communitech is already working with more than 200 start-up firms in the region through its Executive in Residence program and mentoring activities. The Hub also has space for some of the legal and consulting companies that provide services to the high technology sector and serves as the headquarters of the Canadian Digital Media Network. Through the CDMN it is the sponsor of the highly successful Canada 3.0 conferences, which have been held in Stratford for the past three years (Knowles 2011).

These recent initiatives to reposition the region to recover from the current restructuring of its industrial base are an important indication that civic capital in Waterloo is relatively strong and its mobilization is a key factor in the region's resilience. The region is characterized by a high degree of associative activity, civic engagement, personnel overlap and well-developed organizational linkages, and those collaborative networks are being deployed effectively to reposition the local knowledge infrastructure in support of future economic growth. What is most remarkable is that despite the political fragmentation of the region into a number of smaller municipalities, civic capital is highly developed outside of the public sector. Most of the key leaders, groups and initiatives that have been influential in promoting the regional agenda have emerged from the private and higher education sectors, but all of them readily acknowledge the high degree of networking and interaction that exists across the public and private sectors in support of the region's economic future.

CONCLUSION

Applying a socially organized learning approach to the challenge of urban economic development requires an integrated understanding of policy at the 'governance' level – one that involves civic actors and integrates across existing programs, as well as levels of government. The ability to create effective linkages among relevant institutions and actors at the city-region level is a key factor in the development of effective policy and a prerequisite for regional resilience. Much depends on the ability of cities and regions to develop the organizational capacity for formulating and implementing new development strategies. The critical issue concerns the most effective means to alter the conditions that influence the trajectory of growth for a regional or local economy. Successful regions will be those able to engage in strategic management exercises and launch collaborative processes to plan and implement change. These circumstances place new demands on the role of civic leadership at the urban level and their ability to forge cohesive developmental coalitions. Examples abound of city-regions that have launched efforts to alter their prospects for growth through collective efforts to improve their endowment of institutional and cultural factors, in other words through a process of civic engagement and strategic management. The case of Waterloo, Ontario, discussed above, provides one example of how a dynamic urban region with engaged civic leadership has adopted a strategic management approach to build on past successes and create new opportunities for the future. However, the way in which this process occurs in different city-regions varies according to the dynamism of the local civic leadership in place, the relative cohesiveness of the local development coalition and the focus and coherence of the strategic plans that have been developed. There can be no single blueprint for how this should be done in individual city-regions; ultimately, it involves a process of social learning for the civic leadership in each individual case.

REFERENCES

Audretsch, D.B. (2002), 'The innovative advantage of US cities', *European Planning Studies*, **10** (2), 165–76.

Bradford, N. (2003), *Cities and Communities That Work: Innovative Practices, Enabling Policies*, Discussion Paper F/32, Ottawa: Canadian Policy Research Networks.

Bramwell, A. and D.A. Wolfe (2008), 'Universities and regional economic development: the entrepreneurial University of Waterloo', *Research Policy*, **37** (September), 1175–87.

Bramwell, A., J. Nelles and D.A. Wolfe (2008), 'Knowledge, innovation and institutions: global and local dimensions of the ICT cluster in Waterloo, Canada', *Regional Studies*, **42** (1), February, 1–16.

Centre for Knowledge, Innovation, Technology and Enterprise (2007), 'The role of leadership in promoting regional innovation policies in "ordinary regions"', NESTA Working Paper 02, London: National Endowment for Science, Technology and the Arts.

Clarke, S.E. and G.L. Gaile (1998), *The Work of Cities*, Minneapolis: University of Minnesota Press.

Feldman, M. and R. Martin (2005), 'Constructing jurisdictional advantage', *Research Policy*, **34** (8), October, 1235–49.

Futureworks (2004), *Minding Their Civic Business: A Look at the New Ways Regional Business-Civic Organizations Are Making a Difference in Metropolitan North America* (www.futureworks-web.org).

Gertler, M.S. and D.A. Wolfe (2004), 'Local social knowledge management: community actors, institutions and multilevel governance in regional foresight exercises', *Futures*, **36** (1), February, 45–65.

Henton, D., J. Melville and K. Walesh (1997), *Grassroots Leaders for a New Economy: How Civic Entrepreneurs Are Building Prosperous Communities*, San Francisco: Jossey-Bass.

Keating, M. (2001), 'Governing cities and regions: territorial restructuring in a global age', in A.J. Scott (ed.), *Global City-Regions: Trends, Theory, Policy*, Oxford and New York: Oxford University Press, pp. 371–90.

Kenney, M. and D. Patton (2011), 'Does investor ownership encourage university research-driven entrepreneurship? A six university comparison', *Research Policy*, **40** (8), 1100–112.

Knowles, P. (2011), 'Building a better sandbox', *Exchange*, **28** (5), May, 15–18.
Krashinsky, S. (2011), 'Lighting up the screen for a new generation', *The Globe and Mail*, 19 July, B3.
Lorenzen, M. (2007), 'Social capital and localised learning: proximity and place in technological and institutional dynamics', *Urban Studies*, **44** (4), April, 799–817.
Lowe, N. and M. Feldman (2008), 'Constructing entrepreneurial advantage: consensus building, technological uncertainty and emerging industries', *Cambridge Journal of Regions, Economy and Society*, **1** (2), July, 265–84.
Maskell, P. (2000), 'Social capital, innovation and competitiveness', in S. Baron, J. Field and T. Schuller (eds), *Social Capital*, Oxford, UK: Oxford University Press, pp. 111–23.
Montana, J., A. Reamer, D. Henton, J. Melville and K. Walesh (2001), *Strategic Planning in the Technology-Driven World: A Guidebook for Innovation-Led Development*, Washington, DC: Collaborative Economics and the Economic Development Administration, US Department of Commerce.
Nelles, J. (2009), 'Civic capital and the dynamics of intermunicipal cooperation for regional economic development', unpublished PhD thesis, Department of Political Science: University of Toronto.
Paquet, G. (1997), 'States, communities and markets: the distributed governance scenario', in T.J. Courchene (ed.), *The Evolving Nation-State in a Global Information Era: Policy Challenges*, Kingston: John Deutsch Institute for the Study of Economic Policy, Queens' University, pp. 25–46.
Paquet, G. (1999), *Governance Through Social Learning*, Ottawa: University of Ottawa Press.
Peters, G. and J. Pierre (2004), 'Multi-level governance and democracy: a Faustian bargain?', in I. Bache and M. Flinders (eds), *Multi-Level Governance*, Oxford and New York: Oxford University Press, pp. 73–89.
Porter, M.E., Monitor Group, ontheFRONTIER and Council on Competitiveness (2001), *Clusters of Innovation: Regional Foundations of US Competitiveness*, Washington, DC: Council on Competitiveness.
Potapchuk, W.R. and J.P. Crocker Jr. (1999), 'Exploring the elements of civic capital', *National Civic Review*, **88** (3), Fall, 175–201.
Rhodes, R.A.W. (1996), 'The new governance: governing without government', *Political Studies*, **44**, 652–67.
Rodríguez-Pose, A. (2008), 'The rise of the "city-region" concept and its development policy implications', *European Planning Studies*, **16** (8), September, 1025–46.
Safford, S. (2004a), 'Searching for Silicon Valley in the Rustbelt: the evolution of knowledge networks in Akron and Rochester', Working Paper, Cambridge, MA: MIT Industrial Performance Centre.
Safford, S. (2004b), 'Why the garden club couldn't save Youngstown: civic infrastructure and mobilization in economic crises', Working Paper, Cambridge, MA: MIT Industrial Performance Centre.
Safford, S. (2009), *Why the Garden Club Couldn't Save Youngstown: The Transformation of the Rust Belt*, Cambridge, MA and London, England: Harvard University Press.
Scott, A.J. and M. Storper (1992), 'Regional development reconsidered', in H. Ernste and V. Meier (eds), *Regional Development and Contemporary Industrial Response: Extending Flexible Specialisation*, London and New York: Belhaven Press, pp. 3–24.

Scott, A.J., J. Agnew, E.W. Soja and M. Storper (2001), 'Global city-regions', in A.J. Scott (ed.), *Global City-Regions: Trends, Theory, Policy*, Oxford and New York: Oxford University Press, pp. 11–30.

Simmie, J. (2002), 'Trading places: competitive cities in the global economy', *European Planning Studies*, **10** (2), 201–14.

Simmie, J. and P. Wood (2002), 'Innovation and competitive cities in the global economy: introduction to the special issue', *European Planning Studes*, **10** (2), 149–51.

Wolfe, D.A. (2010), 'From entanglement to alignment: a review of international practice in regional economic development', Mowat Centre for Policy Innovation Paper, Toronto: Mowat Centre for Policy Innovation (www.mowat-centre.ca).

Wolfe, D.A. and A. Bramwell (2008), 'Innovation, creativity and governance: social dynamics of economic performance in city-regions', *Innovation: Management, Policy & Practice*, **10** (2–3), December.

Wolfe, D.A. and M.S. Gertler (2002), 'Innovation and social learning: an introduction', in *Innovation and Social Learning: Institutional Adaptation in an Era of Technological Change*, International Political Economy Series, Houndsmill, Basingstoke: Palgrave Macmillan, pp. 1–24.

Wolfe, D.A. and J. Nelles (2008), 'The role of civic capital and civic associations in cluster policies', in C. Karlsson (ed.), *Handbook of Research on Innovation and Cluster Policies*, Cheltenham, UK and Northampton, MA, USA: Edward Elgar, pp. 374–92.

3. Innovation in cities and innovation by cities

Robert D. Atkinson

Innovation is in vogue. Companies want it. Places want it. Why? It is because the success of companies and places depends on innovation more than ever before. Despite its luster, many public and private sector leaders cannot really define innovation and therefore stumble when trying to encourage or harness it. This chapter suggests four challenges that sub-national places face when it comes to innovation:

1. Understanding the integral link between private sector innovation and public innovation policy in economic development;
2. Understanding that innovation comes in many forms and phases of production and development;
3. Focusing on not just innovation in places, but innovation by places, i.e. states and localities must themselves try new policy approaches, and, finally;
4. Creating partnerships between places, especially local places and the national government.

But before discussing these challenges, this chapter first discusses why places should care about innovation.

WHY SHOULD PLACES CARE ABOUT INNOVATION?

Innovation – the creation and adoption of new products, services, processes, and business models – drives economic development, employment and income growth, and the competitiveness of places, especially high-cost, developed places. As the Organisation for Economic Co-operation and Development (OECD) Secretary-General Angel Gurría commented at the release of the OECD's Innovation Strategy in March 2010 (OECD, 2010a), 'Countries need to harness innovation and entrepreneurship to boost growth and employment, for innovation is the key to a sustainable rise in living standards' (Remarks given at launch of OECD Innovation Strategy, May 2010, 'Economics: Innovation'). He could just as easily and accurately have substituted the word 'places' for 'countries.'

In today's knowledge-based, global economy, innovation is becoming the coin of the realm. In recent years, a growing number of economists have come to see that it is not so much the accumulation of more capital that is the key to improving standards of living; rather it is innovation (Helpmann, 2004). When Klenow and Rodriguez-Clare decomposed the cross-country differences in income per worker into shares that could be attributed to physical capital, human capital, and total factor productivity, they found that more than 90 percent of the variation in the growth of income per worker was a result of how effectively capital is used (that is, innovation), with differences in the actual amount of human and financial capital accounting for just 9 percent (Helpmann, 2004). In other words, it is how capital is used that drives countries' long-term economic growth.

Regional economists have, likewise, found that innovation drives growth at the sub-national level. Porter found that differences in patenting intensity account for 30 percent of the variation across regions in the average wage (Porter, 2003). Likewise, Goldstein found that business patenting and business R&D expenditures support greater gains in regional per-worker earnings (Goldstein and Renault, 2004). One reason why technology industries drive income growth is that average wages in high-tech clusters are $63,970 versus $43,180 in non-high tech clusters (Porter, 2003). One key factor that appears to drive higher incomes in a region is a higher share of employment in knowledge-based industries (Grimes and Glazer, 2004). States with higher concentrations of knowledge-based industries, including professional services and high-tech manufacturing, have higher incomes. Weissbourd found that the percentage of a metropolitan area's earnings in the information sector (e.g., business services, IT) had a positive and significant effect on wage growth (Weissbourd and Berry, 2004). Likewise, using the data in ITIF's The 2007 State New Economy Index report, there was a relatively strong correlation between absolute growth in per-capita income between 1999 and 2005 and the share of workers employed in IT occupations (0.47) and high-tech jobs (0.43) (Atkinson and Correa, 2007). Innovation is also supported and enabled by knowledge workers, which is why there is a strong correlation between the share of knowledge workers, particularly workers with a college degree, and per capita income (Porter, 2003). Weissbourd found that for each 2 percent growth in the proportion of college graduates in a metro area, income growth increased by about 1 percent (Weissbourd and Berry, 2004). Gottlieb found that between 1980 and 1997, the metro areas with the best-educated populations enjoyed per-capita income increases two times greater than metro areas with the less well-educated populations (Gottlieb and Fogarty, 2003). In addition, Erickcek and McKinney (2004) found that places with a higher share of college educated residents experienced a greater increase in per-capital income. Moretti found that raising the overall education level of an area increases the wages of all workers in the area and contributes to economic growth (Moretti, 2004). Likewise, Iranzo and Peri found that the share of the workforce with a college degree is a key factor in explaining state economy productivity (Iranzo and Peri, 2009). Bauer found the same relationship between college degrees and relative per-capita personal income (Bauer et al., 2008).

Higher levels of college education also appear to be related to levels of entrepreneurship, new firm formation, and fast-growing firms. One study of metropolitan areas found that the most entrepreneurial regions possess the highest proportion of the population with a college degree (Advanced Research Technologies, LLC, 2005). And these talented workers are more mobile among metropolitan areas: places that have a high proportion of talented workers and can attract more are better poised for economic growth than other places (Cortright, 2005).

One reason why innovation drives growth is that, on average, innovative industries pay higher wages. In the United States, average compensation per employee in innovation-intensive sectors increased 50 percent between 1990 and 2007 – nearly two and one-half times the national average (Rai et al., 2010). These data lead to one conclusion: higher levels of skills and knowledge of workers and the nature of their activities create a virtuous economic cycle in a given region. This is a major reason why so many places around the world compete so vigorously in the race for global innovation advantage; they want to be the home for the next 1,000 high-paying innovation jobs.

Innovation – the wellspring of that 'gale of creative destruction' of which Schumpeter wrote – achieves its outsize economic impact through two principal channels: first, by empowering productivity improvements and second by spurring new activities (and firms) that create higher value. With regard to the former, over the last decade, in industry after industry, firms have adopted computers and software to streamline operations and boost efficiency. As a result, the production and innovative use of IT has been responsible for at least 50 percent of the acceleration in the growth in U.S. total factor productivity between 1995 and 2008, contributing to a U.S. economy that is approximately two trillion dollars larger in terms of annual GDP than it would be otherwise (Brogan, 2009; Atkinson et al., 2010).

With regard to the latter, innovation empowers the creation of new (and ideally more productive and competitive) firms. This turbulent, dynamic process of firm churn and turnover is a vital source of renewal and growth. (Indeed, if innovation were a coin, the other side of that coin would be change, for the two are inextricably linked.) Innovation's demand for constant renewal holds true at both the firm level and economy level. At the firm level, research by Carl Franklin and Larry Keeley suggests that firms that do not replace at least 10 percent of their revenue stream annually with new products or services are likely to be out of business within five years (Keeley, 2003). The emergence of IT has only accelerated this dynamic, across both IT-producing and IT-consuming industries. As Brynjolfsson writes, 'We see much greater turbulence and volatility in the information industries, reflecting the gale of creative destruction that inevitably accompanies disruptive innovation' (Brynjolfsson and Saunders, 2009, p. x). In fact, this has contributed to a dramatic widening since the mid-1990s in the disparity in profits between the leading firms in industries that use technology intensively. Today, leaders truly benefit from innovation while innovation laggards pay a stiff price.

At the national economy level, there is a well-developed literature of the importance of entrepreneurship on regional growth. One review of 87 separate analyses concluded that entrepreneurs engender a sizeable portion of job creation and productivity growth, and produce and commercialize high quality innovations. In addition, entrepreneurial firms produce important spillovers that affect regional employment growth rates of all companies in the region in the long run (Van Praag and Versloot, 2008).

This role of innovation as a key growth factor is very different from historic models in which containing costs was so central. Today, places can no longer rely solely on old economy strategies of keeping costs low and providing incentives to attract locationally mobile commodity-based branch plants or offices. In fact, even places in the United States that traditionally relied on low costs now have a difficult time competing for facilities producing commodity goods and services against nations whose wage and land costs are less than one-fifth of those in the United States. In part, this is because there is much less per-capita income (and by extension wage) divergence between high and low cost places in the United States. For example, in 1958, Alabama's per-capita income was 69 percent of the U.S. average, making it a choice location for industries seeking lower cost production locations. But by 2007, it was just 84 percent of the U.S. average, reflecting its relative increased costs (Bureau of Economic Analysis). Likewise, North Carolina went from 70 to 87 percent of the U.S average over the same period. But per-capita income divergence between the United States and some developing nations is three to four times higher than it was at its peak in the United States between the average and low cost states. For example, in 1958, Chinese per-capita income was just 5 percent of U.S. levels. And while China has made considerable progress in catching up, by 2009 it was just 18 percent of U.S. levels (Penn World Tables). In other words, wages now vary little within the United States but a lot between the United States and other nations, making it clear that we should stop using low labor costs as an economic development tool.

Because of this, a larger share of places in the United States must look for competitive advantage in earlier-stage product (and service) cycle activities, in activities too complex to be done in countries with less skill and technical capabilities, or in activities that can use technology to achieve robust productivity levels to offset lower labor costs overseas. This can mean either fostering new entrepreneurial activities or helping existing firms move up the value-chain to develop higher-value-added products and services that less developed nations simply can't make, at least not as well. This helps them avoid becoming a commodity producer that is, ultimately, interchangeable with other low cost locations. It also includes helping firms lead in process innovation (to automate production and produce more with fewer workers). In short, regions need to be places where existing firms can become more productive and innovative, where new firms can emerge and thrive, and where locationally mobile establishments want to locate because of the rich innovation environment.

As a result, if places are going to meet the economic challenges of the future they will need to make the promotion of innovation a larger part of their economic development policy framework. Fundamentally, places need to be strategic about what sectors they invest in and what kinds of jobs they want to support. The days of economic development strategies of many states and communities being based on 'shoot anything that flies and claim anything that falls' should be banished to the 20th century. Likewise, in a global economy where low value-added, commodity production of goods or services can gain significant competitive advantage in nations with low wages (and artificially depressed currency valuations), places are fighting a losing battle by competing on the low end.

Places need to design their economic development strategies to support on programs and policies that enable firms to gain the factors of competitive advantage that enable them to compete with commodity producers in low-wage nations. Yet, all too often places have not fully revised their economic strategies and policies to reflect this new world. As I discuss next, this is in part because too many places are guided by the wrong economic development doctrine.

AN 'INNOVATION ECONOMICS' DOCTRINE FOR ECONOMIC DEVELOPMENT

In the last decade, many places have put in place new economic develop-ment policies and programs focused on productivity, innovation, and entrepreneurship. But this change has not come without struggle, and despite making inroads, it is not, by far, the predominant approach to economic development in most places. As Atkinson and Audretsch write, 'Innovation policy has gotten short shrift in the U.S. political dialogue largely because the three dominant economic policy models advocated by most economic advisors – and implicitly held by most policymakers – ignore the role of innovation and technology in achieving economic growth in the global, knowledge-based economy of the 21st century' (Atkinson and Audretsch, 2008, p. 1).

It would be one thing if those involved in the strategic management of places were perfectly objective and relied on analysis to shape policy. Then the challenge would be one of simply presenting the evidence of why innovation is key to the economic success of place. But they are not. Not because of some inherent flaws or limitations, but because economics and economic policy are inherently shaped by doctrine. Indeed, virtually all individuals involved in state economic development policy – whether steeped in economics or not, whether in government or not – hold beliefs or economic doctrines that profoundly shape how they view the economy, what they see as important and not important, and, most importantly, what they believe is, and is not, the correct economic development policy. These doctrines or frameworks guide their thinking and deliberations, and help them make sense of an incredibly complex economy that is changing rapidly. Indeed, as John Maynard Keynes once stated, 'Practical men, who believe themselves to be quite exempt from any intellectual influ-ences, are usually the slaves of some defunct economist' (1964, p. 383).

At the sub-national level, three main economic doctrines compete for the attention and allegiance of state policymakers: the conventional economic development doctrine whose guiding philosophy might be boiled down to 'shoot anything that flies, claim anything that falls;' the neo-classical economics paradigm that eschews economic development incentives and programs in favor of just having low taxes on business and few regulations to create a good business climate; and the populist neo-Keynesianism doctrine that advocates policies to directly improve the lives of workers through measures such as more progressive taxes, higher minimum wages, and public spending. None of these doctrines will lead to a robust innovation-based economic development approach. However, the outline of a fourth doctrine, what can be termed innovation

Creating competitiveness

Table 3.1   Economic development doctrines and economic development policy

	Conventional economic development	Neo-classical business climate	Neo-Keynesian populist	Innovation economics
Source of growth	Capital investment	Capital investment	Worker incomes	Innovation and organizational learning
Principal economic development means	Drive down costs through firm-specific subsidies	Drive down costs through lower taxes and reduced regulations	Drive up wages and benefits and foster more progressive taxes and public spending	Spur firm innovation through targeted supports (e.g., research, financing, skills, etc.) and incentives for firms to produce these themselves
Object of policy	Recruitment of out-of-state firms	Recruitment of out-of-state firms	Small business and socially conscious business	High growth entrepreneurs and existing firms
Quality of life	Minor importance	Not important	High importance	Moderately important to attract and retain knowledge workers
Goal	Get big	Get big	Get fair	Get more prosperous

economics, has emerged, with its focus on spurring innovation and growth from within (InnovationEconomics.org) (Table 3.1).

Conventional Economic Development Doctrine

Emerging from post-World War II practice when the competition between states for increasingly mobile economic assets (usually branch plants of factories) began to heat up, the conventional economic development doctrine (CED) is based on the idea that the best way to grow the economy is to attract (or retain) capital (usually establishments of big, multi-state firms) by making specific deals that include tax breaks, loans, and grants. The idea is that these mobile establishments are seeking the lowest costs, and the job of a state is to put forth the best package to attract them. While CED has evolved in the last several decades to encompass a broader array of concerns, such as workforce development and infrastructure, it is still largely about the art of the low-cost deal at its core.

Neo-Classical Business Climate Doctrine

Neo-classical economists are skeptical of the government's ability to pick winners and costs, and they generally look askance at traditional economic development efforts. Rather, they favor eliminating firm-specific subsidies and using the savings to cut taxes for all firms. Unlike holders of the CED, who see some firms and industries as more important to a state economy than others (e.g., traded firms that export outside the state), holders of the neo-classical business climate doctrine (NCBC) believe that state economic policy should not favor any one firm or sector over another, but should support a good overall business climate. Conservative holders of the NCBC doctrine principally define that as low taxes (and few specific incentives) and limited regulation (Atkins and Dubay, 2006). Liberal holders of the NCBC doctrine usually also oppose firm-specific deals and, instead, favor creating a good business climate for all firms through expanding factor inputs like better K-12 education and transportation infrastructure.

Both the CED and NCBC doctrines provide some useful insights. The CED doctrine is right in that, ultimately, if places are to succeed, they have to care about their economies' sectoral composition and target assistance to particular sectors and firms. This is a key component of increasing a place's wealth. Likewise, the NCBC doctrine is right in that places whose taxes and/or regulatory burdens are very high, and who do not at least offset these burdens with world-class public goods (e.g., education system, transportation, etc.) face a disadvantage relative to other places that, in the long run, will hurt their economic success.

Notwithstanding these positive contributions, in many areas these doctrines serve as a flawed guide to economic policy in the new global, innovation-based economy. First, in the new global economy where routinized economic activities now can be done in other nations with dramatically lower cost structures than even the lowest-cost U.S. state, it makes little sense for places to chase the low-cost tiger. In the neo-classical economics paradigm, most firms were seen as having stable production functions and were seeking to produce at the lowest possible cost by reducing the price of factor inputs (e.g., land, materials, labor, and taxes). Accordingly, firms, markets, and entire economies were seen as existing in a rough equilibrium, albeit one occasionally upset by marginal changes in input prices. If, for example, labor costs increased in a region because of stronger demand, labor-intensive production processes would move to regions with lower labor costs until equilibrium was regained. Because firm decisions were seen as highly responsive to marginal changes in prices, the role for state policy was to keep costs low, including by subsidizing business costs. But, in the new global economy, an increasing share of firms' production functions is anything but stable and routine. Rather, they are characterized by innovation and change. In this environment, firms are looking more to adapt and keep at the leading edge, than to simply eking out a few dollars in production costs by moving a routine facility yet again.

Moreover, low costs are not enough to create competitive advantage for innovation-based firms, especially if they come at the expense of the factors that enable firms to innovate and learn: a good education system, research universities, robust broadband telecommunications, a good quality of life to attract and retain knowledge workers, and a dynamic transportation network. This is not to say that places can blithely ignore costs while putting up with inefficient bureaucracies, unreasonable regulations, and very high levels of taxes. However, believing that low costs and not controlling for public services are the major driver of economic well-being is to miss the realities of the New Economy.

Second, the NCBC and CED both premise their views on the idea that the most important goal in economic development is attracting out-of-state business establishments. As such, they give short shrift to helping existing firms grow and helping new firms start up. In the New Economy, entrepreneurship is much more important to economic success than attracting firms. Consider the fact that the number of industrial manufacturing relocations and significant expansions fell from an average of 5,139 per year between 1995 and 2000 to 3,162 in 2005 (Conway Data, Inc., 1991–2005). Assuming that each of these establishments creates 100 jobs, this means that, in any year, they were responsible for creating around 316,000 new jobs. In contrast, small firms (with fewer than 100 employees) created three times as many (946,000) jobs in 2005 (Bureau of Labor Statistics).

Finally, in a world where competitive advantage is created, not inherited, simply reducing the burden of taxes and regulations provides no assurance that a state's economic structure will evolve in ways that provide it with sustainable advantage. Indeed, there is a very slight negative correlation (−0.04) between the increase in per-capita income growth between 1990 and 2005 and overall tax burden as measured by the Tax

Foundation.[1] In other words, overall state tax climate had no effect on per-capita income growth.[2]

Neo-Keynesian Populism Doctrine

Ultimately, the goal of economic development is not to help business; it is to help state residents, including workers. Helping business is the means through which to accomplish this goal. However, for holders of the neo-Keynesian populist doctrine, helping workers directly is not only the goal, it is the means. As such, they focus more on making sure that the wealth generated in a state goes to the people that need it most. They see most economic development issues as boiling down to a question of who gets the benefits: working people, or rich people and corporations. As such, they favor policies that make the state tax code more progressive, expand unemployment insurance and fund affordable housing. They criticize policies that provide incentives for businesses, even if those incentives are targeted on producing innovation (e.g., R&D tax incentives). To the extent that they promote policies to improve economic development directly, they tend to be focused on policies that achieve progressive ends, such as expanding human capital (e.g., universal pre-K, making college more affordable, and workforce training), spurring 'green' infrastructure, investing in transit and high-speed rail, and limiting corporate tax giveaways (Economic Analysis and Research Network, 2008). To the extent they support business development it is often with a focus on helping particular kinds of individuals (micro-enterprise support, minority- and women-owned businesses) and particular kinds of businesses thought to be socially progressive (e.g., green businesses, worker cooperatives, etc.).

The neo-Keynesian populist doctrine also provides some useful insights. Holders of the doctrine are right to call attention to the real goal of economic development – helping workers – and right to criticize economic development practices that lose sight of that. Likewise, they are right to ensure that business incentives be focused on creating good jobs and right to note that workforce development, infrastructure, and quality of life are key components of economic development.

Notwithstanding these positive contributions, in many areas the doctrine serves as a flawed guide to economic policy. Most importantly, as much as they might want to believe otherwise, places are in competition for economic activity, not just with each other but with other places around the world. As such, this new competition imposes practical limits on how far places can go in redistributing wealth before they reduce their attractiveness for private-sector growth. Second, while neo-Keynesian populists are right to call for greater accountability for corporate incentives, not all corporate incentives are the same. There is a significant difference between a tax break given to a low-wage retail firm and an R&D tax credit used by high-tech firms employing high-wage workers making products exported outside the state. The former is usually a waste of public monies, while the latter is a public investment that generates real economic benefits (Atkinson, 2006). Finally, neo-Keynesians put the cart before the horse, forgetting the fact that the main job of economic development is to help the private sector be prosperous in ways that create good jobs, so that social policy can later redistribute some of these gains.

Innovation Economics Doctrine

Holders of the innovation economics doctrine believe that what ultimately determines economic success in a state is the ability of all institutions (private, non-profit, and government) to innovate and change. Because of this, innovation economics focuses less on issues such as the overall business climate or the number of firm-specific deals and more on policies that can spur firm (and entrepreneur) learning and innovation (Cortright, 2001). As a result, when examining how the economy creates wealth, innovation economics is focused on a different set of questions:

- Are entrepreneurs taking risks to start new ventures?
- Are workers becoming skilled and are companies organizing production in ways that utilize those skills?
- Are companies investing in technological breakthroughs? Is government supporting the technology base (e.g., funding research and the training of scientists and engineers)?
- Are regional clusters of firms and supporting institutions fostering innovation?
- Are research institutions, such as universities, transferring knowledge to companies and individuals?
- Are policymakers avoiding imposing protections for companies against more innovative competitors?
- Do individuals and firms have the right incentives and tools to adequately invest in new ideas and commercialize them?
- Are policies supporting the ubiquitous adoption of advanced information technologies and the broader digital transformation of society and the economy?
- And are state and local economic development efforts organized in ways that fit these new realities?

Moreover, adherents of innovation economics do not believe that low costs alone are enough to drive growth or innovation, rather seeing that low costs can come at the expense of public investments in factors like research universities, infrastructure and worker skills, ultimately leading to less, not more, wealth generation. In addition, because innovation is so important, particularly in export-based firms, they believe that there is a role for government to target policies toward innovation (such as R&D tax credits, technology-focused university-industry research centers, and sector-based regional skills alliances). As such 'distorting' the 'free market' when done in these innovation-promoting and growth-promoting ways is an appropriate use of public action (Atkinson, 2011).

Building on the IE doctrine, a new model of economic development has emerged since 2000, focusing less on attracting routinized branch-plant production facilities to states through targeted tax incentives and more on growing entrepreneurial and innovation-based firms in the state through targeted support for innovation. While this new approach to economic development encompasses 'technology-based economic development' (TBED), it also goes significantly beyond it to integrate a focus on innovation into all economic development activities, including support for manufacturing, skills, industrial recruitment, etc. In short, the new economic development model recognizes the fundamental insight that both innovation and entrepreneurship are key, and that both take place in the context of institutions.

This means that the new economic development focuses much more extensively on promoting technological innovation, supporting dynamic acquisition of workforce skills, spurring entrepreneurship, supporting industry cluster and knowledge networks, and lowering business costs, but in ways that, at the same time, boost quality of life. Innovation economics shift the focus of economic policy toward creating an institutional environment that supports technological change, entrepreneurial drive, and higher skills.

This is not to say that some of the insights generated by the other three doctrines are not important. Nor is it to say that simply creating science and technology programs is enough to succeed. It is to say, though, that, ultimately, places will do better if their policies are guided by an innovation economics doctrine, since it better suits the new global economic realities faced by places.

While some may dismiss this discussion of doctrines as ethereal and irrelevant, getting the underlying doctrine or world view is, in fact, critical to getting the right policies and programs in place. For, while the coach may call the plays, the playbook lays out his choices. And the current playbooks in places now limit the plays that the coach (economic policymakers) can call (OECD, 2007). So what are some of the plays and strategies a coach with the innovation economics playbook would use? That is the subject of the next section.

CONCEIVING OF INNOVATION HOLISTICALLY

Innovation has become a central driver of national, regional and local economic wellbeing and competitiveness – and this is why so many places are engaged in the race for global innovation advantage. But to maximize innovation-based economic development, places need to understand and embrace an accurate and holistic definition of innovation. Innovation is a mindset, a philosophy and approach to doing things as much as it is a technical improvement to a new electronic gadget. For too many involved in spurring innovation in places, innovation has been understood in an engineering context, entailing either the creation of new or improved goods, such as the original iPod or its brethren, or enhanced machines or devices, such as lasers or the computer-controlled machine tools by which products are manufactured. In this context, it is often conceived of as something that pertains only to the R&D activity going on at universities, national laboratories, or corporations.

While that is all true, it is much too limiting. Innovation is not just about shiny new products, R&D, and technology, it is about much more. The OECD defines innovation as, 'the implementation of a new or significantly improved product (that is, a physical good or service), process, a new marketing method, or a new organizational method in business practices, workplace organization, or external relations,' (OECD, 2010b, p. 1: Box 1 Key Findings). Indeed, innovation in services has become increasingly important, as service industries now account for more than 80 percent of the U.S. economy (Tekes, 2007). Thus, the understanding of innovation has broadened from a purely scientific and technical focus to include the application of information technologies, evolution of new business models, and creation of new customer experience or service delivery approaches that have transformed virtually all service sectors, from retail, logistics, and hospitality to health care, professional services, and financial services.

Innovations can also arise at many different points in the innovation process, including conception/ideation, research and development, transfer (the shift of the 'technology' to the production organization), production and deployment, or marketplace usage. By definition, all innovations must contain a degree of novelty, whether that novelty is new to the firm, new to the market, or new to the world. It is also important to remember

Table 3.2   The innovation value chain

		Phase of development		
		Conception	Research & development	Transfer	Production/Usage deployment
Type of innovation	Products				
	Services				
	Production process				
	Organizational models				
	Business model				

that an innovation is not just anything new; it must also constitute a viable business concept. Table 3.2 charts the dimensions of potential innovation opportunity in the innovation value chain, revealing implications for both companies and countries alike.

Thus, properly conceived an innovation agenda benefits workers, firms, and regions that depend on manufacturing as well as those that depend on information technology and high school and community college graduates as well as PhDs. Properly conceived, innovation is not just about creating more jobs for engineers and managers in high-technology industries. It is also about providing more and better training for incumbent workers in manufacturing and 'low-tech' services and reorganizing work processes so that their companies can perform better.

Unfortunately, when officials in many places hear the word innovation they think high-tech industry. In fact, many places focus even more narrowly on just a few 'popular' technology industries, particularly ones like biotechnology and clean energy. Too many places want to be the next big hub for a particular industry. Yet, as Cortright argues, not every place can be a biotech hub, for example (Cortright and Mayer, 2002). Places would be better off focusing on a broad range of innovation phases, including helping firms use new process technologies and develop new business models.

INNOVATION BY PLACES

At both the national and regional levels there is increasing evidence that growth is driven by innovation, not by capital accumulation (Easterly and Levine, 2001). The implication for economic development in places is both straightforward and profound. Lower costs and capital attraction can no longer be the principal source of a place's long-term growth. Instead, places need to ensure that their economic environment is conducive to supporting technological change, entrepreneurial drive, and higher skills. This new model of economic development is grounded in the view that it is only through actions taken by workers, companies, industry consortia, entrepreneurs, research institutions, civic organizations, and governments that an economy's productive and innovative power is enhanced.

The keys to success in the new economy now and into the future appear clear: supporting a knowledge infrastructure (world class education and training); spurring innovation (indirectly through universities and directly by helping companies); and encouraging entrepreneurship. Much has been written on this, but places cannot effectively drive an innovation economy if they are not also spurring institutional innovation. In other words, innovation by places is key for innovation in places. Success in the new economy requires that a whole array of institutions – universities, school boards, firms, local governments, economic development agencies – work in new and often uncomfortable ways. At the end of the day, this is a challenge of leadership. Places with leaders who challenge their institutions and businesses, as well as following through with bold new policies focused on innovation, learning, and constant adaptation, will be the ones that succeed and prosper.

Institutional innovation is important because, while the U.S. economy has undergone a transformation to a technology-driven, global new economy, many of its institutions and governing structures have not. This is not unique. Throughout America's history there is a lag between the speed of technological transformation and the corresponding institutional, cultural, political, societal, and individual transformation. Scientists, engineers, and entrepreneurs are often driven to change the world through rapid development of new technologies and development of new business models. The rest of society takes longer to catch up, being committed to old ways of doing things, old investments, old skills, old institutional arrangements, and old attitudes. As a result, during periods when a new techno-economic system is emerging, organizations, institutions, laws, governments, the built environment, and attitudes and culture lag behind. Christopher Freeman notes that as the new technology system emerges, it produces 'major structural crises of adjustment, in which social and economic changes are necessary to bring about a better match between the new technology and the system of social management of the economy' (Freeman and Perez, 1988, p. 38).

If places are to meet these challenges of creating more innovation-based economies, they will need to include 'institutional innovation.' The scope for such far reaching and fundamental innovation is wide ranging, including areas such as transportation, education and training, health care, land use planning and zoning, regulation, transportation and the organization of local government.

Create Different and Better Primary and Secondary Education

States and cities have been focusing on improving K-12 education since the early 1990s because they recognized the importance of higher skills to regional economic success. Yet, the results have been largely disappointing. High schools are unable to retain as many as one in four students through to graduation. Nearly half of the dropouts cite boredom and lack of interest in classes, which is no small surprise since most students have little choice in what they learn as the system is designed for standardization and must, by its inherent nature, ignore the individual needs of individual students (Christensen et al., 2008). Moreover, even the students who do graduate are not well prepared. In one survey, firms reported that 60 percent of applicants with a high school degree or GED were poorly prepared for an entry level job (Lerman, 2008). Respondents to a Conference Board survey rated high school graduates as 'deficient' in 10 skills (including written communications, critical thinking and team work) and excellent in none.

Perhaps it should not be surprising that K-12 'reform' has fallen short of expectations, given that most of it has been not so much about reform but about doing more of the same. Most of the efforts to date have been to get traditional schools to do better, usually by making them more rigorous: more core courses, more standards, more high stakes tests, more hours in the school year, more homework, more teachers getting more pay, and better textbooks. And this all takes place within a K-12 framework premised on standardized curricula, little choice for students, and a focus on being taught particular academic subjects (some with dubious relevance to actual careers).

So long as this is the principal strategy there is little room for innovation; for testing and developing new forms of school and schooling. Rather schools need to move to student-centered, customized learning with a focus on skills rather than on mastering any particular academic content. Success now depends on finding new forms of school and schooling, and in particular shifting education away from its mass production model to a mass-customization model.

This means that states will need to take a risk on embracing fundamental innovation or, in the words of Harvard Business School's Clayton Christensen, policymakers will need to embrace disruptive innovation.

Given the largely poor experience of incumbent businesses at responding to innovation, the likelihood of the existing education sector embracing disruptive innovation is not great. As a result, it is time for places to focus on creating real alternatives. As Ted Kolderie, a founder of the national charter school movement and leader of Education Evolving, argues, 'If the district sector does not – cannot or will not – produce the schools we need then the states will have to get somebody else who will' (Kolderie, 2004, p. 7). In other words, states need to work not only to improve existing schools, but also on creating new entities that will create different and better schools. In short, a one-bet strategy that only tries to change existing schools will not work.

While there are new models popping up that present an alternative to conventional schools, the trend is actually the other way with all schools becoming more alike, all following the academic instruction, test-based model. As a result, states need to work aggressively to provide a wide array of educational options: career academies in high schools, charter schools, vouchers, specialty math and science high schools, entrepreneurial education, and project-based learning high schools (The National Foundation for Teaching Entrepreneurship, 2008). One promising approach, which not only more closely resembles real work life but is often more intrinsically interesting to students, is project-based learning. Rather than focus on 'teaching' every child the exact same information, the focus is on letting students learn in areas that interest them and organized around project-based learning. Perhaps the leading example of this today is Minnesota's New Country School, a public charter school that describes itself, and project-based learning, as

> based upon the idea that students will be most engaged in the learning process when they have a personal interest in what they are learning. Instead of sitting in a teacher-driven classroom all day long, students learn through the exploration of topics that interest them on their own terms, and largely at their own pace. Each student is a member of a team of 12–20 students, managed by an adult advisor who helps to facilitate the learning process. Instead of grades, students receive credit for their work . . .. The process is completely flexible, and can be tailored towards specific learning styles, prior student knowledge, student motivation, etc. (Minnesota New Country School, 2008, page: What is Project Based Learning)

But this is just one type of institutional learning innovation. Another example is Project Lead the Way, which offers engineering and biomedical science curriculum in over 1,500 high schools, often through career and technical education programs (Project Lead the Way, 2008). The program focuses on these two substantive areas, but also on learning how to work as a contributing member of a team; lead a team; use appropriate written and/or visual mediums to communicate with a wide variety of audiences; public speaking; listening to the needs and ideas of others; thinking and problem solving; managing time, resources and projects; researching, data collection and analysis; and going beyond the classroom for answers.

Another approach is to establish high schools with an emphasis on mathematics, science and technology. A number of states have developed such schools, such as the North Carolina School for Science and Mathematics, the Illinois Mathematics and Science Academy, and the Thomas Jefferson High School in Virginia. Texas's T-STEM (Science, Technology, Engineering and Mathematics) initiative seeks to create specialty STEM high school academies throughout the state. These schools are a powerful tool for producing high school graduates with a deep knowledge and strong passion for science and math that translates into much higher rates of college attendance and graduation in scientific fields (Atkinson et al., 2007).

The point is that if places are to make real progress in education, it is time to fundamentally rethink the current model and provide a wide array of types of schools and learning environments. Doing so will take leadership and vision on the part of policymakers.

Create Stronger Incentives for Higher Education to be a Partner in Regional Innovation

A key part of many regions' innovation infrastructure is colleges and universities. In an economy more dependent on innovation, universities and colleges are playing a more active role in spurring innovation and commercialization. Between 1994 and 2004, licensing income increased from $1.96 million per university to $7.06 million, while university-based start-ups increased from 212 in 1994 to 510 in 2007 (AUTM U.S. Survey, Statistics and Metrics Committee, 2004). Further, the number of patent applications filed by universities in the United States increased from 7,200 in 2003 to 11,000 in 2007. And university R&D, as a share of GDP, has increased from 0.055 percent in 1995 to 0.075 percent in 2008 (National Science Foundation). Because of this key role, many places have instituted a range of programs (e.g., research centers of excellence, industry–university grant programs) to spur universities and colleges to be more engaged in economic development. Still other ideas have been proposed, including letting faculty bypass tech transfer offices, letting faculty entrepreneurship count toward their service requirements, and letting successful patent applications count as publications for tenure review purposes (Litan et al., 2007). While these programs are often worthwhile, they do not go to the heart of the problem: higher education and places have different missions and goals. Faculty members are rewarded more for publishing than for working with industry or commercializing discoveries.[3] And to the extent that universities are concerned about knowledge transfer, they are largely focused on maximizing revenues, not enhancing in-state economic growth.

If places are to better align the mission of higher education with state economic development goals, they need to consider more systemic approaches. One is to tie a portion of states' higher education funding to the success of individual institutions at meeting the places' economic development goals. These goals might include doing research related to key industry clusters, providing technical assistance to companies in the region, and transferring technology to companies. Universities and colleges that do well in meeting these goals relative to others would receive a larger share of state funding.

The key to success for such a system would be to develop the right performance metrics. These metrics might include patents received, licensing income, technical assistance provided to industry, and others. One important metric is a university's success in obtaining industry funding. A company's willingness to fund research or license technologies is perhaps the clearest measure of industrial relevance. States might provide public state universities and colleges with one dollar of state funding for every dollar from out-of-state firms and two dollars for every dollar from in-state firms.

One limitation of this metric is that smaller and younger firms are likely to have a harder time generating the funds to support academic research or license intellectual property. States could address this issue in one of two ways. They could establish matching grant programs for small firms along the lines of Maryland's Industrial Partnerships (MIPS) program, Connecticut's Yankee Ingenuity program, and Pennsylvania's Ben Franklin Partnership Programs. For example, MIPS provides funding, matched by participating companies, for university-based research projects that help companies develop new products or solve technical challenges.

A related program is Kentucky's research and development voucher program. The program, which has been copied by Georgia, North Carolina and Puerto Rico, provides a repayable voucher to Kentucky firms that invest in universities in Kentucky to commercialize technology. Firms must invest, in cash and in-kind, one dollar for every dollar of state funds. Alternatively, states could create a more generous R&D tax credit for expenditures by firms at universities, with small firms eligible for a more generous credit (e.g., 50 percent) (Atkinson and Correa, 2007).

The advantage of a performance-based approach is that it would be up to universities and colleges to figure out the best way to be more relevant to the state's economy. Universities might establish external advisory councils made up of industry leaders to provide insight into research trends and entrepreneurial activities. They might make it easier for faculty to work with industry or start new companies. They might streamline intellectual property procedures to make it easier to commercialize innovations. But the bottom line is that universities and colleges would have a much stronger motivation to be more effective economic development partners.

Places should also create new kinds of institutional arrangements to produce trained workers better suited for the innovation economy. Instead of just reflectively spurring more enrollment in higher education, states should focus their efforts much more on expanding apprenticeship programs, school-to-work programs, industry-skills alliances, tax credits for employer-based training, and employer-community college partnerships. A number of states have moved in this direction. Wisconsin and Georgia have strong youth apprenticeship programs. A number of states and local school districts have established career academies within high schools. A number of states have established regional skills alliances – industry-led partnerships that address workforce needs in a specific region and industry sector (NGA Center for Best Practice, 2006). Michigan has provided competitively awarded start-up grants and technical assistance to 25 industry-led regional skills alliances. Pennsylvania's $15 million Industry Partnerships program brings together multiple employers, and workers or worker representatives when appropriate, in the same industry cluster to address overlapping human capital needs. In addition, Pennsylvania has supported a number of specialized industry-led training institutes, such as the Precision Manufacturing Institute, the Advanced Skills Center, and New Century Careers (Precision Manufacturing Institute and William F. Goodling Regional ASC). Other states have established tax credits for company investments in workforce development. California has a deduction for training expenses if a company has spent a certain share of sales on training. Firms in Rhode Island can deduct up to 50 percent of training costs on their corporate income taxes (Rhode Island Economic Development Corporation).

Places should also be focusing on spurring innovation within universities in terms of how pedagogy is organized. Take the case of engineering education. Almost two decades ago a small cadre of visionaries from the corporate and academic sectors got together to examine the state of U.S. engineering education. What they saw gave them pause. Too much of engineering education was rooted in a model of teaching and research that was over one hundred years old. This didn't help students become engineering innovators, nor did it effectively link engineering to businesses. Given the increasingly global and collaborative nature of engineering, this cadre began urging the addition to engineering curricula of teamwork, project-based learning, entrepreneurial thinking, and communication skills, as well as a greater emphasis on social needs and human factors in engineering design.

In 1997, an entirely new college was created in the suburbs of Boston to put that vision into practice. The Franklin W. Olin College of Engineering was created as a highly selective, undergraduate engineering institution designed to prepare students 'to become exemplary engineering innovators who recognize needs, design solutions, and engage in creative enterprises for the good of the world' (Franklin W. Olin College of Engineering Mission Statement). But the founders of Olin realized that they had to completely change the model of engineering education for this to work. They started with perhaps the most radical change: doing away with academic departments and faculty tenure. They made a commitment to diversity with the result that 44 percent of their all-engineering student body is female, compared to approximately 20 percent nationally, and 17 percent is accounted for by minorities. They decided that engineering education had to be interdisciplinary and integrated with hands-on learning and research opportunities for students.

By all measures, Olin has been a tremendous model of institutional innovation. Approximately 80 percent of Olin graduates go into STEM fields; 25 percent of Olin graduates are involved in start-up entrepreneurial enterprises (either full- or part-time), with 10 percent starting their own enterprises. Moreover, on the National Survey on Student Engagement (NSSE), which assembles annual data from first- and senior-year students attending hundreds of colleges and universities, Olin's 'Active and Collaborative Learning' Benchmark Score is among the highest in the nation. Employers of Olin graduates see them as exceptional.

If we want to win the innovation race, it is not enough to create just one Olin, we need hundreds, not only for engineering education, but in area after area of American society: K-12 education, health care, university technology transfer, transportation, electric utilities, government services, social services, etc. Over the years these institutions have become stagnant, bogged down by the weight of convention, tradition, and inertia. We need to be engaged in systemic innovation in our institutions, trying many experiments and widely adopting the ones that work (just like the private sector does). Most importantly, this means that our conception of innovation policy needs to be broadened from its conventional focus on science and technology to include institutions.

CAN PLACES WIN THE INNOVATION RACE ON THEIR OWN?

No man is an island, and no place – city, state, or even nation – can succeed on its own, regardless of how innovative it is. This is particularly true for states and cities. Many in Washington are enamored with the idea of states and cities as the laboratories of democracy for innovation policy, largely because they can be pro-innovation policy without having to embrace federal innovation policy, which may, heaven forbid, look and sound like the dreaded 'industrial policy.' But it is a dangerous illusion to believe that state or city policy actions alone can solve the U.S. competitiveness and innovation challenge. Likewise it is an equally dangerous illusion that places can succeed without a robust national innovation policy.

Unless the federal government develops an effective national innovation and competitiveness strategy, all the state and city actions in the world will not be enough. State and city economic development policies play a necessary, but not sufficient role in national competitiveness. Addressing the competitiveness challenge will require considerably more public investment than states and cities can afford. The resources available to the federal government, even in an era of budget deficits, are considerably more than those available to the states and cities combined. While states might invest several billion dollars in R&D, the federal government annually invests upwards of $70 billion and much of what sub-national places do to spur innovation involves building on this key federal innovation infrastructure. Moreover, while some states provide R&D tax credits and other tax incentives for innovation, federal corporate tax rate incentives for innovation are multiple times greater.

To date, unfortunately, the discussion of the sub-national and federal roles in competitiveness has largely kept them separate. Sub-national governments do their thing while the feds do another. Sub-national governments don't spend time supporting broad collective action (e.g. a robust federal innovation policy); they are too worried about making sure they remain competitive. And with a few exceptions (such as the Economic Development Administration, NIST's Manufacturing Extension Partnership) the federal government largely ignores innovation in places. As such it is time for a new state–federal partnership for innovation and competitiveness.

Both parties bring valuable resources to the table. The federal government is able to marshal resources and drive incentives so that state actions benefit the entire nation, rather than simply redistributing economic resources within the nation. But in an economy where economic policy increasingly must focus on firms, industries, and knowledge-enhancing institutions, as opposed to simply managing the business cycle, states are ideally situated as they are closer to firms, especially small and medium-sized enterprises, and have more control over some innovation infrastructure inputs (such as public higher education).

However, an effective partnership will not be possible unless the federal government begins to see states and regions as important partners. All too often the feds believe that there is one uniform national economy where regional agglomerations are a side show at best. Moreover, to the extent states and regions even have a policy role, it is too often to follow the federal government's lead. A true partnership will require that federal decision makers and program managers understand that states and regions can play an important role and that a top-down, one-size-fits-all federal approach will only stifle the most important role states and regions can play: generating policy innovations and developing policies and operating programs suited to the unique requirements of their regional economies. Given this new understanding, the federal government should expand support for key programs such as the Manufacturing Extension Partnership, the Small Business Innovation Research Program, the Small Business Investment Company Program, and the Technology Innovation Program and create new kinds of industry–university research centers modeled after the German Fraunhofer Institutes (ITIF, 2011).

But even if sub-national places had a real partner in innovation policy in Washington, it would still not be enough. Every place and every globally traded firm faces competition, not just from other places and traded firms, whether within the borders, or elsewhere in the world. To take a recent case, consider the solar energy company, Evergreen Solar, which went bankrupt in 2011. A Massachusetts company that was seen, not just by Massachusetts policymakers but also federal policymakers, as representative of the new fast-growing clean energy economy, Evergreen was provided by the state of Massachusetts with over $40 million in subsidies to build a production facility in the state. However, faced with competition from China, Evergreen shut their plant, eliminating over 800 jobs. It planned to keep open its factory in China, built with a $33 million investment by the local Chinese government. But even with help from Massachusetts and from China, Evergreen couldn't compete with Chinese solar producers who have seen their share of the global market for solar energy soar from 5 to 50 percent between 2001 and 2011. It is not because Evergreen was not an innovative company or because Chinese companies were more innovative. Certainly a major reason for the bankruptcy of Evergreen was that the Chinese government is engaged in massive 'innovation mercantilism,' providing a wide array of subsidies for their solar energy producers, including free electricity, low cost land, cash subsidies, and government procurement preferences. And on top of that Chinese solar producers and all Chinese exporters benefit from at least a 40 percent subsidy on exported products in the form of an undervalued Renminbi currency. As the *Boston Globe* wrote: 'What gave the state's investment in Evergreen Solar its air of futility wasn't the folly of developing solar-energy technology in Massachusetts; it was the idea that little Massachusetts, with its handful of millions in economic-development resources, could compete against China by itself' (*Boston Globe*, 2011). Indeed.

When a country like China is that committed to winning in a key innovation-based industry and is willing and able to engage in a wide array of mercantilist practices, some of which violate global trade agreements, no matter how good the innovation policies of places are, they will not lead to innovation activity. It is only if the federal government takes aggressive and sustained action to combat innovation mercantilism that sub-national places will stand a fighting chance. Helping places win the race for global innovation advantage will require action directed abroad to dramatically reduce unfair and protectionist foreign trade practices. Only the federal government can prosecute a more proactive trade policy that fights foreign mercantilist actions, including currency manipulation, closed markets, intellectual property theft, standards manipulation, high tariffs, forced offsets for market access, and other unfair trading practices (Atkinson and Ezell, 2012).

This gets at what sub-national places should be doing to most effectively spur innovation-based growth in their economies. The most effective action they can take is not to create a new program or policy to generate innovation-based economic activity within their boundaries; it is to educate and lobby Washington on why it has to develop a comprehensive national innovation policy that includes help for sub-national regions.

CONCLUSION

While there are people, companies and public servants all over the country who 'get' the importance of innovation, as a nation the United States does not have a coherent understanding of what innovation is, why it is important to economic development and how to drive innovation with innovation public policy. It has become obvious that successful management of places requires enabling robust levels of innovation in places. But most places are a long way from achieving that goal. They face an array of challenges, such as improving education and worker skill levels, investing in R&D, overcoming established business practices and forging stronger public-private partnerships. Even if they master them all, this is no assurance of success. But without mastering the challenges success is even less likely. Places need to recognize that the economic development 'playbook' they rely on needs to be updated to reflect the new realities of the global innovation race. The tattered playbook of cutting costs and simply letting the market work its magic needs to be tossed aside. Winning the race will require robust 'innovation in innovation policy' – that is, creating new approaches to how places spur innovation. Finally, sub-national places need to recognize that they are not just competing against other places in the United States, or even other places around the world, but rather other sub-national places backed by their national governments. Just as Boeing is competing against China and the Chinese government, San Diego is competing against Shanghai and the Chinese government. Places should no longer assume they can win the race for global innovation advantage on their own and should recognize they are competing against robust national-local partnerships. Places not only need to overhaul their policies, but they must also insist upon regional and national policies that support the overhaul.

NOTES

1. The actual correlation is positive, but a high score on the Tax Foundation index represents low taxes and vice versa. In this regard, there is a negative correlation between per-capita income growth and low taxes.
2. Perhaps one reason for this result is that the Tax Foundation index does not measure actual tax burden, but rather measures like tax rate. In other words, it simply assumes that states with higher rates but more deductions (for example, the R&D credit) are worse than states with lower rates and no deductions. But, from the perspective of the firm, they are the same in terms of amount of taxes paid.
3. For example, Dean Richard Schmalensee of MIT's Sloan School of Management writes that 'Unfortunately, under the current academic reward system, what matters most is having an impact among peers, mainly by getting specialized research published in influential journals. The [university] system isn't designed to evaluate or reward someone who invests significant time in the field learning about industry X and working on its problems, even though that investment may produce a superb observer of what's happening in the field who then brings that direct knowledge to bear on both their teaching and research' (Schmalensee, 2006).

BIBLIOGRAPHY

Advanced Research Technologies, LLC (2005), *The Innovation-Entrepreneurship NEXUS: A National Assessment of Entrepreneurship and Regional Economic Growth and Development*, SBA Office of Advocacy/Edward Lowe Foundation, http://www.sba.gov/advo/research/rs256tot.pdf.
Atkins, C. and C.S. Dubay (2006), *State Business Tax Climate Index*, Washington,

DC: Tax Foundation, 4th edn, http://www.taxfoundation.org/research/show/78. html.

Atkinson, R.D. (2006), 'The research and experimentation tax credit: a critical policy tool for boosting research and enhancing U.S. economic competitiveness', Washington, DC: ITIF, http://www.itif.org/files/R&DTaxCredit.pdf.

Atkinson, R.D. (2011), 'Hearing on tax policy and the high-tech sector,' Testimony Before the California Assembly Committee on Revenue & Taxation, California Congress, http://www.itif.org/files/2011-tax-policy-high-tech-testimony.pdf.

Atkinson, R.D. and D. Audretsch (2008), 'Economic policy and policy differences: why Washington cannot agree on economic policies', Washington, DC: ITIF, http://www.itif.org/files/ EconomicDoctrine.pdf.

Atkinson, R.D. and D.K. Correa (2007), 'The 2007 State New Economy Index: benchmarking economic transformation in the States', Washington, DC: ITIF, http://www.itif.org/files/2007_State_New_ Economy_ Index.pdf.

Atkinson, R.D. and S. Ezell (2012), *Innovation Economics: The Race for Global Advantage*, New Haven, CT: Yale University Press.

Atkinson, R.D., D. Lundgren, M.J. Shapiro, J. Thomas and J. Hugo (2007), 'Addressing the STEM challenge by expanding specialty math and science high schools,' Washington, DC: ITIF, http://www.itif.org/files/STEM.pdf.

Atkinson, R.D., S. Ezell, S.M. Andes, D. Castro and R. Bennett (2010), 'The internet economy 25 years after.com', available at http://www.itif.org/publications/internet-economy-25-years-after-com.

AUTM U.S. Survey, Statistics and Metrics Committee (2004), *AUTM U.S. Licensing Survey: FY 2004*, 16, 24, 28, http://www.autm.org/events/File/04 AUTMSurveySum-USpublic.pdf.

Bauer, P.W., M.E. Schweitzer and S. Shane (2008), *Knowledge Matters: The Long-Run Determinants of State Income Growth*, Washington, DC: Southern Economic Association.

Boston Globe (2011), 'Evergreen Solar's failure shows US weakness in clean energy', editorial, August 18. http://articles.boston.com/2011-08-18/boston-globe/29901685_1_clean-energy-evergreen-solar-renewable-energy (accessed April 19, 2012).

Brogan, P. (2009), 'The economic benefits of broadband and information technology', *Media Law and Policy*, **18**.

Brynjolfsson, E. and A. Saunders (2009), *Wired for Innovation*, Cambridge, MA: MIT Press.

Bureau of Economic Analysis, *Regional Income Accounts*.

Bureau of Labor Statistics, *Business Employment Dynamics*.

Christensen, C.M., C.W. Johnson and M.B. Horn (2008), *Disrupting Class: How Disruptive Innovation Will Change the Way the World Learns*, New York: McGraw Hill.

Conway Data, Inc. (1991–2005), *Year-to-Date New Plant Report*.

Cortright, J. (2001), 'New growth theory, technology and learning: a practitioner's guide', Reviews of Economic Development Literature and Practice 4, U.S. Economic Development Administration, http://www.eda.gov/Image Cache/EDAPublic/documents/pdfdocs/1g3lr_5f7_5fcortright_2epdf/v1/1g3lr_5f7 _5fcortright.pdf.

Cortright, J. (2005), 'The young and restless in a knowledge economy', CEOs for Cities, http://www.ceosforcities.org/rethink/research/files/CEOs_YNR_ FINAL.pdf.

Cortright, J. and H. Mayer (2002), *Signs of Life: The Growth of Biotechnology Centers in the U.S.*, Washington, DC: Brookings Institution, http://www.brookings.edu/reports/2002/06_biotechnology_cortright.aspx.

Easterly, W. and R. Levine (2001), 'It's not factor accumulation: stylized facts and growth models', *World Bank Economic Review*, **15**, 177–219.

Economic Analysis and Research Network, *Economic Development*, (accessed 23 September 2008), http://www.earncentral.org/economic-development.htm.

Erickcek, G.A. and H. McKinney (2004), 'Small cities blues: looking for growth factors in small and medium-sized cities', Upjohn Institute for Employment Research, http://www.upjohninst.org/publications/wp/04-100.pdf.

Franklin, C. (2003), *Why Innovation Fails*, London: Spiro.

Franklin W. Olin College of Engineering Website (2012) *About Olin: Overview*, http://www.olin.edu/about_olin/default.aspx. Accessed April 19, 2012.

Freeman, C. and C. Perez (1988), 'Structural crises of adjustment, business cycles and investment behavior', in G. Dosi, C. Freeman, R. Nelson, G. Silverberg and L. Soete (eds), *Technical Change and Economic Theory*, London: Pinter, pp. 38–66.

Goldstein, H.A. and C.S. Renault (2004), 'Estimating universities' contributions to regional economic development: the case of the U.S.', in *Spillovers and Innovations: City, Environment and the Economy*, Vienna, Austria: Springer-Verlag.

Gottlieb, P.D. and M. Fogarty (2003), 'Educational attainment and metropolitan growth,' in *Economic Development Quarterly*, **17** (4), 325–36.

Grimes, D. and L. Glazer (2004), *A New Path to Prosperity? Manufacturing and Knowledge-Based Industries as Drivers of Economic Growth*, Ann Arbor, MI: Michigan Future Inc. & University of Michigan.

Helpmann, E. (2004), *The Mystery of Economic Growth*, Cambridge, MA: Belknap Press, p. 32.

Iranzo, S. and G. Peri (2009), 'Schooling externalities, technology and productivity: theory and evidence from U.S. states', *Review of Economics and Statistics*, **91** (2), 420–31.

ITIF (2011), *Boosting Competitiveness by Connecting Science and Industry: Insights from Germany's Innovation Model*, Washington, DC, ITIF, http://www.itif.org/media/ boosting-competitiveness-connecting-science-and-industry-insights-germanys-innovation-model#video.

Keeley, L. (2003), 'Innovation heats up', presentation given at Taming of the New workshop, Chicago, IL, USA.

Keeley, L. (2007), *The taming of the new: Larry Keeley workshop on innovation*, Seattle: Puget Sound SIGCHI.

Keynes, John Maynard (1964), *The General Theory*, New York: Harcourt Brace and World.

Kolderie, Ted (2004), *Creating the Capacity for Change: How and Why Governors and Legislatures are Opening a New-Schools Sector in Public Education*, Education Week Press.

Lerman, R. (2008), 'Are skills the problem? Reforming the education and training system in the United States', in *A Future of Good Jobs?*, Kalamazoo, Mich.: W.E. Upjohn Institute for Employment Research.

Litan, R.E., L. Mitchell and E.J. Reedy (2007), 'Commercializing university innovations: alternative approaches', Working Paper Series, http://papers.ssrn.com/sol3/papers.cfm?abstract_id=976005.

Minnesota New Country School Website (accessed 19 April 2012), http://www. newcountryschool.com/.

Moretti, E. (2004), 'Estimating the social return to higher education: evidence from longitudinal and repeated cross-sectional data', *Journal of Econometrics*, **121**, Los Angeles, CA: Department of Economics, UCLA, 175–212.

National Foundation for Teaching Entrepreneurship website (accessed 23 September 2008), http://www.nfte.com/whatwedo/programs/.

National Science Foundation, *Science Indicators*.

NGA Center for Best Practices (2006), 'State sector strategies: regional solutions to worker and employer needs', Washington, DC.

OECD (2007), *OECD Science, Technology and Industry Scoreboard 2007: Innovation and Performance in the Global Economy*, Paris: OECD.

OECD (2010a), *The OECD Innovation Strategy*, Paris: OECD, 20, http://www. oecd.org/ document/15/0,3343,en_2649_34273_45154895_1_1_1,00.html.

OECD (2010b), *Economics: Innovation Central to Boosting Growth and Jobs*, http:// www.oecd.org/document/36/0,3343,en_2649_34273_45324068_1_1_1_1, 00.html.

Penn World Tables, http://pwt.econ.upenn.edu/php_site/pwt_index.php.

Porter, M.E. (2003), 'The economic performance of regions', *Regional Studies*, **37** (6–7), 553–64.

Precision Manufacturing Institute Website, http://www.pmionline.edu/.

Project Lead the Way website (accessed 23 September 2008), http://www.pltw.org/ index.cfm.

Rai, A., S. Graham and M. Doms (2010), 'Patent reform: unleashing innovation, promoting economic growth, and producing high-paying jobs', Department of Commerce, 1, http://2001-2009.commerce.gov/s/groups/public/@doc/@os/@ opa/documents/content/prod01_009147.pdf.

Rhode Island Economic Development Corporation, *Workforce Development*, http://www.riedc.com/riedc/business_services/6/.

Schmalensee, Richard (2006), 'Where's the "B" in B-Schools?', *Business Week*, 27 November. http://www.businessweek.com/magazine/content/06_48/b4011120. htm (accessed April 19, 2012).

Tekes (2007), 'Seizing the white space: innovative service concepts in the United States', *Technology Review* (205), 72–4, http://www.tekes.fi/en/document/43000/ innovative_service_pdf.

Van Praag, M. and P.H. Versloot (2008), 'The economic benefits and costs of entrepreneurship: a review of the research', *Foundations and Trends in Entrepreneurship*, **4** (2), 65–154.

Weissbourd, R. and C. Berry (2004), 'The changing dynamics of urban America', RW Ventures, *CEOs for Cities*, 32.

William F. Goodling Regional ASC Website, http://www.advskills.org/index. html; New Century Careers Website, http://www.ncsquared.com.

4. The strategic recombination of regional innovative capacities: public–private institutions as knowledge bridges

Gerald A. McDermott

Just how a region or state improves the international competitiveness of its firms is nowhere more prescient and challenging than in the emerging market countries, where the norm is often being stuck in some sort of long-term low equilibrium trap. For the past 20 years, scholars and policymakers alike have increasingly focused on how firms and industries in these countries are able to upgrade to compete in the world – shifting from lower to higher value added activities based on a society's innovative capacities (Doner et al. 2005; Giuliani et al. 2005). As Moran and Ghoshal (1999) argue, a key puzzle for development is identifying the institutional conditions, in turn the public policies, which help firms create the 'dynamic capabilities' to continually improve their products, processes, and functions.

Scholars of innovation and regional development have offered three related observations to this problem. First, drawing on evolutionary and knowledge-based views of the firm (Nelson and Winter 1982; Kogut and Zander 1992), they have argued that upgrading improves in large part from a firm's access to a variety of knowledge resources (Fleming 2001). Second, access to this knowledge may depend on whether firms are embedded in rich inter-firm networks, which enable them to build collaborative relationships, gain resources, learn, and coordinate experiments (McEvily and Marcus 2005; Powell et al. 1996). Third, governments can improve upgrading by designing policies that offer economic incentives for domestic or foreign firms to co-locate or 'cluster,' and invest in human capital and R&D (Audretsch and Stephan 1996; Porter 1990).

However, common but problematic interpretations of this research are rooted in assumptions about agglomeration effects and the role of economic and social endowments. The literature on clusters and the spillover effects from foreign direct investment (FDI) reveal that simply the presence or stock of certain firms and knowledge resources (be they know how or advanced technological R&D facilities) often does *not* lead to broad based innovation or gains in productivity and upgrading (Moran et al. 2005; Schmitz 2004). Knowledge is not simply 'in the air' ready to be absorbed and applied by local firms even with well-educated employees. Also, the literature on networks and institutions emphasizes not only the enabling but also the constraining nature of embeddedness. Past firm practices, social structures, and institutions are often slow to change and can constrain access to new knowledge resources (Granovetter 2002; Uzzi 1996). This constraining view presents a particular challenge to arguments about innovation and clusters that rely on conceptions of social capital as stocks or overly structural – i.e., that firms fail to learn and adapt because they are trapped in societies with long histories of weak associationalism and low densities of economic and social organizations (Putnam et al. 1993).

These concerns are prevalent in societies from South Carolina to especially Latin America. Governments have expended significant resources and offered a plethora of economic incentives in an effort to attract new firms and researchers only to see nascent clusters create marginal gains in productivity and limited linkages to local firms, notably suppliers (Gallagher 2007; Pietrobelli and Rabellotti 2011). Moreover, and perhaps most significantly, these are often the very societies that are known for their weak institutions and dysfunctional social capital.

This chapter offers an alternative view about the strategic management of places that can overcome the aforementioned limitations by moving beyond approaches relying on arm's length economic incentives, government largesse, and an overly structural, rigid view of network relationships. This view is grounded in the approach that regional and industry innovation emerges from the ways in which regional and industry leaders are able to create and recombine a diversity of organizational resources. It suggests that while socio-professional relationships are indeed vital for knowledge creation and diffusion, they are malleable. Governments can create institutions with private actors that facilitate new types of relationships and improve the access firms have to diverse knowledge resources.

The logic of the argument has three steps. First, the chapter shows that even where advanced MNCs invest and technology appears highly standardized or 'modular,' the creation and access to new applied knowledge is largely relational but not evenly distributed across firms. Rather, access to this knowledge depends largely on the structural composition of a firm's network and specific relational qualities it has with customers and suppliers, what the literature calls 'pragmatic collaboration.' Second, a firm's access to diverse knowledge resources, and in turn its ability to upgrade its products and processes, depends on being tied not simply to any organization or institution, but rather to those that act as social and knowledge bridges between previously isolated, if not antagonistic, producer communities.

Third, governments can improve upgrading by constructing government support institutions (GSIs) – which run R&D centers, extension services, export promotion programs etc. – with a variety of previously isolated stakeholder groups. To the extent that these new GSIs are constituted with rules of inclusion and participatory governance for the relevant public and private actors, they can anchor new multiplex, cross-cutting ties between producer communities that underpin their ability to offer with a new scale and scope of services and facilitate new problem solving relationships between them. That is, governments and industry leaders together can reshape organizational fields, and in turn knowledge flows by instigating the creation of new public-private institutions that recombine existing social and knowledge resources in new ways and at different levels of society (Campbell 2004; McDermott 2002; Thelen 2003).

I advance this argument by drawing on recent field research and unique quantitative analyses of the transformation of the Argentine autoparts supplier and wine sectors. There are two reasons why these are apt settings for the strategic management of places. First, these are contexts where the starting conditions and the social, technological and economic endowments are in many ways strong test cases for the failures and success of policy and strategy. In short, if sustained upgrading can happen there, it can happen in many other localities. Argentina, and the provinces that house these sectors, are well known for their poor institutions, weak states, and dysfunctional social relations. Prior to the 1990s, these sectors for decades had struggled to create any sort of innovative capacities and had virtually no international presence. Nevertheless, both have witnessed dramatic transformations in their technology, innovation, and international notoriety. Second, given their different technological and organizational characteristics, the common finding about the role of networks and certain institutions facilitating learning and upgrading makes the above argument all the more salient and applicable to different contexts and industries.

The chapter builds the argument and lays out the evidence incrementally. Sections 1 and 2 focus on the policies and strategies of the Argentine automotive industry. After briefly describing the industry, Section 1 shows how mainly domestic suppliers upgraded their products and process not simply due to new FDI-led investments, but particularly due to the composition of their ego-based networks and the qualities of their relationships with customers. Section 2 then takes advantage of an alternative network analysis that includes different types of non-market organizations and GSIs. We find that suppliers learn most when they have multiple strong ties to certain GSIs and industry associations that act as knowledge bridges. Section 3 then builds on these findings through an analysis of the wine sector in the key provinces of Mendoza and San Juan. It shows how Mendoza pioneered new public-private institutions that helped firms accelerate product upgrading for international markets by facilitating new forms of learning. The Mendoza case highlights not only *what* the new institutions can do to facilitate upgrading but also, and perhaps more important for policymakers, *how* they were created and sustained.

1. UPGRADING AND KNOWLEDGE SPILLOVERS – BEYOND PROXIMITY

Following a Schumpeterian approach (Schumpeter 1934), product and process upgrading are particular forms of innovation. Firms focus on the creation of new products for higher value and new processes for greater efficiencies and quality control by experiments with new combinations of existing material and knowledge resources. As Fleming (2001) has argued, this process of recombination is fraught with technological and market uncertainties, demanding that firms gain knowledge and expertise to convert different types of inputs into specific products and processes, to assess the reliability of suppliers, and to learn which types of products can gain traction in different market niches in the short and long run. While firms gain experience from their own in-house activities and human capital, they access a variety of raw and applied knowledge through their peers, customers, and suppliers as well as via non-market actors, such as trade associations and GSIs that promote improvements in skills, R&D, or new market standards (Audretsch et al. 2002; Owen-Smith and Powell 2004; McEvily and Zaheer 1999). Durable social relationships between firms underpin their ability to undertake iterative, joint experiments and participate in the sustained provision of collective resources (McEvily and Marcus 2005; Saxenian 1994).

Although this recombinatory, evolutionary view of knowledge creation and diffusion has gained considerable traction in both research and practice, the dominant views about spillovers from FDI and MNCs as well as within clusters are still wedded to emphases on economic incentives, proximity, and technological determinism. This section address these views and contrasts them with a relational view, first with a brief review of the arguments and then with an empirical example of what we could consider as a 'most likely case' for the knowledge 'in the air' perspective. This is the case of the automotive industry in Argentina, which MNCs entered in the early 1990s to reorganize, giving suppliers strong incentives to adapt or exit. That is, in a context of strong economic incentives and highly standardized or modular technologies, we would expect that knowledge diffusion and upgrading would be relatively even across all surviving suppliers.

The economics literature often depicts innovation occurring in regions that have superior *ex ante* endowments in human, natural, and financial capital or an *ex ante* superior density of firms (Rocha 2004). In this view, knowledge is 'in the air,' readily available for all firms, especially those with high levels of absorptive capacities or knowledge stocks. This view is often coupled in the development literature with institutional views, which emphasize the importance of an *ex ante* system of clear private property rights and clear boundaries between the state and the market. It has also been central to the traditional views about the impact of FDI – once MNCs have reorganized supply lines and allowed market competition to weed out the weak firms, surviving suppliers would in general have similar levels of upgrading (Moran et al. 2005). A similar perspective comes from a variant of the 'modularization view' in the literatures on global supply chains, especially for more traditional manufacturing sectors like automotive vehicles. Each production tier depends on a discreet package of technologies and interfaces, which are increasingly standardized and well codified, such that, in turn, little inter-firm coordination is needed. At its limit, this largely technologically deterministic view understands that once the value chain is established, modularization permits arm's length, market based relationships between suppliers and customers to be sufficient for sustaining global supply chains and increased upgrading (Gereffi et al. 2005; Sturgeon and Florida 2004).

A second type of determinism comes from an endowments view of socio-economic relationships in a cluster. Upgrading is likely to occur in societies historically rich in networks and the attendant social capital that are enduring and manifested in the relative density of associations and cooperatives as well as pre-existing coherent public policies (Putnam et al. 1993).

In contrast, this chapter cuts through these determinisms by building on recent work on innovation (Rocha 2004) and embeddedness (Lin 2001) that increasingly seeks to differentiate the relative impact of a firm's network composition and structure on both its capabilities and performance. Nan Lin (2001) has argued forcefully that an individual's or firm's network is composed of different types of organizations, which, in turn, provide different types of resources and information that can shape the actor's performance in different ways. In particular, Lin argues that researchers should pay closer attention to an actor's *network resources*, which are embedded in one's ego-networks, and not simply to an actor's total number of overall ties or an actor's location in the network. The key insight that I exploit here is whether the focal firm has ties to a certain type of organization (e.g. customer, supplier, trade association etc.) that can lend knowledge resources that are of value for the task at hand. I then push this view further to explore how certain types of relationship emerge through concerted strategies by industry and government leaders.

This view has three important implications for the strategic management of places. First, localities or regions vary in the types of organizations that can provide new knowledge resources. These may be other firms, schools, associations, etc. as well as GSIs.

Second, relational quality may be attached to certain organizations. That is, not all ties are the same, and only a few may offer the active exchange of knowledge. Knowledge transfer and capabilities creation depend on the particular quality and intensity of the relationships that suppliers have with their main customers (Christensen and Bower 1996; Dyer and Hatch 2006; Sako 2004). The underlying idea is that strong ties gradually promote and enhance trust, reciprocity, and a long-term perspective, which in turn helps partners develop joint projects and share tacit knowledge. Researchers on the automotive industry have increasingly focused on these types of customer-supplier relationships, calling them 'pragmatic collaborations' (MacDuffie and Helper 2006; Herrigel 2004), as firms jointly invest in specific routines and interactions that 'permit the transfer, recombination or creation of specialized knowledge' (Dyer and Singh 1998: 665). In this view, new knowledge and capabilities emerge for suppliers when they engage in regular, disciplined discussions with customers about product designs and processes that yield joint experiments and routinized collective problem solving. Such routines tend to develop when customers commit to assisting suppliers in product and process innovations, such as bilateral production programs and focused supplier associations (Dyer and Hatch 2006; Helper and Kiehl 2004).

Third, certain relational and organizational traits of the ties within a community may be dense, but can insulate firms from new information and relationships with members of other communities. As Lin (2001) and Uzzi (1996) have shown, one's ego-network can easily restrict access to different resources and blind one to new information because of the strength of immediate ties and the limited variety of valuable information and resources that its alters (other organizations, firms etc.) can pass on. That is, although a region on aggregate may have a wide variety of resources and experiences that, when combined, could create value, a firm is often embedded in a rather restricted network, be it composed of firms, associations or public agencies (Knoke 2001). Recent work in public policy has sought to show that although a society may contain a plethora of, e.g., professional associations, the attendant social ties and norms that can promote collaboration and collective learning can also be self limiting and exclusionary. To the extent that these groups and localities have different needs and resources, are relatively isolated, and are not incorporated into more encompassing institutions, a diverse socio-economic environment can easily produce a balkanized society that thwarts broad-based inno-vation, knowledge diffusion, and concerted action (Locke 1995; Ostrom 1999; Safford 2007; Schneider 2004; Tendler 1997). The lack of collective goods and coherent policies is rooted not in the absence of social ties but in their insulating qualities and the lack of cross-cutting ties between pro-ducer communities and their respective associations.

To sum up, even when the incentives are clarified and the technology is standardized, implementation demands adaptation, which in turn demands durable inter-organizational relationships to help repackage and transfer tacit knowledge fundamental to experimental process – be it in Japan or Brazil (MacDuffie and Helper 2006; Kotabe et al. 2007). We now turn to a test case of this proposition.

1.1   The Buenos Aires Autoparts Cluster and the Determinants of Upgrading[1]

During the 1990s, Argentina became a leader of pro-market reforms in Latin America, with the cornerstones being a currency board, fiscal stability, price and trade liberalization, and privatization. These efforts brought price stability as well as dramatic increases in growth, trade, and investment. Similar to such countries as Mexico and Brazil, Argentina also sought to revive its automotive industry by using focused policies to attract FDI and enhance trade in both vehicles and autoparts, albeit with little attention on supporting supply-side policies, such as the development of quasi-public institutions for improving R&D and training (Humphrey and Memedovic 2003; Yoguel et al. 1999). The combination of high-powered economic incentives and investment by the automotive MNCs was to lead to increased production as well as improved capabilities for domestic suppliers.

As was the case in many other emerging market countries (Humphrey and Memedovic 2003), the MNCs (i.e., the international assemblers and allied top tier suppliers) took charge of massively reorganizing the indus-try to establish three tiers of suppliers and diffuse the principles of lean production throughout the value chain. The first tier is dominated by foreign firms, which are responsible for complete systems, followed by the second tier (subsystems) and the third tier (components and standard inputs). Suppliers were given strong market incentives to improve quality and reduce costs by incorporating such practices as JIT, TQM, statistical process control, and Six Sigma. Argentine suppliers also had to regularly adapt their products to feed approximately 17–20 different platforms and 24 models, 16 of which were exclusively for the Argentine market and 3 of which changed annually (Kosacoff 1999).

By the late 1990s, these changes allowed for significant increases in sales, investment, and productivity as well as a reduction of the suppliers by about half. Given their ability to survive the turbulence of the 1990s and their similar geographical proximity, the local autoparts suppliers might be viewed as having similar likelihoods of upgrading their processes and products. To the extent they vary, we can discern the relative impact of a firm's internal resources, the composition of its network ties, and the quality of these ties.

McDermott and Corredoira (2010) studied these issues via a unique 1999 survey data set of all surviving suppliers in Buenos Aires province, which accounted for approximately 55 per cent of the sales and employment in the autoparts sector. This study ran two types of quantitative analyses, with the dependent variables as whether the focal firm undertook significant product and process upgrading. The first type of analysis was logistic regressions for each dependent variable. The second type of analysis was the use of the delta method to discern the inter-action effects of type of tie and the tier of the supplier. (Almost all firms in Tiers 2 and 3 were domestic SMEs.) Table 4.1 summarizes the key results from the study.

The results highlight the relative value of a firm's social ties to certain organizations and institutions as well as the importance of collaborative relationships between customers and suppliers. First, the results for the variables measuring the impact of the firm's social and professional ties to different types of organizations suggested that the value of the ties is not uniform, but varies significantly according to the type of organization. Ties to some actors within and outside the value chain, like assemblers, suppliers, and universities, appear to improve the likelihood of process and product upgrading, while ties to other types of organizations and institutions may constrain or offer few relevant resources and information to firms.

Second, it appears that the value a supplier gains from social ties to other firms in the value chain in many ways interacts with its structural position in the value chain or tier. For instance, social ties to assemblers appeared to facilitate more upgrading for suppliers in Tiers 2 and 3 than for Tier 1 suppliers (e.g. mainly the allied MNCs). Tier 1 firms gained greater relative value from ties to one another. These sets of results coincide

Creating competitiveness

Table 4.1   Summary results – type and structure of network ties

Variable	Product upgrading		Process upgrading	
	Effect	Significance	Effect	Significance
Value chain structure (tier)	Negative	p<0.01/0.10	Pos/Neg	ns/ns
Ties to assemblers	Negative	p<0.05	Positive	ns
Ties to customers	Negative	ns	Negative	p<0.01
Ties to suppliers	Positive	ns	Positive	ns
Ties to peers	Positive	ns	Positive	ns
Assemblers X structure*	Positive	p<0.01/0.01	Positive	p<0.05/ns
Customers X structure	Negative	p<0.05/0.05	Positive	p<0.10/0.01
Suppliers X structure	Positive	p<0.05/0.05	Pos/Neg	ns/ns
Peers X structure*	Negative	ns/ns	Negative	ns/p<0.05
Process develop assist	Positive	ns	Positive	p<0.001
Product develop assist	Positive	p<0.05	Positive	p<0.01
Training assist	Negative	ns	Positive	p<0.05

Notes:
* For Product Upgrading, the marginal impact of Ties to Assemblers is significantly greater for firms in Tier 2 than in Tier 1 and for firms in Tier 3 than in Tier 1. The impact of Ties to Peers is significantly greater for firms in Tier 1 than in Tier 3.
Full models included controls for age, size, knowledge stock, sales concentration, FDI, and technology.

with recent research emphasizing the notion that emerging market firms can gain new knowledge from social ties to MNCs and participating in R&D programs in universities, but that their local organizational and institutional environments may be too weak to offer relevant resources and information (Giuliani et al. 2005; Moran et al. 2005). The research on Argentina, especially in the province of Buenos Aires, has shown that the policies of the 1990s largely ignored investment into institutions that provide knowledge resources, particularly those related to manufacturing (Sutz 2000; Casaburi 1999; Casaburi and Angelelli 1999).

Third, the evidence suggested that the quality of inter-firm relationships, and not simply the quantity of social ties, might be especially beneficial for upgrading. The analysis of the marginal effects pointed to diminishing returns on upgrading for the addition of many social ties. For instance, it appeared that it was vital for suppliers from Tiers 2 and 3 to have a few good ties to assemblers rather than many weak ties. Moreover, our variables capturing whether the customer provides training or production assistance programs to suppliers appeared to significantly improve the likelihood of a supplier's ability to upgrade its products and processes. Taking these things together, we see that a few strong ties, grounded in discrete programs that induce pragmatic collaboration, can help firms learn faster than others. Such findings tend to support recent research arguing that collaborative, joint problem-solving relationships rooted in customer initiated assistance programs are likely to facilitate learning and knowledge transfer for suppliers (Dyer and Hatch 2006; MacDuffie and Helper 2006).

These results suggest two important implications for the strategic management of places. First, analysis of relational factors is likely to yield more valuable insights for managers and policymakers in uncertain contexts to the extent it can begin to differentiate the relative impact of different types of inter-organizational relationships on upgrading. Our analysis tried to distinguish the value of relationships according to the type of organization to which a firm is tied and the quality of the tie. We also found that the impact of certain social ties can vary according to one's tier. This approach allows us to identify more consistently how certain types of knowledge resources flow through distinct patterns of relationships and organizations. For instance, in some contexts MNCs might be the key source of knowledge while in others collaborative ties among local firms and their institutions might create relative advantage, regardless of the type of industry.

In the context of the Argentine automotive industry, non-market organizations and institutions appeared weak as supporters of upgrading at the time, while domestic firms appeared more likely to benefit from collaborative relationships with assemblers and their customers. As mentioned above, this is an increasingly common observation from the case-based research in Latin American and other emerging market countries (Blalock and Gertler 2005; Carrillo 2004; Gereffi et al. 2005; Rocha 2004). The issue is not simply whether economic activity is embedded or not in a robust cluster, but rather how network resources vary in an industry or region and what types of firm strategies and public policies can effectively reconfigure them. The following two sections now address this key issue.

2. LOCAL INSTITUTIONS AS KNOWLEDGE BRIDGES – WHEN A LITTLE COLLECTIVE ACTION CAN YIELD LARGE PAYOFFS

The above discussion reinforces the dual notion that even under the most likely conditions favoring the mechanisms of proximity, incentives and modularization, knowledge is not in the air and relationships strongly shape firm learning. But then what could be the role of industry and government leaders in improving firm access to a variety of knowledge resources, be they through collective services or new firm collaboration?

As we noted above, given the Argentine policy in the 1990s of limited support for industry upgrading, local firms acquired new knowledge largely through specific types of ties to other firms, especially from their customers and assemblers. The problem with this finding is that these relationships were not evenly distributed and it makes the local economy dependent on the strategies of the MNCs as the 'gatekeepers' to new markets and technologies. The literature on FDI spillovers has amply shown that MNCs may often not want to deepen backward linkages and knowledge sharing with local firms. In turn, this research has increasingly emphasized how local policies toward innovation systems can shape – positively and negatively – the likelihood that MNCs will engage widely in practices of pragmatic collaboration with domestic actors (Pietrobelli and Rabellotti 2011). The logic is rather straightforward but something of a chicken-and-egg problem: MNCs are more likely to co-invest in more advanced technologies and in broad based upgrading with local firms if domestic actors are investing at the same time in innovative capacities collectively and individually.

At first glance, such conditions for co-investment would seem to be mountainous barriers to upgrading, especially in a context with a lack of coordinated action and weak institutions, such as the Argentine automotive industry. In this section, I explore an initial path to overcome these barriers, by going back to our Argentine autoparts suppliers. The key claim is that even in the absence of a concerted strategy by the government and the MNCs, basic attempts at institutionalizing collective learning can yield significant, initial gains in helping firms access a greater variety of knowledge resources and improve upgrading capabilities.

How could this be? We begin where we just left off. Imagine a world where learning and upgrading depends largely on accessing new knowledge via other firms. What if a few industry leaders and public officials wanted to expand this access – be it through basic training services or re-molding inter-firm knowledge networks? What would these organizational and institutional efforts look like, even where resources were highly constrained and firms had a limited history of knowledge sharing?

An answer emerges from our above discussion of the dual nature of embeddedness – its enabling and constraining features for firms to access and recombine new and old knowledge.

To the extent that upgrading depends on access to a variety of knowledge resources, the isolating effects of a firm's immediate inter-organizational network can be relieved by introducing new alters or nodes into the network that can facilitate such access. The research on networks and innovation has shown that the presence of cross-cutting ties between firms from distinct producer networks or geographical locations can help them overcome these barriers and access new knowledge resources (Uzzi 1996; Zuckerman and Sgourev 2006). Such ties and the attendant knowledge flows appear to occur via organizations or GSIs that act as knowledge bridges. Research suggests that there are two key mechanisms for accelerating the flow of new knowledge and its transfer into the firm (Powell et al. 2011). One is that the organizations offer a set of collective resources or services that the firms would not necessarily have access to, at least at the level and cost that the market would offer (Schmitz 2004). The second is creating programs or forums in which the participating firms begin to learn directly from one another and build new professional ties to one another. McEvily and Zaheer (2004) have called this a 'network facilitator' effect.

In order to capture these effects and identify such organizations and GSIs, Corredoira and I implemented a new survey in 2004–05 of the Argentine autoparts suppliers. We altered the previous approach to the survey in three key ways. First, we expanded the universe of focal firms geographically to include suppliers from different provinces (Cordoba, Santa Fe, and Buenos Aires). Second, we constructed network variables that measure the degree to which the focal firm (supplier) regularly collaborates or gains key information from other firms, schools, banks, GSIs, and associations (including voluntary centers that do not receive government funding). Third, to capture the claim that firms gain access to diverse knowledge resources particularly via mediating alters which themselves are tied to firms from a variety of locations, we decomposed the most salient of above ties (e.g., Ties to GSIs, Ties to Associations, etc.) into those that were the most central and had the highest levels of network geographic diversity and those that did not.[2] We then ran regressions of these variables with a dependent variable of *Process Upgrading*, which our survey yielded to measure the extent to which a firm implemented practices associated with the continuous improvement of efficiencies, adaptation, and quality control. (All regressions included control variables for age, FDI, size, knowledge stock (absorptive capacity), prior intention to upgrade, location, tier and effects from focusing production on a few distinct final assemblers.)

Table 4.2 provides an abbreviated presentation of the results. First, we found that the baseline of network effects – the total size of a firm's network – was negative and not significant. Second, we found that Ties to GSIs and Ties to Associations were the only network variables with positive, significant effects, while Ties to Firms were often negative and not significant. Third, we found that Ties to the Most Central

Table 4.2   Summary results – impact of network ties on process upgrading for Argentine autoparts suppliers (2004–05)

Variable	Effect	Significance
Ties to associations	Positive	$p<0.001$
Ties to GSIs	Positive	$p<0.05$
Ties to other firms	Negative	ns/$p<0.10$
Ties to banks, schools	Negative	ns
Ties to top bridging associations	Positive	$p<0.05$
Ties to top bridging GSIs	Positive	$p<0.05$
Ties to top bridging firms	Negative	ns/$p<0.10$
Ties to top central associations	Positive	$p<0.01$
Ties to top central GSIs	Positive	$p<0.05$
Ties to top central firms	Negative	ns

Note: Full models included controls for age, size, knowledge base, geographic location, FDI, type of assembler, structure of the value chain, and upgrading intent.

and Geographically Diverse GSIs and Associations ('Bridging GSIs or Bridging Associations') the only variables that were consistently positive and significant.

These results suggest that firms achieved relatively higher levels of process upgrading when they have multiple, strong ties not with other firms (!) but with certain associations and GSIs. Moreover, it appears that the associations and GSIs are most effective when they are encompassing and bridging different locations. What is particularly relevant here is that neither the governments (federal or provincial) nor the MNCs had undertaken notable coordinated, coherent efforts to build new institutions or services for the suppliers. Rather, our data and interviews reveal that only a few associations and GSIs were the critical actors, and their efforts came from rather intuitive steps to aid firms. For instance, we find that one of the critical GSIs was INTI, the national institute for industrial technology. Over the 1990s, INTI had consistently been underfunded and understaffed, and had few coordinated programs with major firms and MNCs in Argentina. Under such conditions, a few technicians began speaking with autoparts suppliers to learn of the needs that perhaps INTI could meet. Two of the most common ones were related to basic testing services – testing the safety of components and products as required under the 1998 transportation safety law and testing components to meet the standards of the MNCs (rather than having them sent back to the MNCs' headquarters as was common practice). These services not only saved time and costs, but also accelerated firm learning since the supplier learned from the INTI technicians where the defects were occurring and how they could remedy them.

The role of the associations was not as straightforward for learning, but in many ways reflects the mechanisms for establishing new cross-cutting ties that were emphasized by other scholars in different contexts (Zuckerman and Sgourev 2006; Safford 2007; McEvily and Zaheer 2004). The case in point is AFAC, the Argentine Association of Component Plants, created in 1994. In reorganizing the automotive industry in the 1990s and negotiating with the MNC assemblers for their investment, the federal government had virtually excluded the autoparts suppliers from the process. In turn, AFAC was created first to provide a collective voice for the suppliers in future negotiations and policies. But what was distinct from other trade associations was that AFAC gradually made consistent efforts to provide member firms with domestic and international information that they normally had to gain on their own. AFAC built up a group of experts to collect and organize key industry data on a regular basis. It also created regular meetings or forums in which the members learned about major trends and standards in the industry, regionally and globally, debated their key priorities and activities, and especially learned directly from one another about their respective strategies, practices, and results.

It appears that organizations like INTI and AFAC, despite their limited resources, became vital conduits of new knowledge for suppliers because they acted as social and knowledge bridges in two ways. They became repositories of diverse and important standards and practices with the capabilities to transfer them to the firms themselves. They also helped firms learn directly from one another and build new professional ties.

It is worrisome however that the automotive industry and the government have been slow to expand on these experiences. In many ways, these experiences may well be the exceptions that prove the rule – that concerted public efforts to build domestic support systems and remold knowledge networks fail to overcome the collective action hurdles or the heavy handedness of government bureaucrats.

The next section attempts to bypass this cynicism by turning to the case of the transformation of the Argentine wine industry, which shows in greater detail how public and private actors overcame decades of mistrust to construct new institutions that helped firms access diverse knowledge resources.

3. CONSTRUCTING THE 'ANCHORING INSTITUTIONS'

This section analyzes the transformation of the Argentine wine sector in the two neighboring, dominant winemaking provinces of Mendoza and San Juan. After a long history of backwardness and virtually no international presence, the Argentine wine sector witnessed a dramatic turnaround in the 1990s and now accounts for over 3 per cent of the $16 billion global wine market, and recently overtook Chile to become the fourth largest exporter of wines into the United States in terms of value. This revival has been based on significant innovations in quality control and design of new wines and grapes (McDermott 2007). Mendoza has led this change as the dominant exporter and innovator, pioneering a new constellation of institutions and inter-firm networks that appears to have facilitated widespread product upgrading. San Juan, in contrast, remained a laggard, despite its numerous firms, high density of associations, and policies that ushered in new investment. In turn, by identifying how Mendoza created a new path of innovation so different from its own past and from its neighbor, I can highlight how Mendoza's public and private actors changed key knowledge relationships and created institutional mechanisms that helped firms access a variety of knowledge resources and learn.

I argue here that product upgrading depends on a firm being tied not simply to any or many organizations and GSIs, but rather to those that act as social and knowledge bridges across distinct producer communities and in turn offer firms access to a variety of knowledge resources. In particular, I highlight the ways in which governments can alter the trajectory of product upgrading not simply through largesse or market liberalization but by developing a new set of GSIs with a variety of previously isolated, even antagonistic, stakeholder groups.

The last section noted that firms can overcome the limitations of their immediate socio-economic network or community by participating in organizations and institutions that can act as knowledge bridges. For instance, research on a variety of industries in the United States has shown how certain industry support organizations, be they associations, institutes or GSIs, can bridge socially and geographically isolated groups of firms, legitimize new standards, and promote new forms of joint action (Knoke 2001; McEvily and Zaheer 2004; Owen-Smith and Powell 2004). Policy scholars such as Locke (1995) and Ostrom (1999) suggest that when more encompassing, bridging structures are not historically or organically given, government can find a role to provide them to improve coordination and knowledge diffusion.

This intersection of research has gained increasing traction in policy work on societies noted for their weak state capacities and fragmented, rent-seeking industry groups. First, when confronted with crises, governments can change existing policy by creating new GSIs in partnership with a broader variety of stakeholder groups than in the past (Campbell 2004; Schneider 2004). In acting less as a direct provider and more as a coordinator and empowerer, the government can instigate a process of recombining the resources and information of better-placed actors with its own to facilitate the creation of more effective services and programs (Furman and MacGarvie 2006; Rodrik 2004).

Second, to the extent that these new GSIs are governed by a variety of public and private actors, they have the potential of also reshaping the social and knowledge ties among the government and previously isolated, even antagonistic, producer communities (Locke 1995; Ostrom 1999; Safford 2007). The new GSIs are constituted with rules of empowered inclusion and multiparty governance, whereby participants representing the government and a variety of relevant stakeholder groups, such as trade associations, have rights and responsibilities in defining and evaluating the development of certain industry support programs. As such, they offer participants new structures to engage in collective problem solving, improve mutual monitoring, and build broader strategic considerations on top of their past rent-seeking, mutual hold-up instincts (Sabel 1994; Schneider 2004; Stark and Bruszt 1998; Tendler 1997).

I refer to this sub-group of GSIs as public-private institutions or PPIs (Ostrom 1999; Tendler 1997). My main interest is not their hybrid ownership form per se, but particularly the way their governance principles foster multiplex, cross-cutting ties among previously isolated public and private actors and improve the access firms have to a variety of knowledge resources.

3.1 Comparing Mendoza and San Juan's Approaches to Regional Reform

The relational view of product upgrading is widely embraced in studies of developing countries in general and wine in particular (Giuliani and Bell 2005; Perez-Aleman 2005; Roberts and Ingram 2002; Swaminathan 2001). Upgrading in wine takes several years, beginning with transforming the middle segments of the value chain: state-of-the-art quality control and product development running from careful vineyard maintenance to flawless harvests to fermentation and blending. Enologists work closely with agronomists and growers to introduce, evaluate, and document experiments with new methods of growing and fermentation for different types of varietals and clones. Because of the variation in climates and soils, experimentation is contextualized and knowledge is often tacit, posing barriers to dissemination and application elsewhere. In turn, to accelerate product upgrading, wineries gain a variety of market and applied technical knowledge from other firms as well as collective resources housed in industry associations, schools, and GSIs.

Such coordination and relational-based upgrading is not necessarily forthcoming, however, especially for firms embedded in volatile environments with limited resources and potentially fragmented industry structures. Developing countries, such as Argentina, are widely known for their lack of collective knowledge resources, weak markets, and limited state capacities (Doner et al. 2005; Schmitz 2004). Moreover, although diversity and a decentralized industry structure can be sources of innovation, they can also exacerbate the problems of concerted action and block the widespread diffusion of new practices (Jacobs 1984; Romanelli and Khessina 2005). Mendoza and San Juan have over 100 micro-climates supporting a wide variety of high value grapes and thousands of small vineyards, which typically supply 30–50 per cent of a winery's needs. Both provinces still have over 680 and 170 wineries, respectively, which range from many small and medium family firms to some cooperatives and a few large diversified corporations.[3] Over three hundred wineries export, with relatively low concentration ratios by international standards.

Given the coordination problems associated with product upgrading, our comparison of the two transformation paths focuses on two related questions that link the mechanisms of upgrading with broader policy problems of development. How was a broad set of firms able to upgrade their products and exploit variety rather than being paralyzed by it? What types of new institutional mechanisms were created to help firms access a variety of knowledge resources and learn?

Typical analyses would rely on the inherited economic and social endowments of the two provinces as determinants for the different paths. But in showing in detail the limitations of these approaches, McDermott (2007) revealed how the two provinces had a similar socio-economic structure, which then diverged in the 1990s because of new policies in Mendoza. It is especially noteworthy for the clusters literature that both provinces had similar levels of SME density, natural resources, human resources, and stock measures of social capital. While the two provinces had similar indicators of associationalism and business-government relationships through the 1980s, a key problem for knowledge creation was the fragmented nature of social and political life between producer communities or *Zonas* within the provinces. For instance, while firms within particular *Zonas*, such as the *Zona Primera* and the *Zona Este*, often learned from one another and had their own trade associations to lobby the government

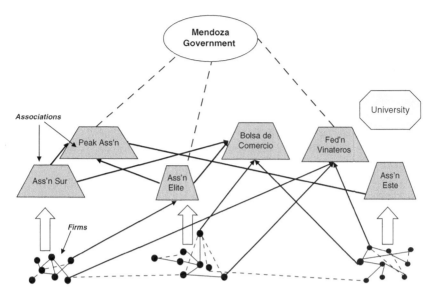

Notes: Figures 4.1 and 4.2: Solid black circles represent firms in different regions in Mendoza. Each region has its main wine business association, as shown by large white arrow. Dashed lines represent weaker links of contracting or communication than solid lines. Solid arrows denote membership and board participation in relevant associations and institutions.

Figure 4.1   Policymaking and strategic ties in the Mendoza wine industry, 1988

for subsidies, they viewed their counterparts in other *Zonas* as rivals, from whom they had little to learn. The traditional policymaking in the provinces of zero-sum games on price supports also reinforced weak horizontal ties between sectoral and zonal associations and ad hoc verti-cal ties between just a few associations and the government (Paladino and Jauregui 2001; Rofman 1999). Figure 4.1 gives a simplified depiction of this structure of policymaking in the wine industry in Mendoza in 1987. One could give a similar depiction of San Juan in both the 1980s and 1990s.

The need for more specific applied knowledge and skills, coupled with regional prejudices and resource inequalities, can create barriers to the processes of aggregation and joint action vital for a sustainable base of innovation. As discussed above, public policy can remedy this problem by initiating a process in which public and private actors create new institutions with governance principles that anchor new horizontal ties between previously isolated producer communities. Such a view shifts the comparative lens of upgrading paths away from the existing economic and social endowments of regions and toward their institution-building processes.

A fruitful comparative analysis, in turn, focuses on how the contrasting policies toward resolving a common crisis in the late 1980s in the two regions led to the formation of different organizational and institutional arrangements in the 1990s. With the Argentine economy stagnating and the wine industry collapsing, the focal points of the crisis were both provinces' respective state-owned, perennial loss-making wineries, Cavic in San Juan and Giol in Mendoza, whose purchasing contracts and inflated prices effectively promoted the production of large volumes of low-quality wine (Azpiazu and Basualdo 2003). San Juan's government sought to insulate itself and rapidly impose high-powered, arm's-length economic incentives on society to induce change. It first chose to rapidly privatize the Cavic to local interests, brushing off the protests of dependent small grape growers and wineries. The firm soon failed again, causing the government to intervene and liquidate it. Then through the 1990s, the government focused on attracting new investment through a federally subsidized tax incentive. By most accounts this policy brought in record levels of investment to the wine industry, but failed to encourage broad based upgrading. The economic benefits remained concentrated among a few large firms that had little interest in incorporating and diffusing new practices along the value chain. The top down approach also exacerbated the fragmentation and animosities among relevant sectoral associations and the state, and perpetuated the old strategies of divide and rule cum rent-seeking. For instance, on several occasions during the 1990s, different sectoral associations proposed new institutions to support training and export promotion. Each attempt failed, with the state and the associations accusing each other of free-riding and attempting to gain control of state resources.

In contrast, Mendoza gradually built a new set of GSIs to provide a variety of new support services and resources in agriculture and especially the winemaking value chain (e.g., hazard insurance, training, R&D, export promotion, etc.). The first experiment came in 1987–88, when the newly elected provincial administration chose to transform Giol into Fecovita, a federation of cooperatives, which were created from the previously dependent thousands of small grape growers and wineries. This experience not only revitalized the cooperative sector, but also initiated a broader effort by the Mendoza government to create Public Private Institutions (PPIs) de novo and then later reform existing GSIs with socio-economic partners over ten years (McDermott 2007).

Table 4.3 gives an abridged description of the most prominent PPIs, their different support activities, and shared governance traits. They are

Table 4.3   Public–private institutions in Mendoza created in the 1990s

Institution	Year of creation or restruc- turing	Governing members	Activities	Resources	Legal form
INTA EEAs	1991; INTA San Juan reformed in 1996	Gov't of Mza, 15 Agro assns, natl and provl institutes and univs	R&D (inputs, plants, tech), extension training, consulting	50% – Govt budget (salaries and overhead); 50% – services, alliances, cooper- adoras	Part of INTA Cuyo; 4 in Mza, 1 in SJ; Public, Non-state, non-profit entity.
Fondo Vitivinicola	1993–94	Govt Mza, 11 wine/ grape assns	Oversees new wine regulations, promotes wine industry/ marketing	Tax on firms from over produc'n of wine	Public, non-state, non-profit entity.
Fondo para la Transfor- macion y el Crecimiento (FTC)	1993–94	Govt Mza, regional advisory councils, assns	Subsidized loans and credit guarantees to SMEs for tech. against extreme weather and for grape conversion	Self- financing; initial capital from govt.	Independent legal entity under authority of governor.
Instituto Desarrollo Rural (IDR)	1994–95	36 founders – INTA Cuyo, Govt Mza, 2 peak assns, various agro sectoral assns	Technical info collection and dissemination; Data base mgmt; R&D, training, consulting	Mza Govt; services; gradual increase of fees from member assns	Non-profit Foundation; with oversight by Min. of Economy

Table 4.3   (continued)

Institution	Year of creation or restruc-turing	Governing members	Activities	Resources	Legal form
Instituto Tecnologico Universi-tario (ITU)	1994	Founders –Govt Mza, Univ Nacional Cuyo, UTN, 2 peak assns	Continuing education for managers and some R&D in mgmt and technology	Founders; fees for services	Non-profit Foundation
Pro Mendoza	1995–96	Govt Mza, 3 peak business associa-tions	Export promotion – organize fairs, delegations, strategic information, training	Govt Mza; peak assns; services	Non-profit Foundation

Notes: INTA – Instituto Nacional de Tecnología Agropecuaria; EEA – Estaciones Experimentales (Sub-regional centers); Mza – Mendoza; Cooperadoras – Non-profit NGOs.

Source: Adapted from McDermott (2007: 123).

public-private in their legal form, governance structures, resources, and membership, which includes representatives from the government and associations of a variety of zones and sub-sectors. As a sub-group of GSIs, they too received at least partial public funding, had state representatives on their boards, and had a public mandate.

But the aforementioned characteristics made the PPIs distinct from the pre-existing GSIs, since the latter were state/bureaucratic centered in their governance and had only ad hoc contact with a few elite groups instead of having governance and resource ties to a variety of associations. They were also distinct from the pre-existing sectoral and zonal associations, since the latter were voluntary organizations with no government representation or resources, were narrow in membership and mission, and had few services other than to lobby the government as mentioned above.

My particular interest is how the distinct governance rules of PPIs anchored their ability to act as multiplex bridges (Padgett and Ansell 1993; Burt 1992) between the public and private domains as well as between the

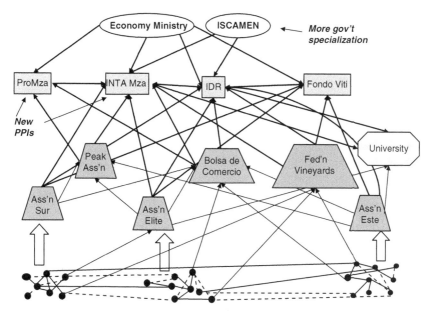

Figure 4.2   Policymaking and strategic ties in the Mendoza wine industry, 2000

relevant producer communities, and in turn create mechanisms to improve firm access to a variety of knowledge resources. Figure 4.2 gives a simplified depiction of this new structure and the role of PPIs in Mendoza in 2000. The combination of these governance rules and network qualities in PPIs fostered three mechanisms to transmit a new variety of applied knowledge to firms. First, in combining the material and informational contributions of the public and private participants, the PPIs gradually built up knowledge resources at a scale, scope and cost that the government and the associations could not have provided individually and did not exist before or in other provinces. For instance, INTA Mendoza, IDR, and ProMendoza pioneered new detailed mappings of the micro-climates for grapes and other agricultural products; data bases on best practices (internationally and sub-regionally), harvests, and product markets; benchmarking and training programs for different sectors and zones; and teams of experienced consultants. The staff acquired such contextualized knowledge from the input of the associations themselves, their own research, and the various service contracts with constituent firms. Similar to the technology centers described by McEvily and Zaheer (2004), these PPIs became public repositories of diverse practices and standards and also of repackaged knowledge to be adapted to particular settings.

Second, PPIs produced services that integrated the needs of their different constituencies with international standards. The leverage of each participant came from its ability to provide or withhold resources as well as its ability to voice proposals and grievances through the board. Third, the PPIs built programs to help firms learn from one another and create new relationships. Both firm managers and directors of these institutions repeatedly told us that one of the most valued qualities of services was the way they helped to diffuse standards, practices, and experiences from one zone or sector to another. A typical example of an indirect method was the use of INTA Mendoza's testing labs and viticulture consultants by a variety of firms, from the most elite to the fragile cooperatives. With this diverse experience, INTA Mendoza began documenting, benchmarking, and teaching practices from the most advanced form of computer monitored drip-watering to new applications of the more traditional orthogonal vine training systems. The most common examples of a more direct method of knowledge transmission and relationship building was the use by INTA, IDR, and ProMendoza of multi-firm training and research programs based on collective problem-solving techniques.

By the end of the 1990s, the overlapping ties and demonstration effects of the new institutions channeled spillovers across policy domains and provinces. Within Mendoza, the older, more archaic institutions and GSIs, such as the regional university, the province's phytosanitary regulator, and the national regulating agency for wine, began to change their programs, standards, and governance structures largely due to their participation in new advisory councils and industry support programs. The Mendoza government and associations also spearheaded the replication of the institutional model at a national level that was signed into law in late 2004. Beginning in 2002, the San Juan government openly criticized the old approach of tax incentives and advocated the creation of new public-private institutional resources for training, R&D, and export promotion. Indeed, the government explicitly mentioned INTA San Juan, INTA Mendoza's satellite center, as an exemplary model (Gobierno de San Juan 2004).

In sum, Mendoza's approach to building new GSIs appears to have helped induce upgrading by improving the access firms had to a variety of knowledge resources and functioning akin to the 'network facilitator' role discussed by McEvily and Zaheer (2004). The rules of inclusion and multi-party governance helped representatives of previously isolated producer communities gradually forge common strategies and a coherent, dynamic set of support policies with the state. Consequently, the programs and services of the relevant institutions helped firms learn how to apply new knowledge with existing natural inputs and build new relationships with one another. With statistical techniques, we now explore the degree to which this new constellation of organizational and institutional ties, once it had taken root, improved a firm's product upgrading.

3.2   Network Composition and Product Upgrading

McDermott et al. (2009) designed and implemented a survey of about 120 wineries in zones of Mendoza and San Juan in 2004–05. The survey had a 90 per cent response rate and focused on measuring the upgrading capabilities of firms, their demographics, and their public-private networks. The cross-sectional nature of our quantitative data impedes us from statistically tracking the changes in a firm's network and product upgrading. It does however allow us to evaluate how the composition and structure of a firm's ego-network impact on its product upgrading, and the plausibility of our key claim that Mendoza's policy approach facilitated firm access to a new variety of knowledge resources by creating new institutions with multiplex bridging qualities that fostered cross-cutting ties between producer communities.

Our previous theoretical and empirical discussions argued that the alters, which appeared most valuable to firms, were those offering a new variety of applied knowledge resources and cross-cutting channels of information and professional contacts between different producer communities, especially the different zones. Mendoza's approach appeared to improve access for firms to a variety of knowledge resources by creating a new set of GSIs, the PPIs, and then reforming the old GSIs to offer new services directly to firms and foster new types of relationships between them. Our qualitative analysis further suggested that wineries benefited most from their interactions with other firms and the GSIs, because these alters, as opposed to the other types, offered the combination of new knowledge resources and inter-active relationships for solving ongoing problems of product development. In contrast, pre-existing organizations, such as schools, banks, associations, and cooperatives were not the repeated recipients of policies to offer new knowledge resources directly for the firm or remained focused in their membership, clientele, and social orientation toward their locality or zone. Furthermore, our discussion above noted that Mendoza's PPIs were especially effective because of the ways in which their governance rules anchored their ability to act as social and knowledge bridges between distinct production communities or *Zonas*. That is, the evidence suggested that alters, be they firms or GSI, could be effective hubs of diverse knowledge resources because they would have ties to many firms from different *Zonas*.

We tested these qualitative claims by regressing a set of control and network variables on a firm's level of *Product Upgrading*, which measures

Creating competitiveness

Table 4.4 *Summary of regression results – impact of network ties on product upgrading of Argentine wineries (full models with controls on firm demographics, locality, all types of ties)*

Variables	Statistical significance
Ties to other firms and to GSIs	Positive, at the 0.01 level
Ties to associations, banks, cooperatives, and schools	Negative or insignificant
Ties to PPIs vs. ties to old GSIs	Positive at the 0.05 level for PPIs
Ties to most central alter firms	Positive, not significant
Ties to most central GSIs	Positive at the 0.05 level
Ties to 'bridging firms' (highest degree of geographic diversity)	Positive at the 0.05 level
Ties to 'bridging GSIs' (highest degree of geographic diversity)	Positive at the 0.05 level

Source: Based on McDermott et al. (2009).

the extent to which the firm implemented practices associated with the introduction of new and higher value wines, experimentation with new blends, varietals and clones, monitoring domestic and foreign markets.[4] The explanatory, network variables measure the degree to which a firm regularly interacts, collaborates, and exchanges information with different types of organizations and institutions, such as other firms, banks, schools, associations, cooperatives, and GSIs. Ties to Firms and Ties to GSIs were then decomposed in two ways. First, the authors decomposed Ties to GSIs into Ties to Old GSIs and Ties to PPIs, which are the new GSIs that Mendoza created in the 1990s. Second, to capture our claim that firms gain access to diverse knowledge resources particularly via mediating alters which themselves are tied to a variety of firms from different locations, they decomposed Ties to Firms and Ties to GSIs into those that were the most central and had the highest levels of network geographic diversity and those that were not. The control variables were: Size, Foreign Ownership, Knowledge Stock, Upgrading Intent, with location dummies for the different zones.

Table 4.4 gives an abbreviated presentation of the results. The only control variables that were consistently significant were Education and Upgrading Intent. The results strongly suggest that product upgrading was greatly enhanced when a focal firm had many, strong ties: (a) to other (alter) firms and to GSIs; (b) to PPIs but not other Old GSIs; (c) to firms and GSIs with the strongest centrality and bridging traits. If access to diverse knowledge is key, then higher levels of upgrading should be associated with ties to alters that have the highest centrality and bridging traits but not with ties to alters that lack these traits. The results appear to broadly confirm our claim, but more so for GSIs than for firms. The combination of these quantitative results and our qualitative analysis suggests that a firm's access to diverse knowledge resources depends on it being tied not just to any or many organizations and institutions but particularly on its being tied to those that excel in centrality and bridging qualities. These results have two important implications for public policy and innovation.

First, to the extent that access to a variety of knowledge resources is vital for firm upgrading, the qualitative and quantitative evidence reframes our notion about which types of alters may facilitate such access. Prior research on innovation has emphasized the importance of firms and associations providing cross-cutting relationships between previously isolated groups of firms (Fleming 2001; Safford 2007; Zuckerman and Sgourev 2006) and the role of GSIs helping diffuse knowledge in providing collective resources and having a public mission to share new knowledge (Breznitz 2007; Owen-Smith and Powell 2004). The evidence here supports a blending of the two views in that the effectiveness of government programs is rooted in the institutionalization of their network qualities. The innovation in Mendoza's approach was developing a new set of GSIs, the PPIs, with rules of inclusion and participatory governance. These rules anchored the multiplex bridging qualities of PPIs that underpinned their ability to provide a new scale and scope of knowledge resources to firms and mold new relationships between them. Hence, this research suggests that firms can improve their access to a variety of knowledge resources and their attendant 'combinatory capacities' (Moran and Ghoshal 1999: 409) if they participate in structures that are constituted with the aforementioned institutional and network qualities.

Second, the evidence in its entirety suggests that organizational fields can be reshaped in different ways, primarily because one component – GSIs – is highly responsive to government policy. This is consistent with growing work on issues ranging from technology diffusion to health care to emerging market corporate governance that shows the impact of government policy in structuring inter-organizational networks (Knoke 2001; Owen-Smith and Powell 2004; Provan and Milward 1995; Stark and Vedres 2006). Hence, a long-term consequence of Mendoza's policy has been to reshape the organizational field in ways that differed significantly from the province's past and from San Juan. For instance, Figure 4.3 offers a UCINET (Borgatti et al. 2002) depiction of the ties between focal firms and the entities we coded as GSIs, comparing the two provinces. An immediate observation is that firms in Mendoza now live in a much richer

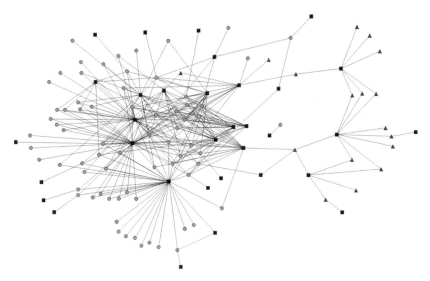

Notes: The circles on the left denote wineries in Mendoza. The triangles on the right denote wineries in San Juan. The squares denote GSIs.

Source: Authors' survey data, 2004–05.

Figure 4.3   Ties between focal firms and GSIs – Mendoza and San Juan, 2005

institutional environment than those in San Juan. Such a view coincides with the increasingly growing argument that locational variables, some of which were significant in our models, should be viewed not simply as proxies for geography and natural resources but as indicators of the different constellations of organizations and institutions, in which a firm is embedded (Granovetter 2002; Locke 1995; Owen-Smith and Powell 2004; Saxenian 1994).

4.   CONCLUDING REMARKS – TOWARDS ORGANIZATIONAL DIVERSITY AND KNOWLEDGE BRIDGES

This chapter has sought to understand how regions and their industries can improve their innovative capacities in the face of high uncertainty and a history of backwardness. The context of inquiry was the autoparts and wine sectors of Argentina – where product and process upgrading improved despite the legacies of limited international exposure, weak institutions and dysfunctional social capital. The cases were chosen not because of their unequivocal success in innovation and international markets. To be sure, these sectors and their regions remained burdened by the uneven patterns of development that plague most emerging market countries (Doner 2009). Rather, the unforeseen, sustained gains in process and product upgrading they have achieved in recent years provided an apt context for generating lessons about the recombination of networks and institutions that can be applied elsewhere.

The arguments and empirical evidence offered here were developed incrementally. The analysis of the transformation of the autoparts supplier sector suggested that access to diverse knowledge resources was neither in the air nor necessarily a function of a region's economic and social endowments. Rather, knowledge flows depended on the composition of a firm's network and the quality of inter-firm relationships. Moreover, we found that even seemingly basic efforts to provide collective learning resources – via non-firm organizations like underfunded associations and research institutes – can have significant impacts on firm level upgrading. In particular, those associations and GSIs that functioned as encompassing, social and knowledge bridges between distinct producer communities could accelerate firm access to diverse knowledge resources because of their services and facilitating new inter-firm learning.

If that analysis helped establish the importance of organizations building new types of network ties and learning, then the analysis of the wine sectors, particularly in Mendoza, helped cement the mechanism at work and offer a roadmap for policymakers in creation and emergence. The new constellation of networks and institutions was not given historically but facilitated through policy approach based on experiments in which public and private actors gradually recombined their existing resources to create a new variety of knowledge assets for firms. There appear to be two key take-aways from this experience.

First, firms improve their access to diverse knowledge resources, in turn their capabilities to upgrade products, to the extent that they have multiple, strong ties not just to any organizations but mainly to those that act as social and knowledge bridges between previously isolated, even antagonistic producer communities. Second, these new pathways and their attendant recombinatory processes can emerge when governments and relevant stakeholder groups collaborate to create new types of GSIs – what I called public-private institutions or PPIs. The PPIs appear to anchor multiplex, cross-cutting knowledge networks to the extent that they are constituted with the principles of inclusion and participatory governance.

The message here is not that regional leaders must follow only the politics of Mendoza or the models of PPIs. Rather, the message is about the key mechanisms that advance knowledge creation and diffusion and the roles of public and private actors in reshaping relevant inter-organizational networks. The seminal work of Woody Powell and his collaborators on the emergence of innovative regions in the life science industries has shown that two critical success factors are organizational diversity and the presence of 'anchor tenants' – organizations, be they public or private, that become the 'scaffolding that assists subsequent connections and field formation' (Powell et al. 2011). On the one hand, this work speaks to the different types of organizations that can become social and knowledge bridges. On the other hand, it coincides with the arguments here about the roles of organizational and institutional bridges both initiating and sustaining firm learning.

Building on these views, this chapter adds a political element. While not universal, the Argentine experiences, and particularly those of Mendoza, suggest that the strategic management of places may begin not simply with the common policies of economic incentives or government outlays for R&D and training. Rather, just as firm product innovation is a process of discovery, so too are experiments in policymaking and institution building. Inclusive, participatory governance can institutionalize problem-solving mechanisms that help public and private actors build new horizontal professional ties and graft broader strategic considerations onto their past rent-seeking, blocking instincts. The new anchoring, bridging institutions are not given but created with distinct rules and governance structures that help them adapt and promote broad-based innovation.

NOTES

1. This section draws heavily from McDermott and Corredoira (2010).
2. To capture the geographic diversity of the alters, we grouped focal firms into seven locations – Cordoba, two regions of Santa Fe, and four regions of Buenos Aires. This division is justified because of the size of the latter two provinces and the ways in which firms in the latter two provinces have clustered geographically into distinct manufacturing districts.
3. On the variety and decentralized structure of wine and grape production, see Cetrangolo et al. (2002) and Ruiz and Vila (2003). According to the data from the Instituto Nacional Vitvinicola (INV), there were still over 16,000 vineyards in Mendoza and 6,000 in San Juan; vineyards in both provinces with less than 25 hectares still accounted for about 92% of the total number and 60% of surface area. According to the 2003 agricultural survey of vineyards in Mendoza, the largest 18 vineyard owners control only 5% of vineyard surface area, and about 1100 owners control 50%. (Authors' calculations for both sets of figures.)
4. The complete discussion of the methods, regressions, and the results can be found in McDermott et al. (2009).

REFERENCES

Audretsch, D.B. and P.E. Stephan (1996), 'Company-scientist locational links: the case of biotechnology', *American Economic Review*, **86** (3), 641–52.

Audretsch, D.B., A.N. Link and J.T. Scott (2002), 'Public/private technology partnerships: evaluating SBIR supported research', *Research Policy*, **31** (1), 145.

Azpiazu, D. and E. Basualdo (2003), 'Industria vitivinicola', *Estudios sectorials: Estudio 1*, EG.33.6, Buenos Aires: CEPAL.

Blalock, G. and P.J. Gertler (2005), 'Foreign direct investment and externalities: the case for public intervention', in T.H. Moran, E.M. Graham and M. Blomstrom (eds), *Does Foreign Direct Investment Promote Development?*, Washington, DC: Institute for International Economics, pp. 73–106.

Borgatti, S.P., M.G. Everett and L.C. Freeman (2002), *Ucinet for Windows: Software for Social Network Analysis*, Harvard, MA: Analytic Technologies.

Breznitz, D. (2007), *Innovation and the State: Political Choice and Strategies for Growth in Israel, Taiwan, and Ireland*, New Haven: Yale University Press.

Burt, R. (1992), *Structural Holes: The Social Structure of Competition*, Cambridge: Harvard University Press.

Campbell, J.L. (2004), *Institutional Change and Globalization*, Princeton: Princeton University Press.

Carrillo, J. (2004), 'Transnational strategies and regional development: the case of GM and Delphi in Mexico', *Industry and Innovation*, **11** (1/2), 127–53.

Casaburi, G. (1999), *Dynamic Agroindustrial Clusters: The Political Economy of Competitive Sectors in Argentina and Chile,* New York: St. Martin's Press.

Casaburi, G. and P. Angelelli (1999), *Estrategias de apoyo a la micro, pequeña y mediana empresa.* Buenos Aires: IERAL.

Cetrangolo, H., S. Fernandez, J. Quagliano, V. Zelenay, N. Muratore and F. Lettier (2002), *El Negocio de los Vinos en la Argentina*, Buenos Aires: FAUBA.

Christensen, C. and J. Bower (1996), 'Customer power, strategic investment, and the failure of leading firms', *Strategic Management Journal*, **17** (3), 197–218.

Doner, R. (2009), *The Politics of Uneven Development*, New York: Cambridge University Press.

Doner, R.F., B.K. Ritchie and D. Slater (2005), 'Systemic vulnerability and the origins of developmental states: Northeast and Southeast Asia in comparative perspective', *International Organization*, **59** (2), 321–61.

Dyer, J.H. and N.W. Hatch (2006), 'Relation-specific capabilities and barriers to knowledge transfers: creating advantage through network relationships', *Strategic Management Journal*, **27** (8), 701.

Dyer, J.H. and H. Singh (1998), 'The relational view: cooperative strategy and sources of interorganizational competitive advantage', *Academy of Management Review*, **23** (4), 660–79.

Fleming, L. (2001), 'Recombinant uncertainty in technological search', *Management Science*, **47** (1), 117–32.

Furman, J. and M. MacGarvie (2006), 'Academic science and the birth of industrial research laboratories in the U.S. pharmaceutical industry', *Journal of Economic Behavior and Organization*, **63**, 756–76.

Gallagher, K.P. (2007), *The Enclave Economy*, Cambridge: MIT Press.

Gereffi, G., J. Humphrey and T. Sturgeon (2005), 'The governance of global value chains', *Review of International Political Economy*, **12**, 78.

Giuliani, E. and M. Bell (2005), 'The micro-determinants of meso-level learning and innovation: evidence from a Chilean wine cluster', *Research Policy*, **34** (1), 47–68.

Giuliani, E., C. Pietrobelli and R. Rabellotti (2005), 'Upgrading in global value chains: lessons from Latin American clusters', *World Development*, **33** (4), 549–73.

Gobierno de San Juan (2004), *Proyecto de fortalecimiento institucional para el desarrollo rural: Provincia de San Juan*.

Granovetter, M. (2002), 'A theoretical agenda for economic sociology', in M.F. Guillen, R. Collins, P. England and M. Meyer (eds), *The New Economic Sociology*, New York: Russell Sage Foundation, pp. 35–60.

Helper, S. and J. Kiehl (2004), 'Developing supplier capabilities: market and non-market approaches', *Industry and Innovation*, **11** (1/2), 89–107.

Herrigel, G. (2004), 'Emerging strategies and forms of governance in high-wage component manufacturing regions', *Industry and Innovation*, **11** (1/2), 45.

Humphrey, J. and O. Memedovic (2003), *The Global Automotive Industry Value Chain: What Prospects for Upgrading by Developing Countries*, in UNIDO (ed.), *Sectoral Studies Series*, Vienna.

Jacobs, J. (1984), *Cities and the Wealth of Nations*, New York: Vintage.

Knoke, D. (2001), *Changing Organizations: Business Networks in the New Political Economy*, Boulder, CO: Westview Press.

Kogut, B. and U. Zander (1992), 'Knowledge of the firm, combinative capabilities, and the replication of technology', *Organization Science: A Journal of the Institute of Management Sciences*, **3** (3), 383.

Kosacoff, B. (1999), *Hacia un mejor entorno competitivo de la produccion automotriz en Argentina*, Buenos Aires: CEPAL.

Kotabe, M., R. Parente and J. Murray (2007), 'Antecedents and outcomes of modular production in the Brazilian automobile industry: a grounded theory approach', *Journal of International Business Studies*, **38** (1), 84–106.

Lin, N. (2001), 'Building a network theory of social capital', in N. Lin, K. Cook and R.S. Burt (eds), *Social Capital: Theory and Research*, New York: Aldine de Gruyter, pp. 3–30.

Locke, R.M. (1995), *Remaking the Italian Economy: Local Politics and Industrial Change in Contemporary Italy*, Ithaca, NY: Cornell University Press.

MacDuffie, J.P. and S. Helper (2006), 'Collaboration in supply chains: with and without trust', in C. Heckscher and P. Adler (eds), *The Firm as Collaborative Community*, New York: Oxford University Press.

McDermott, G.A. (2002), *Embedded Politics: Industrial Networks and Institutional Change in Postcommunism*, Ann Arbor: University of Michigan Press.

McDermott, G.A. (2007), 'The politics of institutional renovation and economic upgrading: recombining the vines that bind in Argentina', *Politics and Society*, **35** (1), 103–43.

McDermott, G.A. and R.A. Corredoira (2010), 'Network composition, collaborative ties, and upgrading in emerging market firms: lessons from the Argentine autoparts sector', *Journal of International Business Studies*, **41**, 308–29.

McDermott, G.A., R.A. Corredoira and G. Kruse (2009), 'Public private institutions as catalysts for upgrading in emerging markets', *Academy of Management Journal*, **52** (6), 1270–96.

McEvily, B. and A. Marcus (2005), 'Embedded ties and the acquisition of competitive capabilities', *Strategic Management Journal*, **26** (11), 1033–55.

McEvily, B. and A. Zaheer (1999), 'Bridging ties: a source of firm heterogeneity in competitive capabilities', *Strategic Management Journal*, **20** (12), 1133–56.

McEvily, B. and A. Zaheer (2004), 'Architects of trust: the role of network facilitators in geographical clusters', in R. Kramer and K. Cook (eds), *Trust and Distrust in Organizations*, New York: Russell Sage, pp. 189–213.

Moran, P. and S. Ghoshal (1999), 'Markets, firms, and the process of economic development', *Academy of Management Review*, **24** (3), 390–408.

Moran, T.H., E.M. Graham and M. Blomström (2005), *Does FDI Promote Development? New Measurements, Outcomes, and Policy Approaches*, Washington, DC: Institute for International Economics.

Nelson, R. and S. Winter (1982), *An Evolutionary Theory of Economy Change*, Cambridge: Harvard University Press.

Ostrom, E. (1999), 'Coping with tragedies of the commons', *Annual Review of Political Science*, 2, 493–535.

Owen-Smith, J. and W.W. Powell (2004), 'Knowledge networks as channels and conduits: the effects of spillovers in the Boston biotechnology community', *Organization Science*, **15** (1), 5–21.

Padgett, J.F. and C.K. Ansell (1993), 'Robust action and the rise of the Medici, 1400–1434', *American Journal of Sociology*, **98** (6), 1259–320.

Paladino, M. and J.M. Jauregui (2001), *La transformacion del sector vitivinicola Argentino*, Argentina: IAE, Universidad Austral.

Perez-Aleman, P. (2005), 'Cluster formation, institutions and learning: the emergence of clusters and development in Chile', *Industrial and Corporate Change*, **14** (4), 651–77.

Pietrobelli, C. and R. Rabellotti (2011), 'Global value chains meet innovation systems: are there learning opportunities for developing countries', *World Development*, **39** (7), 1261–9.

Porter, M.E. (1990), *The Competitive Advantage of Nations*, New York: Free Press.

Powell, W.W., K.W. Koput and L. Smith-Doerr (1996), 'Interorganizational collaboration and the locus of innovation: networks of learning in biotechnology', *Administrative Science Quarterly*, **41** (1), 116–45.

Powell, W.W., K. Whittington and K. Packalen (2011), 'Organizational and institutional genesis: the emergence of high-tech clusters in the life sciences,' in J. Padgett and W.W. Powell (eds), *The Emergence of Organizations and Markets*, Princeton University Press (forthcoming).

Provan, K.G. and H.B. Milward (1995), 'A preliminary theory of interorganizational network effectiveness: a comparative study of four community mental health systems', *Administrative Science Quarterly*, **40** (1), 1–33.

Putnam, R.D., R. Leonardi and R.Y. Nanetti (1993), *Making Democracy Work*, Princeton, NJ: Princeton University Press.

Roberts, P. and P. Ingram (2002), 'Vertical linkages, knowledge transfer and export performance: the Australian and New Zealand wine industries, 1987–1999', unpublished manuscript, Emory University.

Rocha, H. (2004), 'Entrepreneurship and development: the role of clusters. A literature review', *Small Business Economics*, 363–400.

Rodrik, D. (2004), 'Industrial policy for the twenty-first century', KSG Working Paper No. RWP04-047. Available at SSRN: http://ssrn.com/abstract=617544 or http://dx.doi.org/10.2139/ssrn.617544.

Rofman, A.B. (1999), *Desarrollo regional y exclusión social: transformaciones y crisis en la Argentina contemporánea*, Buenos Aires: Amorrortu Editores.

Romanelli, E. and O.M. Khessina (2005), 'Regional industrial identity: cluster configurations and economic development', *Organization Science*, **16** (4), 344–58.

Ruiz, A.M. and H. Vila (2003), 'Structural changes and strategies of the Argentinean wine chain actors', in S. Gatti, E. Giraud-Heraud and S. Mili (eds), *Wine in the Old World: New Risks and Opportunities*, Milano: FrancoAngeli, pp. 215–28.

Sabel, C. (1994), 'Learning by monitoring: the institutions of economic development', in N.J. Smelser and R. Swedberg (eds), *The Handbook of Economic Sociology*, pp. Princeton: Princeton University Press, pp. 137–65.

Safford, S. (2007), *Why the Garden Club Couldn't Save Youngstown: Civic Infrastructure and Mobilization in Economic Crises*, Cambridge: Harvard University Press.

Sako, M. (2004), 'Supplier development at Honda, Nissan and Toyota: comparative case studies of organizational capability enhancement', *Industrial Corporate Change*, **13** (2), 281–308.

Saxenian, A. (1994), *Regional Advantage: Culture and Competition in Silicon Valley and Route 128*, Cambridge: Harvard University Press.

Schmitz, H. (ed.) (2004), *Local Enterprises in the Global Economy: Issues of Governance and Upgrading*, Cheltenham, UK and Northampton, MA, USA: Edward Elgar.

Schneider, B. (2004), *Business Politics and the State in Twentieth-Century Latin America*, Cambridge and New York: Cambridge University Press.

Schumpeter, J.A. (1934), *The Theory of Economic Development*, Cambridge, MA: Harvard University Press.

Stark, D. and L. Bruszt (1998), *Post-Socialist Pathways: Transforming Politics and Property in Eastern Europe*, New York: Cambridge University Press.

Stark, D. and B. Vedres (2006), 'Social times of network spaces: network sequences and foreign investment in Hungary', *American Journal of Sociology*, **111** (5), 1367–411.

Sturgeon, T.J. and R. Florida (2004), 'Globalization, deverticalization, and employment in the motor vehicle industry', in M. Kenney and R. Florida (eds), *Locating Global Advantage: Industry Dynamics in the International Economy*, Stanford, CA: Stanford University Press, pp. 52–81.

Sutz, J. (2000), 'The university–industry–government relations in Latin America', *Research Policy*, **29** (2), 279–90.

Swaminathan, A. (2001), 'Resource partitioning and the evolution of specialist organizations: the role of location and identity in the U.S. wine industry', *Academy of Management Journal*, **44** (6), 1169–85.

Tendler, J. (1997), *Good Government in the Tropics*, Baltimore: Johns Hopkins University Press.

Thelen, K. (2003), 'How institutions evolve: insights from comparative historical analysis', in J. Mahoney and D. Rueschemeyer (eds), *Comparative Historical Analysis in the Social Sciences*, New York: Cambridge University Press, pp. 208–40.

Uzzi, B. (1996), 'The sources and consequences of embeddedness for the performance of organizations: the network effect', *American Sociological Review*, **61** (4), 674–98.

Yoguel, G., V. Moori-Koenig and P. Angelelli (1999), *Los Problemas del Entorno de Negocios: el Desarrollo Competitivo de las PyMEs Argentina*s, Buenos Aires: Miño y Davila Editores.

Zuckerman, E. and S. Sgourev (2006), 'Peer capitalism: parallel relationships in the U.S. economy', *American Journal of Sociology*, **111** (5), 1327–66.

5.   Enhancing economic growth? University technology commercialization

Shiri M. Breznitz and Neela Ram

1.   INTRODUCTION

Local and national governments are putting universities under constant pressure to promote economic growth. Commercialization of technology has been identified as the main mechanism by which universities can do this. Existing studies attempt to find one silver bullet that will work for all universities. However, universities are located in specific geographic environments with their own history, which inevitably affects their ability to commercialize technology. Most studies on commercialization of technology do not take those specific conditions into consideration.

Traditionally, universities have the two roles of teaching and research, so it is important to understand how they became involved in and implemented technology commercialization, in what has become their third role. Adding commercialization to the university's roles began in the nineteenth century. A catalyst in this process was the development of important products and services and the reliance on research during two world wars. The importance of universities' research during that period shifted the view on universities to one as a tool for social change.

In addition, the role of the university has come to include a responsibility for training the work force and working on applied research. The job training aspect was a direct result of changes in modern society. Modern industrial economic growth required a highly trained work force, something universities were in a position to provide (Scott, 1977). Adding to this pressure was the extent of government funding that the universities receive (Russell, 1993). Training a qualified labor force is typically an expensive endeavor and it requires increasingly greater investment. However, no individual company can support such an investment, and even more so, individual companies are not likely to make such an investment, especially if the output benefits other corporations (Kenney, 1986).

Hence, governments became the main source of university research funding. As a result of becoming benefactors of public funding, universities were pressured to make a return to society.

As part of 'paying back the community,' universities make contributions through research and development (R&D), collaborations, and technology transfer to industry (Minshall et al., 2004). In this way, universities become engines of local economic growth through the commercialization of research. The outcome of these efforts can be seen in an analysis of universities' ability to commercialize technology. The many studies on technology commercialization and best practices indicate that this new role of technology commercialization is not performed equally at all universities nor is it equally rewarding everywhere.

This chapter takes the view that there is no silver-bullet method suitable for university technology transfer everywhere and therefore adds the important elements of history and environment in analyzing a critical case study of commercialization of technology at one university: the Georgia Institute of Technology. This university represents a critical case study of a research university that is rapidly growing and developing and a prime example of a university where previous findings regarding best practices for technology transfer should work. We find that to best serve its state as a public university, this relative newcomer to technology commercialization designed and organized its technology transfer activities around its local environment and historical strengths, unlike other universities that tried to follow a general trend in technology commercialization.

2.   WHAT AFFECTS COMMERCIALIZATION AT UNIVERSITIES?

Studies on university technology commercialization best practices found conflicting information (Rothaermel et al., 2007). They mostly overlook the fact that each university operates in a different legislative, financial, and cultural setting and therefore needs to allocate different resources to become successful at commercialization.

External University Factors

External factors that influence the commercialization process are found in the economy and legislation at both national and regional levels (Rahm et al., 2000; O'Shea et al., 2005; Lawton Smith, 2006). Among federal legislation and regulations in the United States, the Bayh–Dole Act of 1990 has had a marked effect on the relationship between university and industry

(Mowery and Sampat, 2001). The law requires faculty members who conduct research using federal grants to disclose inventions created as a result of that research to the Technology Transfer Office (TTO). European countries having seen the impact of the Bayh–Dole Act, especially in regions like Silicon Valley, have tried to replicate this success by creating incentives and a welcoming climate for technology transfer (Lawton Smith, 2006).

The relationship between industry and universities is important in studies of successful technology transfer and commercialization. By viewing these relationships in the context of national and regional innovation systems and the triple-helix theories, the environment in which universities operate as well as the relationship between firms and institutions emerge as important factors in influencing their ability to innovate and bring products to market (Nelson, 1993; Etzkowitz, 1995).

In addition to being obliged to contribute to the national economy, universities also feel the same push at a local level. As a result, these innovation systems are also found at the regional level. Cooke (2002) presents a correlation between the two:

> Clearly, by no means all innovation interaction can or even should occur locally, but the rise of the entrepreneurial university and promotion of the so-called 'triple-helix' of interaction between industry, government and universities as a key feature of the knowledge economy testifies to the practical evolution of interactive innovation process. (p. 136)

Some regions with innovative organizations that are connected through joint research programs, policies, and social networks 'combine learning with upstream and downstream innovation capability' (Cooke and Morgan, 1998, p. 71). These regions are especially important in that firms have easier access to knowledge and ideas. These systems, in which the university is able to operate, have a significant, but not sole, impact on the university's ability to transfer knowledge and ideas to the private market (Morgan, 1997).

Internal University Factors

In addition to the importance of the effect of external factors on the university's ability to commercialize technology, there are internal university factors that can also have an effect. Various studies indicate that the three most important factors are the university's entrepreneurial activity, technology-transfer policy, and technology-transfer organization (Clark, 1998; Etzkowitz, 1998; Bercovitz et al., 2001; Shane, 2004; Link and Scott, 2005; O'Shea et al., 2005; Breznitz, 2011).

Several studies identify university culture as an integral component of technology commercialization. Clark (1998) highlights the importance of the cultural climate of the entire university and asserts that all departments and research centers, not just the leadership, play a vital role in promoting entrepreneurial activity. Moreover, Kenney and Goe (2004) found that the culture within the scientist's department, including individual colleagues, has an effect on his/her entrepreneurial spirit. Moreover, the scientist's university of residence can also direct his or her 'professional entrepreneurship and corporate involvement' (Kenney and Goe, 2004, p. 704) and influence his or her ability to innovate and commercialize technologies (Kenney and Goe, 2004). Bercovitz and Feldman (2007) argue that the likelihood that the scientist will participate in commercialization and technology transfer activities and file inventions will be greater in an atmosphere in which entrepreneurship is encouraged and supported – that is, the department chair and peers within that culture also file inventions. Further studies found that the mission statement of a university in many cases offers a window into the commercialization culture and organization of the institute. For technology commercialization especially, mission statements indicate an institution's commitment to economic development in general and technology and research commercialization in particular (Breznitz, 2011).

Another factor that affects technology transfer and output is the physical organization and management of the university – in particular, the university's Technology Transfer Office (TTO) or, in some universities, the Technology Licensing Office (TLO). Moreover, studies indicate that the characteristics of the university TTO influence the level of spinout activity for that institution (Bercovitz et al., 2001; Owen-Smith and Powell, 2001; Shane, 2004; Chapple et al., 2005; Lockett and Wright, 2005; O'Shea et al., 2005). O'Shea et al. (2005) found that historical background and past technology transfer success predict a university's future capability and options with regard to spinout formation. The quality and number of personnel at a TTO, which reflect its resources, influence the flexibility and trust of the university. If a TTO has a highly credentialed and knowledgeable staff, inventors and investors will be more willing to work with it (Shane, 2004; Lockett and Wright, 2005; O'Shea et al., 2005). Studies by Clarysse et al. (2005) and Lockett and Wright (2005) found that the TTO's business development capabilities have a positive influence on startup formation. The use of outside lawyers can also affect output. Siegel et al. (2003) found that resources dedicated to outside counsel reduce the number of licensing agreements but increase revenues from the agreements made. Breznitz (2011) found that the concentration of commercialization activities in one unit within the university, policy clarity, and professional staff are important factors that promote prompt and productive technology commercialization.

Several studies have explored the importance of academic policies that affect the relationship between universities and industry. In particular, they have examined the effects of intellectual property rights (IPR) with regard to patents, licenses, and spinout companies and how they influence the effect of technology transfer on that relationship. IPR policies at universities refer to copyright on academic publications, such as journals and books, or to patents filed by the university for inventions that were created as a result of research there. Ownership of these inventions shapes the analysis of IPR policies in general, not only because the definitions change from one university to another but also because of the differences between TTOs in culture, history, and organization. For instance, one university might wholly own inventions while at another ownership is determined by the source of funding (Siegel and Phan, 2005). One factor that encourages and enhances technology licensing is assigning a higher share of royalties to the inventor. According to Link and Seigel (2005), 'Universities that seek to enhance licensing should allocate a higher share of royalties to faculty members' (p. 179). Another important policy influence on technology transfer and commercialization is the university's willingness to contribute equity for patenting and licensing expenses. Di Gregorio and Shane (2003) state that universities that are willing to take on this expense have a higher rate of spinning out companies than universities that are not. Further studies by Shane (2004) indicate that a university's policies have a marked influence on its spinouts. He finds that the following factors are important in determining the rate of creating spinout companies: allowing exclusive licensing, allowing a leave of absence, permitting the use of university resources, the size of the share of royalties allocated to inventors, and providing access to pre-seed-stage capital.

3.　METHODS

This is an empirical case study of the factors that affect commercialization of technology at a university. The specific case examined here is the Georgia Institute of Technology (Georgia Tech) and the steps it took as a university, new to commercialization, that let it become one of the top ten commercializing universities in the United States.[1] This study collected data through two sources that support such data: the Patent Board and the Association of University Technology Managers (AUTM). First, the selection of the case study and comparable institutes was based on the patent scorecard for 2009. The Patent Board, which is a private business, provides information regarding the technology and patent strengths of each university.[2]

Second, the authors used the AUTM licensing surveys, which provided information regarding public and private investment, spinout companies, and licenses for each of the institutions (AUTM, 2005, 2009). In particular, the authors used the 2009 survey to compare the data to the patent scorecard of 2009. The 2005 licensing survey was added to allow an historical perspective. Third, university web sites revealed information regarding their technology commercialization policies and organization. Fourth, the researchers conducted interviews with Georgia Tech administrators, including directors and managers. These interviews provided an in-depth look into the operations and organization of technology commercialization at the university and how commercialization was achieved using various university resources.

This study compares Georgia Tech to the other institutions listed in the top ten (out of a ranking of 124 institutions)[3] 'University Leaders in Innovation' by the Patent Board (Oldach, 2009): California Institute of Technology, Cornell University, Massachusetts Institute of Technology, Stanford University, University of Michigan, University of North Carolina – Chapel Hill, University of Texas – Austin, and University of Wisconsin – Madison. These universities made the list because of the 'relative strengths of their patent portfolios' in terms of both overall quantity and quality.

4.   THE CASE OF GEORGIA TECH

This section analyzes and compares Georgia Tech by using the factors identified in the literature review. We start by examining the historical and environmental factors in which the university operates. The following section reviews internal university factors: culture, organization, and policy to commercialize technology and Georgia Tech.

External University Factors at Georgia Tech

The Georgia Institute of Technology was established in 1885 as the Georgia School of Technology as part of an attempt to reconstruct the South and create the 'New (Industrial) South' (O'Mara, 2005; McMath, 1985; Youtie and Shapira, 2008).[4] The Georgia School of Technology, which was built on land donated by the state, originally trained students by using model factories to help develop agricultural technologies (O'Mara, 2005). Initial conversations regarding the pursuits of the school focused on whether its curriculum would use a practical approach, based on that of the Worcester Free Institute, or a more academic approach, similar to the model used by the Massachusetts Institute of Technology. The school's formation committee, which was created by Georgia's state legislature and headed by two former Confederate soldiers, decided that the institute would combine both approaches and provide a well-rounded education in a post-Civil War South. The state of Georgia appropriated $65,000 for buildings, land, and other costs associated with operating the school for one year (Georgia Tech, The Hopkins Administration).

Georgia's congressional representation played a heavy role in contributing to Atlanta's industrial growth, especially in the 1950s and 1960s, during the Cold War era. Because two Georgians played influential roles on the House Armed Services Committee during that critical period, Georgia was the recipient of many military contracts, and its industrial capacity grew exponentially. By 1960, the state was home to fifteen new military installations (O'Mara, 2005). Georgia Tech benefited from these contracts in the form of not only increased federal R&D grants for military objectives but also new relationships with the private sector. These interactions created the need for a university liaison to foster beneficial relationships between the various entities, and, to that end, the Engineering Experiment Station (EES)[5] created the 'Industrial Associate Program.' By paying a standard fee of $15,000 every three years, corporations could fund research at EES and help direct how the money was used, and, in turn, EES would offer the services of its research staff to those firms (O'Mara, 2005).

By 1969, a survey of Atlanta firms indicated that Georgia Tech and its resources were responsible for creating 29 companies, which generated over $23 million in sales and employed 1,400 workers (O'Mara, 2005). The promise of such growth spurred discussions by city officials regarding the creation of a science park. In the early 1960s, Paul Duke, a prominent alumnus, offered a large swath of land in the northern part of the city. Though the land is located more than 10 miles away from the main campus, city officials thought that it was a prime location for the skilled workers it was hoping to attract (O'Mara, 2005). That is, the location offered insulation from the racial and economic tensions that surrounded Georgia Tech's campus. Following its institution's mission statement, the Georgia Tech administration, under the leadership of President Edward Harrison, thought that university-related development should be focused on urban renewal projects in areas proximate to the campus, and it withdrew support of the park's development. Technology park development went ahead without any university partnership. In 1982, it was home to 40 companies, which employed more than 2,500 people (O'Mara, 2005).

The state of Georgia developed a series of programs to help elevate its status as a destination for firms related to high technology industry (Youtie and Shapira, 2008). In 1990, the Georgia Research Alliance (GRA) was created as a collaborative partnership among the six research universities in the state. These universities, Clark Atlanta University, Emory University, Georgia Institute of Technology, Georgia State University, Georgia Health Sciences University, and the University of Georgia, were brought together to help foster economic development through their research capabilities (Georgia Research Alliance, 2011). The GRA has leveraged $225 million in state funding to generate more than $2.5 billion in federal and private investment in its first twenty years. By promoting partnerships between business, government, and the universities, the alliance's primary aim was to build a technology-driven economy (Georgia Research Alliance, 2011).

In 2002 the GRA created the Georgia Research Alliance Venture Fund. The fund invests in the six research universities to allow inventions to leave the lab and develop into a commercial product. The fund's investors are the state of Georgia, private individuals, corporations, and foundations. Research enterprises can go through four stages of investment. Phases I and II provide commercialization grants for a university lab totaling $150,000.[6] Firms that receive the funds are required to go through the GRA VentureLab education program, which at Georgia Tech is managed by the Advanced Technology Development Center (ATDC). Researchers are expected to collaborate with the ATDC and apply to the GRA for funding. A committee made up of representatives from the six universities then considers the proposal. In Phase III, the company can apply for a loan up to $250,000. The request is then considered by the GRA committee as well as an outside committee made up of lawyers, venture capitalists, and entrepreneurs. The loan has favorable terms, with 4 per cent APR up to seven years. In Phase IV, as limited partnerships, firms that have completed the VentureLab program can apply for to up to $1 million from the fund. The application is considered at the investor level only. There is no university involvement.

By helping universities attract intellectual talent, invest in infrastructure, and provide funding to advance commercialization of the new technology, the GRA aimed to fulfill its mission of creating economic opportunity through university-based innovation (Georgia Research Alliance, 2011). Though the GRA was funded primarily through grants from private foundations and industries, investments were part of the state budget and were approved by the legislature (Georgia Research Alliance, 2011). Current economic conditions have threatened the funding of the organization – the current governor, Nathan Deal, proposed cutting the organization's annual funding from $17 million to less than $4 million for fiscal year 2012 (Stuart, 2011).

In addition to the GRA, Georgia's Traditional Industries Program (TIP) was created in 1994 as a partnership among the state government, the University System of Georgia, and the state's three traditional industries – paper, food processing, and textiles. Since its beginnings, TIP has conducted more than 200 R&D projects in these three areas across the state. More than $80 million has been invested in R&D since the program's inception to help close the gap between research and practice and to increase these sectors' competitiveness within the state and beyond (Economic Development Institute).

At the federal level, the Bayh–Dole Act of 1980 has been influential in incentivizing cooperation between industries and institutions. By allowing the institution to elect to retain title to inventions related to federally funded work, this law has allowed universities to market inventions and benefit from their inventions and innovations (AUTM, 2011). The Office of Technology Licensing has stated that, as a result of the Bayh–Dole Act, Georgia Tech secured 786 patents and 592 active licenses by 2011. In addition, the university has been able to increase its sponsored funding and recruit top faculty and researchers, and in 2010, it secured a record $557 million in awards (Georgia Tech, 2011).

The varied technology commercialization history and environment, especially at the state level, have shaped Georgia Tech's view and ability to transfer knowledge and commercialize technology. Inconsistent support at the state level, coupled with the original mission of the university to create jobs for the state, had a significant impact on building up the industrial infrastructure of the university. Moreover, public-private partnerships gained importance with the increase in federal funding. Though the state's financial contribution to the university decreased in the second half of the twentieth century, it provided support through the creation of programs that encouraged public-private partnerships. These programs helped facilitate intra-university collaborations and helped partner industry with firms. These collaborations, which were further strengthened by the discriminatory development plans implemented by city officials in the 1960s, allowed the university to optimally employ the support from the federal and state government, strengthen its ties with private industry, and build up its commercialization services.

Internal University Factors

Existing studies show that internal university factors strongly affect the ability of a university to commercialize its technology. In particular, studies refer to a university's culture, policy, and technology commercialization organizational structure. This section examines internal university factors at Georgia Tech and finds that Georgia Tech's commercialization is based on its creation as a public university with a goal of contributing to the local economy. Hence, knowledge transfer and technology policy focuses on industrial collaboration and university spinout companies.

University commercialization culture at Georgia Tech
Georgia Tech's mission statement focuses on the state of Georgia as the main beneficiary of its innovation and teaching. In particular, the university's mission is 'to provide the state of Georgia with the scientific and technological base, innovation, and workforce it needs to shape a prosperous and sustainable future and quality of life for its citizens' (Georgia Tech, 2010c). Though Georgia Tech was not established as a land-grant university, the university's early years were dedicated to workforce development and training. As Atlanta strived to move beyond recovering from the Civil War, the school sought to abandon the model factories in favor of technology research and engineering projects around the state. This desire to shift direction had little support from state officials, and the school continued to promote the regional economy by providing technological training through the end of the nineteenth century (O'Mara, 2005).

Another indicator of a university's entrepreneurial culture is its close ties with industry. Historically, industrial research at Georgia Tech was conducted mainly through the Georgia Tech Research Institution (GTRI) (previously the Engineering Experiment Station, EES).[7] The establishment of the EES in 1919, which was authorized by the state assembly, was a response to the school's frustrations regarding expansion of its academic program. However, it was mostly a symbolic move; in its early years the state neglected to fund the program. Sixteen years after its inception, the state finally allocated $5,000 toward programs that addressed engineering problems with a stated connection to Georgia's economic interests (GTRI, 2009c; O'Mara, 2005). This effort, coupled with 'Forward Atlanta,' a 1920s economic development campaign that rebranded Atlanta as a regional business center (O'Mara, 2005), marked a new era of using the school, its resources, and Atlanta's location to attract out-of-state firms and corporations. The 'Forward Atlanta' initiative and the EES contributed to a strong business community that heavily influenced the growth and direction of Atlanta's economy.

In the 1950s, innovators at the EES wanted to capitalize on the technologies and inventions that emerged from the work performed there. This resulted in the creation of Scientific Atlanta, a firm that produced telecommunications products based on technologies developed at the EES. This move was not supported by members of Georgia Tech's administration, who feared the possibility of conflicts of interest that could interfere with

Table 5.1   Georgia Tech's industrial relationship strength

University	Industrial expenditure ($)	Industrial impact*
MIT	79,783,825	1.94
Cal Tech	21,362,988	1.46
Georgia Tech	45,112,899	1.40
Stanford	52,541,458	1.34
UNC – Chapel Hill	18,002,543	1.13
UT – Austin	38,701,273	1.09
Cornell	24,131,895	1.02
Michigan	38,617,528	0.94
UW – Madison	3,118,440	0.83

Note: *Based on the Patent Board's 2009 patent scorecard (Oldach, 2009).

the work of the EES. In addition, they thought that contracts that would normally be awarded to the EES were being assigned to Scientific Atlanta (GTRI, 2009d). Scientific Atlanta was a major producer of telecommunication products that was acquired by Cisco in 2006 (Cisco, 2011). As the Cold War came to an end, defense research spending in the federal budget decreased, markedly so during the administration of Bill Clinton. Georgia Tech adapted to this change by adapting the GTRI's mission, strengthening its industrial partnerships, especially in the areas of transportation, medical technology, and modeling, simulating, and testing (GTRI, 2009b). In 1984, on its fiftieth anniversary, the EES officially became the Georgia Tech Research Institute (GTRI, 2009a).

Compared to other top research universities, Georgia Tech has established relatively strong connections with industry. This is especially evident in the amount of funding the university receives from private industry and also in terms of the number of patents it holds. The university has received, on average, $45 million from private industry every year. Though it does not fare as well as peer institutions (see Table 5.1) in terms of both government and overall research expenditures, Georgia Tech has won more awards from industry. Moreover, the patent scorecard reveals that Georgia Tech's patented innovations are more likely to be built upon than those of most other institutions.[8]

In addition to the university's strong relationship with industry, Georgia Tech encourages innovation among its students. The InventurePrize@ GeorgiaTech, a competition created by the faculty and aimed at undergraduate students at Georgia Tech, is a high-profile event that seeks to create an entrepreneurial and innovative climate at the university using a bottom-up approach:

The goal ... is to encourage an interest in invention, innovation, and entre-preneurial lifestyle amongst GT students and create an infrastructure, culture, and focus that galvanizes, captures, and highlights student inventiveness and inventorship. (Georgia Tech, 2010d)

This competition contributes to the entrepreneurial culture of Georgia Tech by fostering innovation and technological advancement at the undergraduate level. Contest entries are judged on their innovation, marketability, size of the market for the innovation, probability of success of the business idea, and the drive of the inventor. The winner is awarded a $15,000 cash prize and is offered patent counsel through the GTRC, and, if applicable, the GTRC will file a patent on the winner's behalf and assume any associated costs (Georgia Tech, 2010b). Additional benefits include having access to business counsel and other resources that could help increase the marketability of the invention and opportunities for raising capital to support the idea (Georgia Tech, 2010b).

The Business Plan Competition, which was started in 2001, is a similar program administered by the College of Management and aimed at both Georgia Tech students and alumni. The competition has been credited with building up the local community and economy:

The Business Plan Competition is an important contributor to the expansion of entrepreneurship locally, regionally, nationally, and internationally. Each year, the competition draws from 60 to 70 leading venture capitalists, entrepreneurs, and business people to participate as judges and workshop presenters. (Georgia Tech, 2010a)

The competition guidelines state that entrants must develop a business plan that is both viable and sustainable; plus built on the idea that the technology or service has a viable market. There are both cash and service prizes awarded to the top winners in the competition (Georgia Tech, 2010a).

University commercialization organization at Georgia Tech
There are two pathways to commercialize technology transfer at Georgia Tech. The first is through the GTRC, which contains the Office of Technology Licensing (OTL), and the second is through the Enterprise Innovation Institute (EII), which contains the ATDC. The GTRC is primarily concerned with patents and licensing. The EII in general and the ATDC in particular are responsible for incubating firms and spinning out companies that promote the technologies being developed on campus. That said, all contracts for spinout companies must go through the OTL and the GTRC. Moreover, the EII supports technology partnerships and economic development and connects companies to R&D, education, and other resources at Georgia Tech.[9]

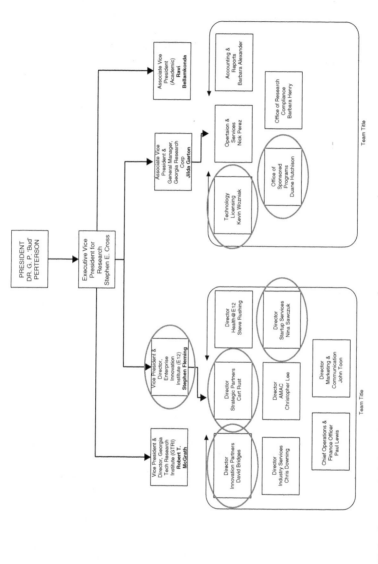

Note: Technology transfer is based in two parts of the institute: at the Enterprise Innovation Institute and at the Georgia Tech Research Corporation. Marked in circles are all the units involved with technology commercialization.

Source: Georgia Tech organizational chart (Gatech, 2011).

Figure 5.1 Technology commercialization at Georgia Tech

The GTRC, established in 1937 as the Industrial Development Council, was created to 'stimulate industrial development, to promote the fullest utilization of natural resources, and to foster research invention and discovery so as to provide a constantly improving technique in that behalf.'[10] The organization is primarily concerned with applying the technological innovations developed at Georgia Tech through technology transfer and fostering relationships with public and private sectors.[11] The GTRC is the body through which funding from different funding agencies is channeled into Georgia Tech.

> GTRC serves as the contracting entity for the academic colleges of Georgia Tech. GTRC supports and promotes research through its stewardship of the funds for sponsored research and the financial support of research activities. GTRC is the owner of intellectual property created at Georgia Tech, and its Office of Technology Licensing (OTL) is responsible for the protection, licensing, and management of the intellectual property portfolio. The E-Commerce and Training Division within OSP [Office of Sponsored Programs] is responsible for implementation and administration of electronic proposal submission systems, sponsored programs data, and the administration of electronic commerce functions. The Office of Research Compliance promotes the responsible conduct of research and manages regulatory requirements for human subjects, the use of animal models, the application of export controls, compliance with the conflicts of interest policy, and administration of recombinant DNA regulations. (GTRC, 2011)

The GTRC provides administrative support to faculty, staff, and students with regard to research administration, contracting, and intellectual property management. The technology commercialization is handled by two units at the GTRC: (1) the OTL, which was founded in 1990, a decade after the passage of the Bayh–Dole Act, is responsible for university licensing and tracking of expenses and royalties; it owns all intellectual property that results from research activities and works closely with industry and government to sponsor research at the university; (2) the EII, which provides support for startups and spinout companies.

Studies show that the size and quality of OTL employees, the use of outside attorneys, and past success are indicators of the office's commercialization ability. The OTL at Georgia Tech has ten full-time employees (seven professionals and three support staff). The seven professionals in this office are focused in the biological and physical sciences and all have advanced degrees (MBA, MS, JD, etc.). Moreover, two out of the seven professionals are attorneys. The office uses outside attorneys mostly for patenting. However, outside counsel is used as needed for other contractual and transactional needs. Georgia Tech has not earned revenues in the hundreds of millions of dollars. However, the office does receive about $500,000 a year from some deals. Excluding the deals in biomedical fields, Georgia Tech compares favorably with Stanford in terms of the level of royalties.

The second avenue through which technology commercialization occurs is in several units within the EII. Spinout and startup activity is encouraged through the Startup Services Unit, where we find the ATDC. The Strategic Partners Unit provides industrial liaison for large corporations seeking to collaborate with Georgia Tech researchers. The Innovation Partners Unit at the EII provides economic development services to Georgia's communities, technology-transfer consulting to smaller universities in the region, collaboration with the National Aeronautics and Space Administration (NASA), and Small Business Innovation Research (SBIR) assistance. Funding for university spinouts and startup companies is managed mainly through the office of the vice president and director of the EII, Stephen Fleming.

In 2011 three new programs were created to foster entrepreneurship and innovation at Georgia Tech. GT:IPS provides an expedited license from the OTL and a support system from the ATDC in particular and across campus in general. To receive these benefits, firm founders are required to go through an education program regarding conflict of interest, legal affairs, licensing, and patenting procedures. The second organization is Flashpoint at Georgia Tech. This program, together with the Flashpoint venture capital fund, will invest and provide assistance to firms' leaders while they take a semester to learn more about how to build and run their firm. The third program is the Bio-impact Commercialization Team (BCT). This program works closely with faculty members to commercialize translational research in biomedicine.

The organizational structure at Georgia Tech historically supported technology commercialization. Until 2010, both the ATDC and the OTL reported to the vice provost, who reported to the provost, who reported to the president of the university. In 2010, with a structural change at the university, Georgia Tech continued to show its commitment to technology commercialization by eliminating one reporting level. As of 2011, both the ATDC and the OTL report to their directors, who report to the executive vice president of research. This organizational structure demonstrates support for these programs by allowing both units direct access to top-level administration.

University Commercialization Policies at Georgia Tech

Existing studies show that intellectual property ownership, royalty share, equity, and exclusive licensing all have an impact on a university's commercialization ability.

IPR policy

Georgia Tech retains all rights to intellectual property developed under federally funded research. Until recently, the GTRC afforded the same right to private sponsors; however, this severely limited the marketability of the innovation. As a result, the GTRC now retains title to the invention and also gives the industrial sponsor the right of first refusal in licensing the technology. Also, when Georgia Tech releases the title to intellectual property, there is usually a stipulation that allows it to continue to use or practice the property for academic or research purposes.[12]

> All full or part-time faculty and staff shall, as a condition of employment with the Institute, execute an Assignment of Rights Form, assigning all rights, title and interest, to the extent prescribed in this policy, in any Intellectual Property to the Georgia Tech Research Corporation. Students shall not be required to execute an Assignment of Rights Form except in the cases where they are employees of the Institute. This policy shall, however, be applicable to them and shall be set forth in the General Catalog and Student Handbook. (GTRC, 2011)

Georgia Tech's OTL provides exclusive licensing and, even more importantly, nonexclusive royalty-free licenses, especially for industry-sponsored research deals. These deals are a major part of the reason for the large proportion of Georgia Tech's industrial expenditures (see Figure 5.2). Royalty shares at Georgia Tech favor the university (Table 5.2).[13] Georgia Tech frequently takes equity in firms; a factor that studies indicate has a positive impact on spinout creation.

Table 5.2 summarizes the breakdown of distribution after the initial payment.

Spinout policy

The ATDC, an organization within the EII, provides startup services. It is a startup accelerator that seeks to launch tech entrepreneurs and create successful businesses. The ATDC has helped launch more than 120 companies since its inception in 1980. Companies at the ATDC are

Table 5.2   Distribution of net licensing income (%)

	Next $500k	$501,000–$1 million	>$1 million
Creator	33	33	33
Unit	17	27	33
GTRC	50	40	34

Source: Office of Faculty Career Development Services, 2008.

divided into four categories: Stage I, Concept; Stage II, Prototype; Stage III, Production; and Stage IV, Expansion. The ATDC provides assistance to firms in writing a business plan, designing a financing strategy (VC, angels, SBIR), and recruiting employees.

The ATDC also provides incubator and accelerator services. As of 2011, out of 400 firms served by the ATDC, 40 were in the ATDC's incubator. Georgia Tech provides incubator space at three locations: two on Georgia Tech's campus in Atlanta and one in Savannah. Recently, the ATDC merged with the VentureLab program and the SBIR assistance program[14] and expanded its services to companies across the development spectrum – from the conception stage to well-established firms.[15] Because the ATDC is fully funded by the state of Georgia, it offers these services to all Georgia firms.

In addition to the GRA venture fund, funding for university spinouts and for local startups is provided at Georgia Tech through the following funds and programs:

ATDC seed fund   The ATDC seed fund was created in 1999 by the state of Georgia and is managed by EII director Stephen Fleming. Because the purpose of the fund was to enhance the creation of jobs in Georgia, the fund invests in startups located in or moving to the state. The maximum funding per company is $1 million. However, the ATDC is restricted in its ability to invest in companies. The fund can invest only $1 for every $3 in private investment. Moreover, the state has not made a contribution to the fund since 2010.[16]

Georgia Tech Edison Fund   This fund, created in 2008, invests in Georgia Tech-related companies.[17] Managed directly by Stephen Fleming, the fund was created from private donations, including the Charles Edison Fund in New Jersey. The fund invests $10,000–$25,000 in each firm.

Flashpoint at Georgia Tech   In 2011 following a change in leadership at Georgia Tech, the university launched Flashpoint at Georgia Tech. The program's mission is to identify early-stage companies with Georgia Tech connections. Like the GRA venture fund, the program is based on a venture fund and an education program. Based in Atlanta, the venture fund is a new private firm called Flashpoint Investments, and it is headed by Sig Mosely, president of Imlay Investment. Flashpoint Investments will invest in selected startups that go through the Flashpoint at Georgia Tech educational program. Nina Sawczuk, the general manager of the ATDC, and Merrick Furst, from the College of Computing, will manage the education program at Georgia Tech. The program will last one semester.

5. DISCUSSION: HOW DOES GEORGIA TECH COMPARE?

At Georgia Tech commercialization of technology might not exactly follow what studies call 'best practices,' but that accentuates its success in bringing technologies to market. Georgia Tech's ability to commercialize its technology successfully is especially apparent when the results there are compared with those at other peer institutions. Georgia Tech's TTO has one of the shortest histories but is still very competitive with other, more established TTOs. Figure 5.2 illustrates a comparison of the commercialization performance of Georgia Tech and other universities in terms of the age of their TTOs.

University Commercialization Culture

Working with industry is extremely important at Georgia Tech. Thus, as with the MIT Lincoln Laboratory and SRI International (originally called Stanford Research Institute), with state support the university has created a separate unit, the GTRI, dedicated to industrial research and collaboration with local and national businesses. Its commercialization culture is also reflected in its student invention competitions. Students' invention competitions at Georgia Tech, like those at the universities with the most spinouts, such as MIT and Stanford, show that the culture at Georgia Tech is oriented toward applied research and inventions. Students can compete at both the undergraduate and the graduate level and promote their inventions with the goal of commercialization. Moreover, the students receive the full support of the institute to patent and commercialize their technologies.

Georgia Tech is one of the leading universities in its positive and supportive attitude and culture toward commercialization. In 2011 alone, the university developed three new programs to support technology commercialization. In many ways Georgia Tech is at the cutting edge of the industry university spectrum, working very closely with industry, a situation that has both advantages and disadvantages.[18]

University Commercialization Organization

Georgia Tech has two main units that work on technology commercialization: the ATDC under the EII and the OTL under the GTRC. Six of the nine universities on the patent scorecard have only one office dedicated to technology commercialization. Georgia Tech is competitive with these universities in terms of the number of spinouts and licenses, which might imply that the number of units does not matter.

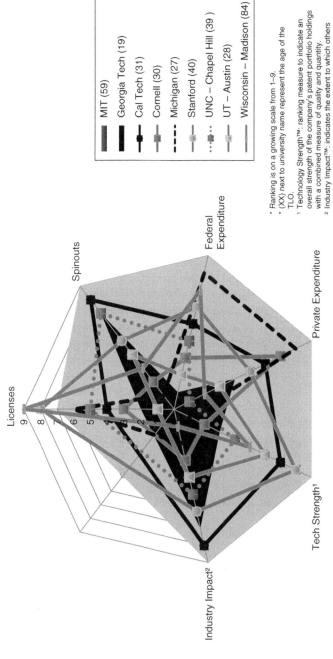

MIT (59)

Georgia Tech (19)

Cal Tech (31)

Cornell (30)

Michigan (27)

Stanford (40)

UNC – Chapel Hill (39)

UT – Austin (28)

Wisconsin – Madison (84)

Spinouts

Federal
Expenditure

Licenses

Private Expenditure

9
8
7
6
5
4
3
2

Tech Strength¹

Industry Impact²

* Ranking is on a growing scale from 1–9.
* (XX) next to university name represent the age of the
  TLO.
¹ Technology Strength™: ranking measure to indicate an
  overall strength of the company's patent portfolio holdings
  with a combined measure of quality and quantity.
² Industry Impact™: indicates the extent to which others
  are building upon a portfolio of issued US utility patents as
  compared to a total set of patents.

Note: Of the universities on the patent scorecard, MIT leads in terms of commercialization ability. Georgia Tech performs well in terms of the number of spinouts and industry impact, considering the age of the technology licensing office and its research expenditure.

Source: Patent Board, Patent Scorecard (Oldach, 2009).

Figure 5.2   Georgia Tech technology commercialization performance in comparison to other universities

Table 5.3   Universities ranking by number of technology transfer offices

University	Number of technology commercialization-related offices
Cal Tech	1
Cornell	1
MIT	1
Stanford	1
UNC – Chapel Hill	1
UW – Madison	1
Georgia Tech	2
Michigan	3
UT – Austin	3

Note: Georgia Tech is one of three universities in the patent scorecard that has more than one unit working on technology commercialization.

While its OTL is comparatively young and has a smaller number of employees than other TTOs, Georgia Tech does well in terms of the number of patents and licenses (AUTM, 2009).[19] Comparing Georgia Tech's commercial output with that of the other universities on the patent scorecard, we find a positive correlation between the number of employees in a TTO and the university's income from licenses. This implies that the size of a TTO matters. Previous studies found contradictory results regarding the size of the TTO. However, studies agree that the professionalism of a TTO affects its ability to transfer technology. Data on the professionalism of the employees in the universities studied in addition to Georgia Tech were not available. Large offices might have more funding, employ more experienced employees, use outside lawyers, and be better able to evaluate technologies. As a result, larger TTOs commercialize technology that brings in more revenue.

Comparing the scorecard universities using the AUTM data from 2005 and 2009 (Table 5.4), we find different results with regard to the number of employees versus the number and income from licenses. Cal Tech, UNC – Chapel Hill and Georgia Tech have the fewest full-time employees dedicated to licensing technology – ranging from five to seven. However, UNC has the highest number of licenses issued, and Georgia Tech ranks in the top half of the universities analyzed. In contrast, the income received from the licenses tells a different story – UNC and Georgia Tech rank lowest in terms of the level of income received, which corresponds to the number of employees dedicated to licensing. However, this is not the case with Cal Tech. The University of Wisconsin, MIT, and Stanford all earn the highest

Table 5.4   Universities' TTO ranking by number of employees

University	Number of employees	Age of TTO (2009)	Number of licenses	Income from licensing ($ million)	Presence of medical school
Cal Tech	5	31	26	47	No
UNC – Chapel Hill	6	39	72	3	Yes
Georgia Tech	7	19	59	2.4	No
Michigan	9	27	22	18	Yes
Cornell	11	30	64	5.1	Yes
Stanford	16	40	62	65	Yes
MIT	20	59	71	66.4	No
UW – Madison	26	84	40	56	Yes

Note: This table indicates that smaller offices perform just as well in the number of licenses compared with larger offices but do not perform as well in evaluating licensing income.

Source: AUTM (2009).

licensing income and have some of the largest TTOs (with 26, 20, and 16 employees, respectively).

The comparatively low income from licenses at Georgia Tech might have several explanations, but most are related to the university's mission, which is geared toward relations between university and industry and the commercialization of technology. The majority of big successes in technology commercialization are related to medical research. The scorecard indicates that Georgia Tech is one of the few that does not have a medical school. Moreover, commercialization of nonmedical technology is usually based on royalty stacking.[20] Most products require more than one patent; hence, the royalty per patent is low. Also, inventions in nonmedical fields tend to be product or process improvements, which also have lower returns. Moreover, Georgia Tech has a proportionately high number of nonexclusive royalty-free licenses. As mentioned above, these licenses do not earn any revenue for the university yet it views such licenses as an important component of a positive relationship with industry.

University Commercialization Policies

IPR policy at Georgia Tech is similar to that of other universities in that the university retains rights to faculty and staff inventions (Breznitz and Feldman, 2010). Moreover, Georgia Tech's division of royalties favors the

Table 5.5   Universities' royalty shares policies and average spinouts

University	Royalty share for inventor	Average number of spinouts
UNC – Chapel Hill	40% for tangible property and 70% for copyright[a]	2.60
Cornell	1/3 of royalty[b]	4.20
Wisconsin – Madison	20% for patents and non-copyrightable inventions	4.80
UT – Austin	50%[c]	6.00
Michigan	50% up to $200,000 and 30% after that amount[d]	8.80
Stanford	1/3 of royalty[e]	7.75
Georgia Tech	1/3 of royalty	8.80
Cal Tech	25% of royalty[f]	14.20
MIT	1/3 of royalty[g]	21.00

Note: Conflicting results regarding the impact of royalty share on the ability to license technology and spin out companies.

Sources:
[a] http://intranet.northcarolina.edu/docs/legal/policymanual/500.2.pdf;
[b] http://www.cctec.cornell.edu/inventors/techtransferprocess.php;
[c] http://www.otc.utexas.edu/publications/8StepsOfTechCommercialization.jsp;
[d] http://www.techtransfer.umich.edu/resources/inventors/royalties.php;
[e] http://otl.stanford.edu/inventors/inventors_policies.html?headerbar=1#royalty;
[f] https://www.ogc.caltech.edu/forms/documents/patentpolicy;
[g] http://web.mit.edu/tlo/www/community/guide4.html#4.8; AUTM (2005, 2009).

university, which, as with other universities on the scorecard, has a positive effect on its ability to spin out companies.

It is difficult to compare universities' policies regarding the creation of spinouts. These usually involve case-by-case studies. However, studies show that Georgia Tech's spinout policies are similar to those of MIT, Stanford, and Yale. These studies show that a supporting infrastructure in the form of business education, assistance with business plans, employee recruitment, and funding for university spinouts encourages innovation and leads to an increase in university-related firms (Breznitz, 2007; Breznitz, 2011; Breznitz et al., 2008; Saxenian, 1994; Shane, 2002).

6.   DISCUSSION AND CONCLUSIONS

Studies on university commercialization culture highlight the importance of the university's mission statement, the research and commercialization of peer employees, and the administration's attitude toward commercialization. An examination of Georgia Tech finds a university that, from its inception, took its role as a public university as a guide in its focus on technology commercialization. This culture is evident in the extent to which the university collaborates with industry, works on applied research, and encourages faculty and students to innovate. Georgia Tech's commercialization policy is similar to that of many highly ranked universities. The university owns the intellectual property, has a royalty share in support of spinout creation, and provides assistance for technology licensing and spinout creation.

Studies on the organization of TTOs stress the importance of focusing university efforts through one office that has had success in commercializing technology (i.e., had an innovation go through the process of commercialization and earn royalties). Moreover, studies view the size of the office and the use of an outside legal team as harbingers of success. At Georgia Tech, several units deal with technology commercialization. However, most of the work is done at two units: startup services (ATDC) and the OTL. The ATDC focuses specifically on the creation of startup firms, and decision making regarding patenting and licensing is based at the OTL. The university has not had a big success in its licensing income compared to Yale with Zerit™ or Stanford and UCSF with Recombinant DNA. The university has a relatively small technology licensing office and does not use outside lawyers. These facts alone, according to existing studies, should have impaired the university's ability to commercialize technology; however, the results of this study show the opposite.

Georgia Tech has had notable success in technology commercialization. The university ranks among top universities in terms of the number of patents and licenses. In the past decade, Georgia Tech has been consistently rated as one of the top ten public universities in the United States by *US News & World Report*. Considering the pressure that public universities are facing to make a contribution to the economy, *Forbes* magazine named Georgia Tech one of the best incubators and accelerators of technology firms. Moreover, in view of the size and age of the institution, the amount of its industry-sponsored research and industry collaboration is unprecedented. Because of a clear university mission statement and strong support from its administration, Georgia Tech has been able to make a substantial contribution to Georgia's economy. Georgia Tech's policies, culture, and organization are focused on this goal, allowing the university to create an educated workforce, provide an incubator for new firms, and foster industrial collaboration. In the words of one of our interviewees:

If you want to know what I think [is the reason for Georgia Tech's success] it is three things: the fact that we have no med school and all the expenses related to it; the fact that we lost the Civil War, which created an agenda to build factories and create jobs; and the fact that we are well aware that we are not Silicon Valley, and that is why we have to do more than other places do.

This chapter reinforces studies regarding university culture and policy. Policies regarding intellectual property rights, royalties, and spinout companies, as well as a strong entrepreneurial university culture have positive impacts on university technology commercialization. However, the case of Georgia Tech does not conform to studies on university TTOs and organization. In this way, the chapter supports former studies that contravene the existence of 'one formula' or 'the right sauce' to achieve knowledge transfer and technology commercialization. Every university must consider its own historical and environmental context as well as its own resources and capacity.

ACKNOWLEDGEMENTS

The authors would like to thank David Audretsch, Dan Breznitz, Stephen Fleming, Mary Walshok, Kevin Wozniak, and the participants of the Strategic Management of Places Conference in the University of California, San Diego for helpful comments and suggestions. Special thanks are extended to the interviewees in the project; their insight provides the foundation of this chapter.

NOTES

1. According to the 2009 patent scorecard.
2. The score for each institution is based on five categories (Oldach, 2009): Technology Strength™: indicates overall strength of the company's patent portfolio holdings with a combined measure of quality and quantity. Industry Impact™: indicates the extent to which other institutions are building upon a portfolio of issued US utility patents, compared with a total set of patents. Science Linkage™: indicates the degree to which a portfolio cites scientific publications. Innovation Cycle Time™: indicates whether a patent or patent portfolio builds on previous innovations. The number of US patents granted in a given year.
3. The score-card includes the University System of California. Since this system includes a number of universities we chose to remove it from our comparison.
4. It was renamed the Georgia Institute of Technology in 1948.
5. EES, which later became GTRI. More about GTRI can be found in the section on internal university factors.
6. The funding goes directly to the university while the faculty involved must participate in the training.

7. Read more about GTRI/EES in the section on Georgia Tech external factors.
8. The reference to patents that are 'more likely to be built upon' is based on the patent scorecard factor 'Industry Impact'. As indicated in the method section, Industry Impact™ indicates the extent to which other institutions are building upon a portfolio of issued US utility patents as compared with a total set of patents.
9. http://innovate.Georgia Tech.edu/about-us/a-message-from-the-vice-provost/.
10. http://www.gtrc.Georgia Tech.edu/history/.
11. http://www.gtrc.Georgia Tech.edu/mission/.
12. http://www.osp.gatech.edu/intellectual-property/.
13. http://www.academic.Georgia Tech.edu/handbook/Georgia_Institute_of_Technology_-_Faculty_Handbook_Sep2008.pdf.
14. *About SBIR Assistance Program of Georgia*
'The state of Georgia has one of the nation's leading SBIR/STTR assistance programs which, since being established in 2005, has educated and helped hundreds of Georgia entrepreneurs access these sources of federal funds. With the program's direct assistance, 150 companies have submitted one or more proposals resulting in more than $30 million in federal awards. By merging into ATDC, the program will be able to interact with more entrepreneurs across the state, including those who may have never considered applying for federal grants, and bring more of these awards into Georgia's startup ecosystem.'
About VentureLab
'In 2001, Georgia Tech became a founding member of VentureLab, a program of the Georgia Research Alliance (GRA). VentureLab helps build spinout companies around cutting-edge university research. With its emphasis on technologically-grounded business analysis, access to early-stage funds, and recruitment of experienced management, Georgia Tech's VentureLab has launched more than two dozen successful companies and serves as a model for other universities seeking to commercialize their discoveries. GRA's VentureLab Program now extends to four other research universities in Georgia; with an investment of some $13 million from GRA, more than 150 Georgia-based startups have been created around university intellectual property in the state. GRA also recently launched a new venture fund to make equity investments into these spinout companies' (Fleming, 2009).
15. http://atdc.org/about.
16. The state actually removed $5 million in 2010.
17. Georgia Tech-related companies are companies with strong relationships to tech developed at the university. They include both spinouts and local companies that hire tech students, faculty, and alums from the university.
18. Many studies reflect on the negative impact on universities by working 'too close' to industry (Russell, 1993). However, this chapter does not focus on these aspects.
19. See Table 5.4.
20. In royalty stacking a product is based on more than one patent.

REFERENCES

Audretsch, D.B. and E.E. Lehmann (2005), 'Does the knowledge spillover theory of entrepreneurship hold for regions?', *Research Policy*, **34**, 1191–202.
AUTM (Association of University Technology Managers) (2005), AUTM Licensing Activity Surveys.
AUTM (2009), AUTM Licensing Activity Surveys.
AUTM (2011), Bayh–Dole Act (Online), available at: http://www.AUTM.net/Bayh_Dole_Act.htm.
Bercovitz, J., M. Feldman, I. Feller and R. Burton (2001), 'Organizational structure as a determinant of academic patent and licensing behavior: an exploratory

study of Duke, Johns Hopkins, and Pennsylvania State Universities', *Journal of Technology Transfer*, **26**, 21–35.

Bercovitz, J.E.L. and M.P. Feldman (2007), 'Fishing upstream: firm innovation strategy and university research alliances', *Research Policy*, **36**, 930–48.

Breznitz, S.M. (2007), 'From ivory tower to industrial promotion: the development of the biotechnology cluster in New Haven, Connecticut', *Revue d'Economie Industrielle*, no. 120 115–34.

Breznitz, S.M. (2011), 'Improving or impairing? Following technology transfer changes at the University of Cambridge', *Regional Studies*, **45**, 463–78.

Breznitz, S.M. and M.P. Feldman (2010), 'The engaged university', *Journal of Technology Transfer*, online version.

Breznitz, S.M., R.P. O'Shea and T.J. Allen (2008), 'University commercialization strategies in the development of regional bioclusters', *Journal of Product Innovation Management*, **25**, 129–42.

Chapple, W., A. Lockett, D. Siegel and M. Wright (2005), 'Assessing the relative performance of U.K. university technology transfer offices: parametric and non-parametric evidence', *Research Policy*, **34**, 369–84.

Cisco (2011), 'Scientific Atlanta is now part of Cisco', available at: http://www.cisco.com/web/about/ac49/ac0/ac1/ac259/scientificatlanta.html.

Clark, B.R. (1998), *Creating Entrepreneurial Universities: Organizational Pathways of Transformation*, Oxford: Pergamon Press.

Clarysse, B., M. Wright, A. Lockett, E. Van De Elde and A. Vohora (2005), 'Spinning out new ventures: a typology of incubation strategies from European research institutions', *Journal of Business Venturing*, **20**, 183–216.

Cooke, P. (2002), 'Regional innovation systems: general findings and some new evidence from biotechnology clusters', *Journal of Technology Transfer*, **27**, 133–45.

Cooke, P. and K. Morgan (1998), *The Associational Economy: Firms, Regions, and Innovation*, Oxford: Oxford University Press.

Di Gregorio, D. and S. Shane (2003), 'Why do some universities generate more start-ups than others?', *Research Policy*, **32**, 209–27.

Economic Development Institute, 'What is the Traditional Industries Program', available at: http://www.gatip.org/program.html.

Etzkowitz, H. (1995), 'The triple helix – university–industry–government relations: a laboratory for knowledge based economic development', *EASST Review*, **14**, 9–14.

Etzkowitz, H. (1998), 'The norms of entrepreneurial science: cognitive effects of the new university–industry linkages', *Research Policy*, **27**, 823–33.

Fleming, S. (2009), 'VentureLab merges with ATDC', available at: http://blog.gtventurelab.com/.

Gatech (2011), *Fact Book Online*.

Georgia Research Alliance (2011), 'Georgia's 'deal maker' for university research', available at: http://www.gra.org/AboutGRA.aspx.

Georgia Tech The Hopkins Administration, 1885–1895, 'The building of Georgia Tech at the turn of the 20th century, 1888–1908', available at: http://www.library.gatech.edu/gtbuildings/hopkins.htm.

Georgia Tech (2010a), 'Background', available at: http://scheller.gatech.edu/fac_research/centers_initiatives/bpc/bpc_back.html.

Georgia Tech (2010b), 'Competition', available at: http://inventureprize.gatech.edu/competition.

Georgia Tech (2010c), 'General information: vision and mission', available at: http://www.catalog.gatech.edu/general/mission.php.
Georgia Tech (2010d), 'Vision', available at: http://inventureprize.gatech.edu/vision.
Georgia Tech (2011). 'About', available at: http://otl.gtrc.gatech.edu/about/.
GTRC (2011), 'Research administration at Georgia Tech', available at: http://www.gtrc.gatech.edu/research-administration/.
GTRI (2009a), 'EES shapes new image and gets new name', available at: http://www.gtri.gatech.edu/gtri75/our-75-years/ees-shapes-new-image-and-gets-new-name.
GTRI (2009b), 'GTRI builds industry relationships', available at: http://www.gtri.gatech.edu/gtri75/our-75-years/gtri-builds-industry-relationships.
GTRI (2009c), 'Introduction: solving problems for 75 years', available at http://www.gtri.gatech.edu/gtri75/our-75-years/introduction-solving-problems-75-years.
GTRI (2009d), 'Researchers form Scientific Atlanta', *GTRI 75 Years.*
Kenney, M. (1986), *Biotechnology: The University–Industrial Complex*, New Haven: Yale University Press.
Kenney, M. and R.W. Goe (2004), 'The role of social embeddedness in professional entrepreneurship: a comparison of electrical engineering and computer science at UC Berkeley and Stanford', *Research Policy*, **33**, 691–707.
Lawton Smith, H. (2006), *Universities, Innovation, and the Economy*, Abington: Routledge.
Link, A.N. and J.T. Scott (2005), 'Opening the ivory tower's door: an analysis of the determinants of the formation of US university spin-off companies', *Research Policy*, **34**, 1106–12.
Link, A. and D. Siegel (2005), 'Generating science-based growth: an econometric analysis of the impact of organizational incentives on university–industry technology transfer', *European Journal of Finance*, **11**, 169–81.
Lockett, A. and M. Wright (2005), 'Resources, capabilities, risk capital and the creation of university spin-out companies', *Research Policy*, **34**, 1043–57.
McMath, R.C. (1985), *Engineering the New South: Georgia Tech, 1885–1985*, University of Georgia.
Minshall, T., C. Druilhe and D. Probert (2004), 'The evolution of "Third Mission" activities at the university of Cambridge: balancing strategic and operational considerations', 12th High Tech Small Firms Conference, University of Twente, The Netherlands.
Morgan, K. (1997), 'The learning region: institutions, innovation and regional renewal', *Regional Studies*, **31**, 491–503.
Mowery, D.C. and B.N. Sampat (2001), 'University patents and patent policy debates in the USA, 1925–1980', *Industrial & Corporate Change*, **10**, 781–814.
Nelson, R.R. (1993), *National Innovation Systems: A Comparative Analysis*, New York: Oxford University Press.
O'Mara, M.P. (2005), *Cities of Knowledge*, Princeton and Woodstock: Princeton University Press.
O'Shea, R.P., T.J. Allen, A. Chevalier and F. Roche (2005), 'Entrepreneurial orientation, technology transfer and spinoff performance of US universities', *Research Policy*, **34**, 994–1009.
Office of Faculty Career Development Services (2008), *Faculty HandBook*, Georgia Institute of Technology.
Oldach, Scott (2009), *The Universities Patent Scorecard™ – 2009 University Leaders in Innovation*, Intellectual Property Today: Patent Board™, 2009.

Owen-Smith, J. and W. Powell (2001), 'To patent or not: faculty decisions and institutional success in academic patenting', *Journal of Technology Transfer*, **26**, 99–114.

Rahm, D., J. Kirkland and B. Bozeman (2000), *University–industry R&D Collaboration in the United States, the United Kingdom, and Japan*, Dordrecht, The Netherlands: Kluwer Academic Publishers.

Rothaermel, F.T., S.D. Agung and L. Jiang (2007), 'University entrepreneurship: a taxonomy of the literature', *Industrial and Corporate Change*, **16**, 691–791.

Russell, C. (1993), *Academic Freedom*, London: Routledge.

Saxenian, A. (1994), *Regional Advantage: Culture and Competition in Silicon Valley and Route 128*, Cambridge, MA: Harvard University Press.

Scott, P. (1977), *What Future for Higher Education*, London: Fabian Tracts.

Shane, S. (2002), 'Selling university technology: patterns from MIT', *Management Science*, **48**, 122–37.

Shane, S. (2004), *Academic Entrepreneurship: University Spinoffs and Wealth Creation*, Cheltenham, UK and Northampton, MA, USA: Edward Elgar.

Siegel, D.S. and H.P. Phan (2005), 'Analyzing the effectiveness of university technology transfer: implications for entrepreneurship education', in D.G. Libecap (ed.), *University Entrepreneurship and Technology Transfer: Process, Design, and Intellectual Property*, Amsterdam: Elsevier.

Siegel, D.S., D. Waldman and A. Link (2003), 'Assessing the impact of organizational practices on the relative productivity of university technology transfer offices: an exploratory study', *Research Policy*, **32**, 27–48.

Stuart, J. (2011), 'Research Alliance funding cut by 75% in proposed budget', GPB News.

Youtie, J. and P. Shapira (2008), 'Building and innovation hub: a case study of the transformation of university roles in regional technological and economic development', Research Policy, **37** (8), 1188–1204.

6. Academic entrepreneurship: lessons learned for university administrators and policymakers

Donald S. Siegel

1. INTRODUCTION

There has been a substantial rise in the commercialization of publicly funded research at research universities in the US (Siegel et al. 2007) and Europe (Wright et al. 2007). In the academic literature, considerable attention has been devoted to the rise in university technology transfer, via patenting, licensing, research joint ventures and sponsored research, and the formation of startup companies. However, we have also witnessed a dramatic increase in investment in incubators/accelerators, science parks, and other property-based institutions that facilitate the transfer of technology from universities to firms. Examples of key technologies transferred from universities to firms include the famous Boyer–Cohen 'gene-splicing' technique that launched the biotechnology industry, diagnostic tests for breast cancer and osteoporosis, Internet search engines (e.g., Google), music synthesizers, computer-aided design (CAD), and green technologies.

There has also been a concomitant rise in commercialization efforts at national laboratories (Link et al. 2011) and federal agencies (Siegel and Wessner 2011), which are often tied to research universities. I refer to this wide range of activity as 'academic entrepreneurship,' since the goal of these efforts is to commercialize innovations developed by scientists at universities or federal labs.

In this chapter, I review and synthesize recent selected studies of academic entrepreneurship. The remainder of this chapter is organized as follows. In Section 2, I consider empirical evidence on academic entrepreneurship, especially the literature on university-based startups. Section 3 synthesizes these findings and identifies some key recommendations for university administrators and policymakers.

2.   REVIEW OF SELECTED PAPERS ON ACADEMIC ENTREPRENEURSHIP

As noted in Siegel et al. (2003), university scientists are the 'suppliers' of new technologies, in the sense that they discover new knowledge while conducting funded research projects (typically for a federal agency). However, before a university-based innovation can be commercialized, several hurdles must be surmounted. Key issues are whether researchers have sufficient incentives to disclose their inventions, how to induce researchers' cooperation in further development in bringing IP to market and whether it is possible to overcome asymmetric information problems relating to the value of university inventions.

Invention disclosures to the university constitute the critical input in the technology transfer process. In the US, the Bayh–Dole Act requires that academics who are funded by a federal research grant disclose their inventions to their university's technology transfer office. In Europe, there are notable differences across countries in the ownership of university intellectual property, although it is possible to discern some convergence. Based on extensive interviews with faculty members in the US, Siegel et al. (2004) reported that many faculty members are not disclosing their inventions to their university. Survey research by Thursby et al. (2001), Jensen and Thursby (2001), confirms this finding. Markman et al. (2005a, 2005b) recently documented that many technologies are indeed 'going out the back door.'

The failure of many academics to disclose inventions to their university highlights the problems university technology licensing officers have in eliciting disclosures. Although the Bayh–Dole Act stipulates that scientists must file an invention disclosure, this rule is difficult to enforce. Instead, the university needs to have proper incentive schemes in place, specifying an adequate share for the inventors in royalties or equity. The importance of this revenue in securing researchers' cooperation in technology licensing has been analyzed by Macho-Stadler et al. (1996), Lach and Schankerman (2004), and Link and Siegel (2005). All of these models focus on licensing instead of commercialization through startups. Nevertheless, empirical studies of startup formation by universities have demonstrated the importance of royalty regimes of the university, even on the rate of spin-off creation at universities (DiGregorio and Shane 2003; O'Shea et al. 2005).

If a faculty member files an invention disclosure, the university technology transfer office (which, in most countries, owns the intellectual property) decides whether the invention should be patented, usually in consultation with a committee of faculty experts. In making this decision, the university technology transfer office typically attempts to assess the commercial potential of the invention. Sometimes, firms or entrepreneurs have already expressed sufficient interest in the new technology to warrant filing a patent. If industry expresses little interest in the technology, universities may be reluctant to file for a patent, given the high cost of filing and protecting patents. When a patent is filed and awarded, the university typically attempts to 'market' the invention, by contacting firms that can potentially license the technology or entrepreneurs who are capable of launching a startup firm based on the technology.

Faculty members may also become directly involved in the licensing agreement as technical consultants or as entrepreneurs in a university spin-off. Jensen and Thursby (2001) show that faculty involvement in the commercialization of a licensed university-based technology increases the likelihood that such an effort will be successful. In order to provide incentives for faculty involvement, licensing agreements should entail either upfront royalties or royalties at a later date. For spin-offs, Macho-Stadler et al. (2007) demonstrate how the optimal contract between the university technology transfer office, the researcher and the venture capitalist, entails the allocation to the researcher of founder shares to secure her involvement in the venture. It may also require the researcher to be financially involved in the project as a way to give her incentives to provide effort. The creation and development of a spin-off may generate higher financial returns to universities than licensing. However, we shall see in the next section that university technology transfer offices may encounter numerous challenges in pursuing entrepreneurial activities.

Asymmetric Information and Valuation of Inventions

Even when the disclosure and researcher involvement problem is remedied through appropriate incentive schemes, not all potentially viable inventions will be patented and licensed by the university. This relates to the problem of asymmetric information between industry and science on the value of the inventions. Firms typically cannot assess the quality of the invention *ex ante*, while researchers may find it difficult to assess the commercial profitability of their inventions. This problem has been examined by Macho-Stadler et al. (2007), who advance a reputation argument for a university technology transfer office to alleviate the asymmetric information problem. The authors demonstrate that larger technology transfer offices may have an incentive to shelve some of the projects in order to build a reputation for delivering good projects, thus raising buyers' beliefs on expected quality. Their results support the importance of a critical size for a university technology transfer office to be successful. The authors also predict that establishing a technology transfer office may result in fewer license agreements, but higher average license revenues.

Siegel et al. (2003) were the first to note that the traditional emphasis of the university technology transfer office is on licensing and patenting. There is, however, increased attention devoted to the creation of spin-off firms by university scientists. Scholars examine university technology commercialization and entrepreneurship, typically focusing on the 'performance' of university technology transfer offices, while also analyzing agents engaging in commercialization, such as academic scientists and entrepreneurs. Several authors evaluate the antecedents and consequences of faculty involvement in technology commercialization, such as the propensity of academics to patent, disclose inventions, co-author with industry scientists, and form university-based startups.

The Association of University Technology Managers (AUTM, 2007) reports that the number of startup firms at US universities rose from 35 in 1980 to 652 in 2010. This rapid increase in startup activity has attracted considerable attention from scholars. Some researchers focus on the university, firm, or project as the unit of analysis, while others analyze entrepreneurial agents (either academic or non-academic entrepreneurs).

Studies using the university as the unit of analysis typically focus on the role of university policies in stimulating entrepreneurship. Roberts and Malone (1996) speculate that Stanford generated fewer startups than comparable institutions in the early 1990s because the institution refused to sign exclusive licenses to inventor-founders. Degroof and Roberts (2004) examine the importance of university policies relating to startups in regions where environmental factors (e.g. technology transfer and infrastructure for entrepreneurship) are not particularly conducive to entrepreneurial activity. A taxonomy of four types of startup policies was derived from their analysis: (1) an absence of startup policies; (2) minimal selectivity/support; (3) intermediate selectivity/support; and (4) comprehensive selectivity/support. Consistent with Roberts and Malone (1996), they find that comprehensive selectivity/support is the optimal policy for generating startups that exploit knowledge with high growth potential. However, such a policy is an ideal that may not be feasible, given resource constraints. The authors conclude that while spinout policies do matter in the sense that they affect the growth potential of ventures, it may be more desirable to formulate these policies at a higher level of aggregation than the university.

Table 6.1 summarizes some key papers on academic entrepreneurship. DiGregorio and Shane (2003) directly assess the determinants of

Table 6.1   Selected empirical studies of academic entrepreneurship

Author(s)	Data sets	Methodology	Key results
Siegel et al. (2003)	AUTM, NSF, and US census data, interviews	Total factor productivity (TFP) of university licensing, stochastic frontier analysis and field interviews	University technology transfer offices exhibit constant returns to scale with respect to the no. of licenses; increasing returns to scale with respect to licensing revenue; organizational and environmental factors have considerable explanatory power
Link and Siegel (2005)	AUTM, NSF, and US census data, interviews	TFP of university licensing, stochastic frontier analysis	Land grant universities are more efficient in technology transfer; higher royalty shares for faculty members are associated with greater licensing income
Lach and Schankerman (2004)	AUTM, NSF, NRC	Regression analysis	Higher royalty shares for faculty members are associated with greater licensing income
Thursby et al. (2001); Jensen and Thursby (2001)	AUTM, authors' survey	Descriptive analysis of authors' survey/ regression analysis	Inventions tend to be disclosed at an early stage of development; elasticities of licenses and royalties with respect to invention disclosures are both less than one; faculty members are increasingly likely to disclose inventions
Bercovitz et al. (2001)	AUTM and case studies, interviews	Qualitative and quantitative analysis	Analysis of different organization structures for technology transfer at Duke, Johns Hopkins, and Penn State; differences in structure may be related to technology transfer performance

Table 6.1 (continued)

Author(s)	Data sets	Methodology	Key results
Chapple et al. (2005)	UK-NUBS/ UNICO survey-ONS	Data envelopment analysis and stochastic frontier analysis	UK TTOs exhibit decreasing returns to scale and low levels of absolute efficiency; organizational and environmental factors have considerable explanatory power
DiGregorio and Shane (2003)	AUTM survey	Count regressions of the determinants of the no. of startups	Two key determinants of startup formation: faculty quality and the ability of the university and inventor(s) to take equity in a startup, in lieu of licensing royalty fees; a royalty distribution formula that is more favorable to faculty members reduces startup formation
O'Shea et al. (2005)	University-based startups	AUTM survey/count regressions of the determinants of the no. of startups	A university's previous success in technology transfer is a key determinant of its rate of startup formation
Franklin et al. (2001)	TTOs and university-based startups	Authors' quantitative survey of UK TTOs	Universities that wish to launch successful technology transfer startups should employ a combination of academic and surrogate entrepreneurship
Lockett and Wright (2005)	TTOs and university-based startups	Survey of UK TTOs/ count regressions of the determinants of the no. of startups	A university's rate of startup formation is positively associated with its expenditure on intellectual property protection, the business development capabilities of TTOs, and the extent to which its royalty distribution formula favors faculty members

Table 6.1   (continued)

Author(s)	Data sets	Methodology	Key results
Clarysse et al. (2005)	TTOs and university-based startups	Interviews and descriptive data on 50 universities across 7 European countries	Five incubation models identified. Three match resources, activities and objectives: low selective, supportive and incubator. Two do not: competence deficient and resource deficient
Markman et al. (2005a)	TTOs and university startups	AUTM survey, authors' survey/linear regression analysis	The most attractive combinations of technology stage and licensing strategy for new venture creation – early stage technology and licensing for equity – are least likely to be favored by the university (due to risk aversion and a focus on short-run revenue maximization)
Markman et al. (2005b)	TTOs and university-based startups	AUTM survey, authors' survey/linear regression analysis	There are three key determinants of time to market (speed): TTO resources, competency in identifying licensees, and participation of faculty-inventors in the licensing process
Bercovitz and Feldman (2008)	Medical school researchers at Johns Hopkins and Duke	Determinants of the probability of filing an invention disclosure	Three factors influence the decision to disclose inventions: norms at the institutions where the researchers were trained and the disclosure behaviors of their department chairs and peers
Lowe and Gonzàlez-Brambila (2007)	Faculty members	150 faculty members from 15 universities/ regression analysis	Faculty members are more productive researchers than observationally equivalent colleagues before they established their firms. The

Table 6.1 (continued)

Author(s)	Data sets	Methodology	Key results
			research productivity of these academics did not decline in the aftermath of their entrepreneurial activity
Zucker et al. (1998b)	Relationships involving 'star' scientists and US biotech firms	Scientific papers, data on biotech firms from the North Carolina Biotechnology Center (1992) and Bioscan (1993)/count regressions	Location of star scientists predicts firm entry in biotechnology
Zucker et al. (2000)	Relationships involving 'star' scientists and US biotech firms	Scientific papers reporting genetic-sequence discoveries, /count regressions	Collaboration between star scientists and firm scientists enhances research performance of US biotech firms, as measured using three proxies: no. of patents granted, no. of products in development, and no. of products on the market
Zucker and Darby (2001)	Relationships involving 'star' scientists and Japanese biotech firms	Data on biotechnology firms and the Nikkei Biotechnology Directory	Collaboration between star scientists and firm scientists enhances research performance of Japanese biotech firms, as measured using three proxies: no. of patents granted, no. of products in development, and no. of products on the market
Vanaelst et al. (2006)	Startups and entrepreneurial team members	Interview data and comparative univariate analysis	Some researchers actively involved in the first phase of the spin-off exit; new members enter, especially those with commercial human capital; some

Table 6.1   (continued)

Author(s)	Data sets	Methodology	Key results
			faculty remain with university but work part-time in a technology development role for spin-off
Link and Ruhm (2009)	National Institutes of Health SBIR project and firm-level data	Logit regressions of the determinants of commercial success	University involvement in research enhances the probability of successful commercialization
Siegel and Wessner (2011)	Department of Defense SBIR project and firm-level data	Tobit and negative binomial regressions of the determinants of commercial success	Startups with ties to universities achieve higher levels of commercial success, especially for patenting and licensing

startup formation using AUTM data from 101 universities and 530 startups. Based on estimates of count regressions of the number of university-based startups, the authors conclude that the two key determinants of startups are faculty quality and the ability of the university and inventor(s) to assume equity in a startup in lieu of licensing royalty fees. Interestingly, the availability of venture capital in the region where the university is located and the commercial orientation of the university (proxied by the percentage of the university's research budget that is derived from industry) are found to have an insignificant impact on the rate of startup formation. The authors also find that a royalty distribution formula that is more favorable to faculty members reduces startup formation, a finding confirmed by Markman et al. (2005a). DiGregorio and Shane (2003) attribute this result to higher opportunity costs associated with launching a new firm, relative to licensing the technology to an existing firm.

O'Shea et al. (2005) extend these findings in several ways. First, they employ a more sophisticated econometric technique, also employed by Blundell et al. (1995), on innovation counts, which accounts for unobserved heterogeneity across universities due to 'history and tradition.'

This type of 'path dependence' would seem to be quite important in the university context. Indeed, the authors find that a university's previous success in technology transfer is a key explanatory factor of startup formation. Consistent with DiGregorio and Shane (2003), they also find that faculty quality, commercial capability, and the extent of federal science and engineering funding are also significant determinants of higher rates of university startup formation.

Franklin et al. (2001) analyze perceptions at U.K. universities regarding entrepreneurial startups that emerge from university technology transfer. The authors distinguish between academic and surrogate (external) entrepreneurs and 'old' and 'new' universities in the U.K. Old universities have well-established research reputations, world-class scientists, and are typically receptive to entrepreneurial startups. New universities, on the other hand, tend to be weaker in academic research and less flexible with regard to entrepreneurial ventures. They find that the most significant barriers to the adoption of entrepreneurial-friendly policies are cultural and informational. The universities generating the most startups (i.e., old universities) are those that have the most favorable policies regarding surrogate (external) entrepreneurs. The authors conclude that the best approach for universities that wish to launch successful technology transfer startups is a combination of academic and surrogate entrepreneurship. This would enable universities to simultaneously exploit the technical benefits of inventor involvement *and* the commercial know-how of surrogate entrepreneurs.

In a follow-up study, Lockett et al. (2003) find that universities generating the most startups have clear, well-defined strategies regarding the formation and management of spinouts. These schools tend to use surrogate (external) entrepreneurs, rather than academic entrepreneurs, to manage this process. It also appears that the more successful universities have greater expertise and vast social networks that help them generate more startups. However, the role of the academic inventor was not found to differ between the more and less successful universities. Finally, equity ownership is more widely distributed among the members of the spinout company in the case of the more successful universities.

Based on an extended version of the same database, Lockett and Wright (2005) assess the relationship between the resources and capabilities of U.K. technology transfer offices and the rate of startup formation at their respective universities. In doing so, the authors apply the resource-based view (RBV) of the firm to the university. RBV asserts that an organization's superior performance (in the parlance of strategic management, its 'competitive advantage') is related to its internal resources and capabilities. They are able to distinguish, empirically, a university's resource inputs from its routines and capabilities. Based on estimation of count regressions (Poisson and negative binomial), the authors conclude that there is a positive correlation between startup formation and the university's expenditure on intellectual property protection as well as the business development capabilities of technology transfer offices and the extent to which its royalty distribution formula favors faculty members. These findings imply that universities wishing to spawn numerous startups should devote greater attention to recruitment, training, and development of technology transfer officers with broad-based commercial skills. These results are important for the following section of this chapter.

Markman et al. (2005b) develop a model linking university patents to new-firm creation in university-based incubators, with university technology transfer offices acting as intermediary. They focus on universities because such institutions are responsible for a substantial fraction of technology-oriented incubators in the US. While there are some qualitative studies of technology transfer office licensing (e.g. Bercovitz et al. 2001; Siegel et al. 2003; Mowery et al. 2001), these are based on data from elite research universities only (e.g. Stanford, UC Berkeley, and MIT) or from a small sample of more representative institutions. These results may not be generalizable to the larger population of institutions, which often do not enjoy the same favorable environmental conditions. To build a theoretically saturated model of technology transfer offices' entrepreneurial development strategies, the authors collected qualitative and quantitative data from virtually the entire population of university technology transfer offices.

A surprising conclusion of Markman et al. (2005b) is that the most 'attractive' combinations of technology stage and licensing strategy for new venture creation, i.e. early stage technology, combined with licensing for equity, are *least* likely to be favored by the university and thus are not likely to be used. That is because universities and technology transfer offices typically focus on short-term cash maximization, and are extremely risk-averse with respect to financial and legal risks. Their findings are consistent with evidence presented in Siegel et al. (2004), who find that technology transfer offices appear to do a better job of serving the needs of large firms than small entrepreneurial companies. The results of these studies imply that universities should modify their technology transfer strategies if they are serious about promoting entrepreneurial development.

In other studies the authors use the same database to assess the role of incentive systems in stimulating academic entrepreneurship and the determinants of innovation speed, or time to market (Markman et al. 2004, 2005a). One interesting result of Markman et al. (2004) is that there is a positive association between compensation to technology transfer office personnel with both equity licensing and startup formation. On the other hand, royalty payments to faculty members and their departments are either uncorrelated or even negatively correlated with entrepreneurial activity. This is consistent with DiGregorio and Shane (2003).

In Markman et al. (2005b), the authors find that speed matters, in the sense that the 'faster' the technology transfer office can commercialize technologies protected by patents, the greater the returns to the university and the higher the rate of startup formation. They also report that there are three key determinants of speed: technology transfer office resources, competency in identifying licensees, and participation of faculty-inventors in the licensing process.

Nerkar and Shane (2003) analyze the entrepreneurial dimension of university technology transfer, based on an empirical analysis of 128 firms founded between 1980 and 1996 to commercialize inventions owned by MIT. They begin by noting that there is an extensive literature in management that suggests that new technology firms are more likely to survive if they exploit radical technologies (e.g. Tushman and Anderson 1986) and if they possess patents with a broad scope (e.g., Merges and Nelson 1990). The authors propose that the relationships between radicalness and survival with scope and survival are moderated by both market structure and level of concentration in the firm's industry. Specifically, they assert that radicalness and patent scope increase the probability of survival more in fragmented industries than in concentrated sectors. They estimate a hazard function model using the MIT database and find empirical support for these hypotheses. Thus, the effectiveness of the technology strategies of new firms may be dependent on industry conditions.

Several studies focus on individual scientists and entrepreneurs in the context of university technology transfer. Audretsch (2000) examines the extent to which entrepreneurs at universities differ from other entrepreneurs. He analyzes a dataset on university life scientists in order to estimate the determinants of the probability that they will establish a new biotechnology firm. Based on a hazard function analysis, including controls for the quality of the scientist's research, measures or regional activity in biotechnology, and a dummy for the career trajectory of the scientist, the author finds that university entrepreneurs tend to be older and more scientifically experienced.

There is also evidence on the importance of norms, standards, and culture in this context. Based on a qualitative analysis of five European universities that had outstanding performance in technology transfer, Clark (1998) concludes that the existence of an entrepreneurial culture at those institutions was a critical factor in their success. Roberts (1991) finds that social norms and MIT's tacit approval of entrepreneurs were critical determinants of successful academic entrepreneurship at MIT.

Louis et al. (1989) analyze the propensity of life-science faculty to engage in various aspects of technology transfer, including commercialization. Their statistical sample consists of life scientists at the 50 research universities receiving the most funding from the National Institutes of Health. The authors find that the most important determinant of involvement in technology commercialization was local group norms. They report that university policies and structures had little effect on this activity.

The unit of analysis in Bercovitz and Feldman (2008) is also the individual faculty member. They analyze the propensity of medical school researchers at Johns Hopkins and Duke to file invention disclosures, a potential precursor to technology commercialization. The authors find that three factors influence the decision to disclose inventions: norms at the institutions where the researchers were trained; disclosure behaviors of their department chairs; and the disclosure behavior of their peers.

The seminal papers by Lynne Zucker and Michael Darby, with various collaborators, explore the role of 'star' scientists in the life sciences on the creation and location of new biotechnology firms in the US and Japan. In Zucker et al. (2000), the authors assess the impact of these university scientists on the research productivity of US firms. Scientists either resigned from the university to establish a new firm or kept their faculty position but worked very closely with industry scientists. In the life sciences, a star scientist is one who has discovered more than 40 genetic sequences, and affiliations with firms are defined through co-authoring between the star scientist and industry scientists. Research productivity is measured using three proxies: number of patents granted, number of products in development, and number of products on the market. Ties between star scientists and firm scientists is found to have a positive effect on these three dimensions of research productivity, as well as other aspects of firm performance and rates of entry in the US biotechnology industry (Zucker et al. 1998a; Zucker et al. 1998b).

In Zucker and Darby (2001), the authors examine detailed data on the outcomes of collaborations between 'star' university scientists and biotechnology firms in Japan. Similar patterns emerge in the sense that they find that such interactions substantially enhance the research productivity of Japanese firms, as measured by the rate of firm patenting, product innovation, and market introductions of new products. However, they also report an absence of geographically localized knowledge spillovers resulting from university technology transfer in Japan, a contrast to the US, where they found that such effects were strong. The authors attribute this result to institutional difference between Japan and the US in university technology transfer. In the US, it is common for academic scientists to work with firm scientists at the firm's laboratories, but in Japan, firm scientists typically work in the academic scientist's laboratory. Thus, according to the authors, it is not surprising that the local economic development impact of university technology transfer appears to be lower in Japan than in the US.

Networks of academic scientists who become entrepreneurs may be important influences on the performance of university startups. Mustar (1997) classified startups depending on their cooperation arrangements with other public and/or private bodies and highlighted the relationship between the breadth of the social network, the growth trajectory, and the attrition rate. Nicolaou and Birley (2003) recognized that differences in the embeddedness of academics in a network of ties external or internal to the university may be associated with different growth trajectories.

Siegel and Wessner (2011) conduct an empirical analysis of project-level data from a key federal government program designed to provide financial assistance to firms during the initial stages of their development: the Small Business Innovation Research (SBIR) program. They have a simple research question: do SBIR startups with a connection to a university tend to be more successful than comparable SBIR startups without such a connection? This is a key extension of empirical work on university-based startups, since there has been little direct, systematic empirical analysis of the role that universities play in enhancing the success of entrepreneurial ventures. Most researchers (e.g., DiGregorio and Shane 2003; O'Shea et al. 2005) address this issue by estimating regressions of counts of the number of university-based startups. The unit of observation in such studies is typically the university. The use of numerical startup counts at the university level is problematic for three reasons. First, startup counts are only one metric through which one can gauge the extent of academic entrepreneurship at a university. Second, it is also not clear how well this approach measures the market value or outcomes of such activity. Finally, the proper unit of analysis is not the university, but rather the university-based startup, which should be followed over time to determine whether it is successful.

To address these concerns, the authors constructed a rich and unique database of Department of Defense SBIR projects and firms, with multiple direct measures of the commercial success of entrepreneurial ventures, including actual sales of products, processes, and services, expectations of future sales, domestic and foreign agreements, and job creation. SBIR is a 'set-aside' program, which requires key federal agencies (e.g., Department of Defense) to allocate 2.5 percent of their research budget to small firms that attempt to commercialize new technologies. Based on estimation of

Tobit and negative binomial regressions of the determinants of commercial success, the authors find that startups with closer ties to universities achieve higher levels of performance.

These results complement additional SBIR findings reported by Link and Ruhm (2009), who examined commercialization activity resulting from research projects funded through the National Institutes of Health's SBIR program. They estimated the determinants of the probability of commercialization, where commercialization is defined as a dichotomous variable, which is equal to one if a project resulted in a commercialized product, process, service or sales of the rights to a technology or licensing revenue. The authors report that university involvement in research enhances the probability of commercialization.

3.   SYNTHESIS AND RECOMMENDATIONS

The burgeoning scholarly literature on academic entrepreneurship yields several key insights for university leaders and policymakers. These 'lessons learned' are especially important, given that many cities, states, and regions are increasingly viewing the research university as an engine of new firm creation and economic growth. A key lesson is that the university president or provost must formulate and implement a rational technology commercialization strategy. The first step in the formulation of such a strategy is the determination of strategic priorities. Before addressing the important aspects of incentives and culture, the university administration must first make it clear that technology commercialization is a key strategic priority of the institution. This strategic choice should be reflected in resource allocation patterns; e.g., hiring individuals with strong technical, commercial, and entrepreneurial backgrounds to staff the technology transfer office and devoting additional resources to stimulating university-industry partnerships.

The university must also decide which mode of technology commercialization to stress: whether it is licensing, startups, sponsored research or other mechanisms of technology transfer focused on directly stimulating economic and regional development, such as incubators and science parks. Institutions choosing to stress the entrepreneurial dimension of technology transfer need to address skill deficiencies in technology transfer offices, reward systems inconsistent with enhanced entrepreneurial activity, and education/training for faculty members, post-docs, and graduate students relating to interactions with entrepreneurs. Business schools at these universities can play a major role in addressing these skill and educational deficiencies through the delivery of targeted programs to technology licensing officers and members of the campus community wishing to launch startup firms.

Administrators also need to make sure that the technology transfer office is working closely with the university's technology incubator/ accelerator and research/science park, especially if startup creation is a key strategic goal. Licensing and sponsored research generate a stream of revenue, while equity from startups can generate large payoffs in the long term. Universities wishing to stress economic and regional development (as many public universities might do) should focus on startup creation, since these companies can potentially create jobs in the local region or state. Note also that while a startup strategy entails higher risk, since the failure rate of new firms is quite high, it also can potentially yield higher returns if the startup goes public. It is also important to note that a startup strategy entails additional resources if the university chooses to assist the academic entrepreneur in launching and developing their startup.

A review of the literature also reveals the high potential opportunity cost of commercialization and the need to modify promotion and tenure requirements to reflect the growing importance of commercialization. Specifically, universities placing a high priority on technology commercialization should modify their promotion and tenure guidelines to place a stronger positive weight on technology transfer activities in the promotion and tenure decision. This will require a great deal of tenacity on the part of academic administrators since there will be resistance from conventional academics to this change. The extant literature also indicates that having department chairs and deans who support technology commercialization is critical to overall success. Some institutions are currently actively recruiting such individuals to stimulate this activity. I believe that such changes are warranted at institutions that wish to stress academic entrepreneurship, although I do not underestimate the difficulty of changing norms, standards, and values among entrenched tenured faculty. Finally, a switch from standard compensation to incentive compensation for technology licensing officers could also result in more licensing agreements.

It has also been difficult for universities to attract and retain technology transfer office personnel with the appropriate skill sets to support an aggressive commercialization strategy. Traditionally, there is an emphasis in technology transfer offices on legal skills, with an eye toward protecting the university's intellectual property portfolio. However, an expansion of technology commercialization will require the creation and development of university-based startups, which means that technology transfer office employees must also be adept at opportunity recognition, marketing, finance, and other aspects of commercialization. They also need to be adept at interacting with venture capitalists and angel investors.

As universities increasingly emphasize startup creation, the role of courses, programs, and a full-fledged technological entrepreneurship curriculum becomes critical. Such a curriculum, while commonly encountered in business schools, can also be delivered to key technology transfer stakeholders. These include academic entrepreneurs, technology transfer officers, incubator and science park managers, small firm licensees, and anyone else involved in startup formation. Dimensions of such a curriculum include not just courses and programs in entrepreneurship, but also idea labs, internships with entrepreneurial firms, technology familiarization, business plan competitions, and venture forums.

Academic research has revealed that successful entrepreneurs have cognitive routines that allow them to recover quickly from failure. Although such entrepreneurs still fear failure, this does not hinder their desire to launch new ventures. Studies have also shown that serial entrepreneurs are, on average, more successful. This finding underscores the importance of learning and knowledge accumulation of the 'how to' aspects of new venture creation. Thus, entrepreneurship courses designed for technology transfer office stakeholders should focus both on the mechanics of launching a venture and on the economic/strategic implications of the technologies being commercialized. Finally, for the technology transfer officer or entrepreneur who is not familiar with the specifics of the technology, technology survey courses, taught by faculty scientists, are recommended.

We should not lose sight of the fact that the primary source of knowledge creation regarding university startups is the researcher (faculty, student, or post-doc). Thus, incentives should be created for those involved in the research enterprise to expand their research domains to include questions related to innovation and entrepreneurship from a technological or business perspective. Universities should also consider establishing a formal program that allows successful faculty entrepreneurs to serve as role models and mentors for faculty, students, and post-docs who wish to engage in new venture creation. The implication of such an initiative is that the entrepreneurship curriculum must be driven from the top of the hierarchy and embedded in the institutional priorities, design principles, and measurement systems of the university.

Courses can be designed and taught by faculty members across divisions of the university with the appropriate experience or knowledge set. Ideally, such programs should be managed by top-level university administrators. Syracuse, Wake Forest, and Rensselaer Polytechnic Institute have recently created top-level administrative positions in entrepreneurship (e.g. a Vice Provost for Entrepreneurship). Such an action highlights the importance of these initiatives within the university and also sends an important signal to other stakeholders (e.g. faculty, donors) that the university places a high value on such activities.

REFERENCES

Audretsch, D.B. (2000), 'Is university entrepreneurship different?', mimeo, Indiana University.

AUTM (Association of University Technology Managers) (2007), *The AUTM Licensing Survey*, Fiscal Year 2006.

Bercovitz, J.E.L. and M.P. Feldman (2008), 'Academic entrepreneurs: organizational change at the individual level', *Organization Science*, **19** (1), 69–89.

Bercovitz, J.E.L., M.P. Feldman, I. Feller and R. Burton (2001), 'Organizational structure as determinants of academic patent and licensing behavior: an exploratory study of Duke, Johns Hopkins, and Pennsylvania State Universities', *Journal of Technology Transfer*, **26** (1–2), 21–35.

Blundell, R., R. Griffith and J. Van Reenen (1995), 'Dynamic count data models of technological innovation', *Economic Journal*, **105** (429), 333–44.

Chapple, W., A. Lockett, D.S. Siegel and M. Wright (2005), 'Assessing the relative performance of university technology transfer offices in the U.K.: parametric and non-parametric evidence', *Research Policy*, **34** (3), 369–84.

Clark, B.R. (ed.) (1998), *Creating Entrepreneurial Universities: Organizational Pathways of Transformation*, Oxford: Pergamon.

Clarysse, B., M. Wright, A. Lockett, E. van de Elde and A. Vohora (2005), 'Spinning out new ventures: a typology of incubation strategies from European research institutions', *Journal of Business Venturing*, **20** (2), 183–216.

Degroof, J.J. and E.B. Roberts (2004), 'Overcoming weak entrepreneurial infrastructure for academic spin-off ventures', *Journal of Technology Transfer*, **29** (3–4), 327–52.

DiGregorio, D. and S.A. Shane (2003), 'Why do some universities generate more startups than others?', *Research Policy*, **32** (2), 209–27.

Franklin, S., M. Wright and A. Lockett (2001), 'Academic and surrogate entrepreneurs in university spin-out companies', *Journal of Technology Transfer*, **26** (1–2), 127–41.

Jensen, R. and M. Thursby (2001) 'Proofs and prototypes for sale: the licensing of university inventions', *American Economic Review*, **91** (1), 240–59.

Lach, S. and M. Schankerman (2004), 'Royalty sharing and technology licensing in universities', *Journal of the European Economic Association*, **2** (2–3), 252–64.

Link, A.N. and C.J. Ruhm (2009), 'Bringing science to market: commercializing from NIH SBIR Awards', *Economics of Innovation and New Technology*, **18**, 381–402.

Link, A.N. and D.S. Siegel (2005), 'Generating science-based growth: an econometric analysis of the impact of organizational incentives on university-industry technology transfer', *European Journal of Finance*, **11** (3), 169–81.

Link, A.N., D.S. Siegel and D.D. Van Fleet (2011).'Public science and public innovation: assessing the relationship between patenting at US National Laboratories and the Bayh–Dole Act', *Research Policy*, **40** (8), 1094–9.

Lockett, A. and M. Wright (2005), 'Resources, capabilities, risk capital and the creation of university spin-out companies', *Research Policy*, **34** (7), 1043–57.

Lockett, A., M. Wright and S. Franklin (2003), 'Technology transfer and universities' spin-out strategies', *Small Business Economics*, **20** (2), 185–201.

Louis, K.S., D. Blumenthal, M.E. Gluck and M.A. Stoto (1989), 'Entrepreneurs in academe: an exploration of behaviors among life scientists', *Administrative Science Quarterly*, **34** (1), 110–31.

Lowe, R. and C. Gonzàlez-Brambila (2007), 'Faculty entrepreneurs and research productivity', *Journal of Technology Transfer*, **32** (3), 173–94.

Macho-Stadler, I., X. Martinez-Giralt and D. Pérez-Castrillo (1996), 'The role of information in licensing contract design', *Research Policy*, **25**, 43–57.

Macho-Stadler, I., D. Pérez-Castrillo and R. Veugelers (2007), 'Licensing of university innovations: the case of a technology transfer office', *International Journal of Industrial Organization*, **25**, 483–510.

Markman, G., P. Phan, D. Balkin and P. Gianiodis (2004), 'Entrepreneurship from the ivory tower: do incentive systems matter?', *Journal of Technology Transfer*, **29** (3–4), 353–64.

Markman, G., P. Phan, D. Balkin and P. Gianiodis (2005a), 'Entrepreneurship and university-based technology transfer', *Journal of Business Venturing*, **20** (2), 241–63.

Markman, G., P. Phan, D. Balkin and P. Gianiodis (2005b), 'Innovation speed: transferring university technology to market', *Research Policy*, **34** (7), 1058–75.

Merges, R. and R.R. Nelson (1990), 'On the complex economics of patent scope', *Columbia Law Review*, **90** (4), 839–916.

Mowery, D.C., R.R. Nelson, B. Sampat and A.A. Ziedonis (2001), 'The growth of patenting and licensing by US universities: an assessment of the effects of the Bayh–Dole Act of 1980', *Research Policy*, **30** (1), 99–119.

Mustar, P. (1997), 'Spin-off enterprises: how French academies create hi-tech companies: the condition for success or failure', *Science and Public Policy*, **24** (1), 37–43.

Nerkar, A. and S. Shane (2003), 'When do startups that exploit academic knowledge survive?', *International Journal of Industrial Organization*, **21** (9), 1391–410.

Nicolaou, N. and S. Birley (2003), 'Social networks in organizational emergence: the university spinout phenomenon', *Management Science*, **49** (12), 1702–25.

O'Shea, R., T. Allen and A. Chevalier (2005), 'Entrepreneurial orientation, technology transfer, and spin-off performance of US universities', *Research Policy*, **34** (7), 994–1009.

Roberts, E.B. (ed.) (1991), *Entrepreneurs in High Technology, Lessons from MIT and Beyond*, New York: Oxford University Press.

Roberts, E. and D.E. Malone (1996), 'Policies and structures for spinning off new companies from research and development organizations', *R&D Management*, **26** (1), 17–48.

Siegel, D.S. and C. Wessner (2011), 'Universities and the success of entrepreneurial ventures: evidence from the small business innovation research program', *Journal of Technology Transfer*, forthcoming.

Siegel, D.S., D. Waldman and A.N. Link (2003), 'Assessing the impact of organizational practices on the relative productivity of university technology transfer offices: an exploratory study', *Research Policy*, **32** (1), 27–48.

Siegel, D.S., D. Waldman, L. Atwater and A.N. Link (2004), 'Toward a model of the effective transfer of scientific knowledge from academicians to practitioners: qualitative evidence from the commercialization of university technologies', *Journal of Engineering and Technology Management*, **21** (1–2), 115–42.

Siegel, D.S., R. Veugelers and M. Wright (2007), 'Technology transfer offices and commercialization of university intellectual property: performance and policy implications', *Oxford Review of Economic Policy*, **23** (4), 640–60.

Thursby, J.G., R. Jensen and M.C. Thursby (2001), 'Objectives, characteristics and outcomes of university licensing: a survey of major US universities', *Journal of Technology Transfer*, **26** (1–2), 59–72.

Tushman, M. and P. Anderson (1986), 'Technological discontinuities and organizational environments', *Administrative Science Quarterly*, **31** (3), 439–65.

Vanaelst, I., B. Clarysse, M. Wright, A. Lockett, N. Moray and R. S'Jegers (2006), 'Entrepreneurial team development in academic spinouts: an examination of team heterogeneity', *Entrepreneurship: Theory and Practice*, **30** (2), 249–91.

Wright, M., B. Clarysse, P. Mustar and A. Lockett (eds) (2007), *Academic Entrepreneurship in Europe*, Cheltenham, UK and Northampton, MA, USA: Edward Elgar.

Zucker, L.G. and M.R. Darby (2001), 'Capturing technological opportunity via Japan's star scientists: evidence from Japanese firms' biotech patents and products', *Journal of Technology Transfer*, **26** (1–2), 37–58.

Zucker, L.G., M.R. Darby and J. Armstrong (1998a), 'Geographically localized knowledge: spillovers or markets?' *Economic Inquiry*, **36** (1), 65–86.

Zucker, L.G., M.R. Darby and M.B. Brewer (1998b) 'Intellectual human capital and the birth of US biotechnology enterprises', *American Economic Review*, **88** (1), 290–306.

Zucker, L.G., M.R. Darby and J. Armstrong (2000), *University Science, Venture Capital, and the Performance of US Biotechnology Firms*, mimeo, UCLA.

7. Driving regional growth: the growing role of policies to promote clusters

Charles W. Wessner and Sujai Shivakumar

Ever since Silicon Valley and Boston's Route 128 gained global attention as fountains of dynamic new high-technology companies, state and local governments across the United States have tried to create innovation clusters of their own (Katz et al., 2010). These innovation clusters are regional concentrations of large and small companies that develop creative products and services, along with specialized suppliers, service providers, universities, and associated institutions.[1] To this end, state and local governments have sought to attract a critical mass of skills and talent. Seeking to promote a high level of interaction among entrepreneurs, researchers, and innovators, they have invested in science parks, business incubators to nurture start-ups, and an array of research collaborations between universities and private industry (Muro and Katz, 2010).

The federal government has traditionally played an important though largely supportive role in the development of regional innovation clusters.[2] Federally funded research and military procurement have been instrumental in the emergence of clusters that have formed around major research universities.[3] Through legislation, such as the Bayh–Dole Act of 1980, Congress has encouraged universities and national laboratories to commercialize federally funded research.[4] Unlike many Asian and European nations, however, the United States has not generally adopted explicit national policies that promote development of particular industries in specific regions.[5]

The federal role is now evolving. In recent years, support has grown in Washington for a more direct federal role in assisting and accelerating regional innovation clusters.[6] In part, the impetus for this change has come from a National Academy of Sciences Report, *Rising Above the Gathering Storm*, which warned that the US is in danger of ceding global leadership in technology and innovation to nations with more ambitious and comprehensive policies to enhance their competitiveness (National Academy of Sciences et al., 2007). Citing this report, Congress in 2007 passed, and in 2010 reauthorized, the America COMPETES Act, which includes provisions to boost the development of innovation clusters.[7] The impetus for more focused development activity has also come in response to the recent economic downturn and its severe impact on manufacturing employment.

GROWTH IN NATIONAL CLUSTER POLICIES FOR REGIONAL GROWTH

This shift in the United States reflects a global trend. Governments around the world have recognized the powerful competitive advantages of strong regional innovation clusters.[8] This recognition has been accompanied with a new perspective on how clusters merge and develop.[9]

In the past, regional economic strategy tended to be about compensating for economic disparities. National governments often acted like Robin Hood, taking funds from rich locales and giving them to poorer ones. Many governments also provided subsidies to small business entrepreneurs. Typically, these reallocation efforts not only failed to erase regional disparities, they also subsidized companies that never achieved the scale or ability to sufficiently differentiate their products so they could compete globally (Pezzini, 2003).

In what Mario Pezzini calls 'a new paradigm in regional policy,' national governments are increasingly calling on their regions to identify their comparative advantages and are focusing on strengthening university research, workforce training, and small-business mentoring (Pezzini, 2012). These investments are viewed as infrastructure that communities can use to build innovation-driven economies.

To this end, local, regional and national governments around the world are implementing programs and policies to create, develop, and strengthen locally focused networks among businesses, universities, research and development organizations, and philanthropic foundations.[10] A recent study by the Brookings Institution documents national cluster development programs in Japan, the Republic of Korea, and 26 nations in the European Union.[11] Interestingly, many of the new initiatives that the US now looks to as a source of policy guidance, represent efforts by other nations to emulate the success of Silicon Valley.

The Development of French Innovation *Pôles*

The French *pôles de compétitivité* are a key example of this focus on cluster-based development. The program's goal is to strengthen the competitiveness of the French economy by developing localized synergies between research institutes, firms and education organizations. Traditionally, French technology and innovation policies were directed by the central government and performed and implemented by large national companies. Over the past decade, however, French efforts have increasingly focused on realizing the potential of small and medium-sized enterprises to innovate, and on the transfer and commercialization of research results generated in universities, and public scientific and technological research organizations – a decidedly more bottom-up approach (Duranton et al., 2010).

The French initiative to develop productive interlinkages among France's research institutes, universities and industry was launched in September 2004. Cluster members were encouraged to collaborate with each other through incentives in the form of direct aid, tax deductions, and access to sources of funding. From more than 100 proposals from competing regions, 66 competitiveness clusters were selected in 2005, of which six were labeled *pôles de compétitivité mondiaux* and ten *pôles de compétitivité à vocation mondiale*. The project was launched with a budget of €1,500 million for the first three years and ministries were encouraged to allocate around 25 per cent of their funds to collaborative projects (Muller et al., 2009). More recently, these efforts have been complemented by significant university reforms designed to link academia more closely to industry.[12]

Support at the European Level

In the Europe Union, such national initiatives are supported at the supra-national level. The European Union's Regions of Knowledge initiative, implemented under the Seventh Framework Programme, aims to strengthen the research potential of European regions by encouraging the development of research-driven clusters associating universities, research centers, enterprises and regional authorities and supporting their cooperation.[13] The European Commission's Regions for Economic Change initiative, which assists trans-national networks of regions in their efforts to improve their regional innovation systems, complements this program.[14]

Building Clusters in China

National development programs to support regional efforts to develop innovation clusters are also under way in the world's emerging economies. China, notably, has now constructed over fifty research parks, many from scratch, as a part of a coordinated strategy for developing innovation clusters. China's research parks vary in size and mission, with many very large examples. For example, the Zhongguancun Science Park in Beijing hosts over 20,000 enterprises, employs nearly a million people, and has earned about $124 billion in income in recent years (Tan, 2006; Tzeng, 2010; National Research Council, 2009).

RECENT FEDERAL CLUSTER INITIATIVES

Until recently, the United States had no similar coordinated national effort under way to build new research parks or develop new innovation clusters.[15] Traditionally, state and local governments and, in some cases, private foundations and other regional organizations, have singularly or in combination sought to stimulate the development and growth of clusters. In many cases, however, state and local efforts lack critical mass in terms of funding and facilities and, in some cases, the sustained policy support needed for success.

To address this apparent gap and to adjust to the changing international competitive environment, some advocates have called for the federal government to play a more active role in supporting the development of local innovation clusters.[16] Andrew Reamer of the Brookings Institution and Jonathan Sallet of the Center for American Progress are among those who have urged federal agencies to make more effective and efficient use of resources they already deploy in stimulating the development of innovation clusters.[17]

Identifying three principles to guide federal participation, a recent Brookings report calls on the federal government to support the development of regional innovation clusters (Mills et al., 2008):

Bottom-up First, federal programs should be flexible, bottom-up, and collaboration-oriented, rather than top-down, prescriptive, and input-focused.

Incentive-based Second, the government should use a kit of diverse tools to improve market information and incentivize entrepreneurship through the selective use of grants.

Appropriately funded Third, a federal effort should be funded at a level appropriate to need.

The Brookings report further states that any federal effort to support the growth of innovation clusters should build on the capacities of state and regional organizations. To serve as effective local catalysts, it notes that federal policy should also link, leverage, and align existing federal programs that support regional economic development (Mills et al., 2008).

Drawing on this research, and recognizing clusters as important catalysts for growth and employment, the Obama Administration has actively sought to develop federal-regional partnerships to foster their development. As we see next, key initiatives to develop regional innovation clusters are being led by the Department of Energy, the National Institute for Standards and Technology, and the Small Business Administration.

The Energy Department's Energy Regional Innovation Clusters

The Energy Regional Innovation Cluster (E-RIC) program is a new initiative led by the Department of Energy to develop regional clusters in solar power, energy-efficient buildings, nuclear energy, and advanced batteries for storing energy. The Energy Department has announced that the first regional innovation hub will focus on developing more energy-efficient buildings, given that buildings consume 40 per cent of energy generated in the United States. This hub will also draw the participation of related industries such as appliance manufacturers, building supply manufacturers, and construction companies.[18]

E-RIC also expects to draw on support from other federal agencies in coordinating with an array of regional partners such as colleges, workforce training programs, private companies, non-government organizations, and local and state development agencies. Describing the scope of the initiative at a National Academy of Sciences symposium, Ginger Lew, then of the White House National Economic Council, noted that: the Labor Department can team with community colleges to make sure a region has enough engineers and skilled workers to meet project demand for a cluster; the National Institute for Standards and Technology (NIST) can work with university-industry research centers to accelerate development of core technologies; and the SBA can provide seed capital for qualifying start-ups (Lew, 2012). While observing that getting so many federal bureaucracies to work together is a significant challenge, she noted that a major goal of the E-RIC initiative is to fine-tune the collaboration model so that it could eventually be used as a template to accelerate other federal efforts to support the development of regional innovation clusters (Lew, 2012). The costs in time and effort to coordinate these very diverse programs and procedures remain, nonetheless, a major constraint.

The Economic Development Administration's Regional Innovation Strategies Initiative

The Commerce Department's Economic Development Agency (EDA) has launched a Regional Innovation Strategies Initiative, which serves as a framework for its economic development activities. In remarks at a National Academy of Sciences symposium, EDA Administrator John Fernandez stated that his agency is realigning all its programs to support this initiative, adding that staff members are developing a rich data base of innovation cluster activities across the country and new metrics to evaluate their performance (Fernandez, 2012). He noted that EDA programs also offer technical assistance and disseminate best practices to economic-development practitioners. For example, the agency offers an online, self-paced curriculum called 'Know Your Region' that explains the benefits of regional planning, data on employees and companies in each county that could contribute to a cluster, and tools to formulate regional strategies.[19]

Finally, EDA is expanding the scope of its public works program to include critical infrastructure needs of the 21st century, such as research parks, incubators, and better access to capital. Assistant Secretary Fernandez also reported that the EDA is supporting proof-of-concept and workforce training centers that are custom-designed to act as catalysts for specific technology clusters and to serve the needs of communities (Fernandez, 2012).

The National Institute for Standards and Technology's Nanoelectronics Research Initiative

NIST's Rapid Innovation and Competitiveness initiative, launched in 2007, seeks to increase the nation's return on its scientific investment through the development of innovation clusters. Its first pilot program, the Nanoelectronics Research Initiative (NRI), draws together industry, government, and academia to work toward the development of semiconductor technologies that eventually will replace CMOS.[20]

NIST relies heavily on industry input to define technology roadmaps for next-generation semiconductors. The alliance includes corporations such as IBM, Advanced Micro Devices, Freescale, Micron Technology, and Texas Instruments, as well as 35 universities.

Under the NRI initiative, four nanotechnology research centers have been set up at different universities around the country. The largest, an 11-university consortium called Index, is based at the State University of New York-Albany. Other centers are located at the University of Texas-Austin, the University of California-Los Angeles, and Notre Dame

University. NIST contributes $2.75 million annually to the centers.[21] Given the importance of the semiconductor industry to US growth and competitiveness, one wonders if more robust funding would be in order.[22]

These efforts are however, in many cases, being complemented by investments by state governments. NIST's initial investments in the Albany cluster, for example, are dwarfed by those of the state of New York, which has provided grants, tax breaks and other subsidies of more than $1 billion to encourage big-company investments and foster the birth of small start-ups in the Albany cluster (Haldar, 2011).

The Small Business Administration's Support for Clusters

SBA is broadening its traditional role of providing advice, loan guarantees, and grants to small businesses to provide support for clustered development.[23] According to SBA Administrator Karen Mills, the agency has a $90 million loan portfolio, 68 field offices, and 900 Small Business Development Centers across the nation that can be harnessed to support the growth of clusters across the nation. The SBA also is affiliated with SCORE, a small-business mentoring program with 350 chapters and 14,000 counselors (Mills, 2011). SBA's efforts to foster regional clusters began with the Michigan robotics cluster. According to Karen Mills, the agency saw an opportunity to help struggling automotive suppliers meet the Department of Defense's need for unmanned military vehicles for use in detecting roadside bombs. The Detroit area's advantages include an advanced manufacturing supply base, automated tool suppliers, expertise in sensor technologies, and robotics R&D at Oakland University. SBA helped organize a two-day meeting of DOD procurement officers and 200 Michigan businesses.[24] SBA also is helping organize similar cluster initiatives in Hampton Roads, Virginia (in robotics, unmanned systems, port security, sensors, modeling, and simulation) and in Hawai'i (to develop unmanned vehicles to detonate unexploded ordnance.) The SBA expects to fund additional clusters in robotics and other technologies around the country.[25]

ADDITIONAL FEDERAL-STATE SYNERGIES FOR CLUSTER DEVELOPMENT

Federal efforts to support the growth of regional innovative clusters go well beyond these recent initiatives. Federal-state synergies for cluster development have also developed from research parks built around the hub of a national laboratory, from the early-state innovation funding awarded by the Small Business Innovation Research Program (SBIR) and by the outreach and technical advice provided by the Department of Commerce Manufacturing Extension Partnership.

The Case of the Sandia Research Park

Beginning in the 1980s, Congress sought to encourage national laboratories, rich reservoirs of scientific and applied technological research, to commercialize their technology and encourage regional growth. The Federal Technology Transfer Act of 1986 required every federal laboratory to actively transfer technology to industry, universities, and state and local governments.[26] This process accelerated in the 1990s with policy measures and funding for CRADA.[27] Bureaucratic resistance and the reduction of funding for CRADA reduced the level of activity substantially. Provisions of the 2005 Energy Policy Act again sought to commercialize technologies based on research conducted at national laboratories, again with mixed response.[28]

In some quarters, progress was made. For example, Sandia National Laboratories in Albuquerque, New Mexico, was among the first national laboratories to expand its mission beyond national security and systematically seek to commercialize government-sponsored research. One focal point of this effort has been Sandia's now well-established science park.[29] While not at the scale of many foreign parks, it is now home to over 30 high-tech companies, employing over 2,000 people in industries as diverse as solar energy and software to nano-materials and semiconductor manufacturing equipment. The park continues to expand, and hopes to draw in an additional 4,000 jobs over the course of this decade (Rottler, 2012).

Sandia's 'Separation to Transfer Technology' program has been an important element in the success of its cluster development efforts. The program allows scientists who work at Sandia National Laboratory to take leave of absence for up to two years to join or help start up companies. If a business venture doesn't work out, the scientists can return to their jobs. Since 1994, 138 Sandia scientists and engineers have left the laboratory in New Mexico and its California affiliate, Lawrence Livermore National Laboratory, to enter business. At least 91 companies have been started or expanded as a result.

Seed Capital for Innovation: The Role of SBIR

The largest early-stage innovation program in the United States, the Small Business Innovation Research (SBIR) offers $2.5 billion a year in competitions and awards to stimulate technological innovation among small private-sector businesses while providing government agencies new, cost-effective, technical and scientific solutions to meet their diverse mission needs.

The challenge of incomplete and insufficient information for investors can pose substantial obstacles for new firms seeking seed capital. Given that attracting investors to support an imperfectly understood, as yet-to-be-developed innovation is especially daunting – the term 'Valley of Death' has come to describe the period of transition when a developing technology is deemed promising, but too new to validate its commercial potential and thereby attract the capital necessary for its continued development.[30] This means that inherent technological value does not lead inevitably to commercialization; many good ideas perish on the way to the market, often for the lack of sufficient funds.

In a recent comprehensive assessment of the program, the US National Academies found that SBIR encourages the entrepreneurship needed to bring innovative ideas from the laboratory to the market by providing scarce pre-venture capital funding on a competitive basis (National Research Council, 2008). Further, by creating new information about the feasibility and commercial potential of technologies held by small innovative firms, SBIR awards aid investors in identifying firms with promising technologies. SBIR awards thus appear to have a 'certification' function, acting as a stamp of approval for young firms and allowing them to obtain resources from outside investors (Lerner, 1999). Recognizing the potential of this federal program, several states have sought to leverage SBIR to accelerate regional growth. The One North Carolina Small Business Program, for example, awards state matching funds to North Carolina businesses that have received funding from SBIR.[31] Some states have also initiated 'Phase 0' programs to increase the chances of local firms submitting a successful SBIR proposal.[32] In all of the regional development clusters programs, the dearth of early stage capital often remains a major obstacle to technology commercialization and small firm development; SBIR addresses this need.

Practical Advice for Manufacturers: The Role of MEP

Organized under the National Institute of Standards and Technology (NIST), the US Manufacturing Extension Partnership (MEP) is a decentralized network of 59 centers, more than 300 local offices, and more than 1,000 professional specialists in all 50 states. The partnership provides 'pragmatic assistance, appropriate to state and local conditions, with business services, quality systems, manufacturing systems, information technology, human resources, and engineering and product development ("soft" business practices)' (Shapira et al., 2010, 260).

Collaborating with other MEP centers, with other NIST programs, and with other public and private organizations, the partnership addresses the technological and business needs of companies, most of which are small and mid-sized companies. MEP's decentralized organization supports this approach by allowing each center, within certain operational and performance parameters, to customize its organizational model, service offerings, and delivery based on the needs of its clients and the institutional capabilities within its service region (Shapira, 2001).

The Potential of the Fraunhofer Model

While technical expertise extended through MEP is helpful to small firms in developing regional clusters, a key question is whether the program – at $125 million a year – is at sufficient scale to make a significant contribution in an economy as large and far-flung as the United States. Other nations have major institutions focused on applied and translational research aimed at enabling domestic companies to develop manufacturing processes and marketable products. Large, well-funded public-private partnerships such as Germany's Fraunhofer-Gesellschaft have proven successful at helping large and small domestic manufacturers translate new technologies into products and production processes and remain globally competitive. This has led some to call for similar institutions that are dedicated to helping small and mid-sized manufacturers across the nation's regions to translate emerging technologies into production processes and new products.

The Fraunhofer-Gesellschaft is one of the world's largest and most successful applied technology agencies. Fraunhofer's 60 research institutes and centers both within Germany and around the world employ some 17,000 people – 4,000 of them with Doctoral and Master's degrees – and has a $2.3 billion (€1.62 billion) annual budget.[33] The society's mission is to act as a 'technology bridge' to German industry.[34] Although Fraunhofer researchers publish scientific papers and secure patents – they filed 685 applications in 2009 – their primary mission is to disseminate and commercialize technology. Serving over 5,000 corporate clients, Fraunhofer engineers develop intellectual property on a contract basis, hone product prototypes and industrial processes, and work with manufacturers on the factory floor to help implement new production methods. The institutes in the Fraunhofer network also can conduct market research and offer consulting services. Some *Mittelstand* manufacturers – the small and medium-sized enterprises that are the backbone of Germany's high-value export sector – have been Fraunhofer clients for generations. Nearly one-third of clients have 250 or fewer employees.[35]

Fraunhofer's strength and durability – key assets – are based on its diverse funding base, which enables its institutes to perform their own in-house research, remain engaged in strategic national and EU innovation programs, and collaborate with industry. Federal government funding, which covers one-third of its budget, has been stable and has steadily increased, enabling Fraunhofer to plan for the long term. Another third of Fraunhofer's revenue comes from manufacturing clients. Fraunhofer's 59 Institutes of Applied Research in Germany collaborate closely with manufacturers in 16 different clusters. The federal government generally matches funds raised from industry. Half of the industry contracts are with small and medium-sized enterprises. When contracted to perform research, institutes agree to meet deadlines, milestones, and deliverables. Customers own the intellectual property. The remaining third comes from publicly funded research projects that it wins on a competitive basis from the German government and the European Union.[36] These help keep Fraunhofer at the forefront of developing technologies meeting national and European Union priorities. On the other hand, some users find the Fraunhofer system to be heavily bureaucratic and less adaptive to the needs of emerging sectors.[37]

THE ROLE OF STATE AND REGIONAL PLAYERS

While the federal government has expanded its support in recent years, industry cluster strategies remain chiefly a concern of states, regions, and metropolitan areas. Many state and regional governments have taken a pragmatic approach to fostering innovation clusters, targeting industries such as semiconductors, batteries, flexible electronics, and robotics. Michigan, Ohio, and Kansas are among states that have intervened actively to support innovation-based growth by fostering productive collaboration among private industry, universities, and government. Their initiatives have moved well beyond the traditional incentives long used by states to attract large factories and corporate headquarters, such as tax breaks, free work training, and low-cost land and utilities. As we see in the examples below, these states are providing grants and early-stage capital to stimulate and grow high-tech start-ups. They are also co-investing with universities, industry, and federal agencies to establish major research centers devoted to core applied technologies.

The experience of three states, Michigan, Ohio, and Kansas are briefly reviewed below, demonstrating the importance of local leadership, dedicated institutions, a sectoral focus, and complementary investments by the federal government in developing regional innovation clusters.

Building Michigan's Advanced Battery and Electric Vehicles Clusters

Michigan has been one of the boldest states in subsidizing new investment to renew and diversify its industrial base. Led by then Governor Granholm, the state legislature took a number of initiatives to develop new technological clusters that leveraged existing local strengths in engineering knowhow and automobile manufacturing to develop new industries in renewable energy and electric transportation.

The state offered some of the nation's most generous financial incentives for opening manufacturing facilities. It invested in start-ups through a 21st Century Jobs Fund and provides loans and grants to help larger companies commercialize manufacturing and green-energy technologies (National Research Council, *Building the US Battery Industry*, forthcoming). The state also offered a variety of refundable tax credits, including special programs for companies that manufacture advanced batteries and solar-power equipment, companies that invest in smaller Michigan companies, and companies that invest at least $350,000 for new strategic innovation relationships.

The Michigan Economic Development Commission (MEDC) has worked with the private sector, universities, and federal agencies to identify emerging industries where the state enjoys strategic advantages and the opportunity to be competitive globally. From this process, MEDC selected the advanced energy-storage systems, equipment for wind and solar power, and bio-fuels industries. These sectors were seen to leverage Michigan's strengths in manufacturing, natural resources, existing parts and materials suppliers, and extensive university and corporate R&D (Shreffler, forthcoming). The state in partnership with industry also funded a university-based research program called 'Centers of Energy Excellence' to support clusters in these technologies.[38]

Michigan's new advanced battery cluster illustrates the potential of state-federal synergies. Michigan's own substantial efforts to build a battery cluster were supported by $1.3 billion in federal funds for companies such as A123, General Motors, Johnson Controls, XTreme Power, and South Korea's LG to build lithium-ion cell or battery-pack factories in the state (Zanardelli, forthcoming). This federal investment has encouraged private companies to invest a further $5.2 billion, with the hope of creating up to 40,000 new jobs by 2017 and attracting out-of-state manufacturers of related technologies. Growing demand by the military for electrified transportation is helping to reinforce the growth of this new industry but there remain many questions concerning the adequacy of demand for these high cost, unproven vehicles (Zanardelli, forthcoming).

Building Ohio's Renewable Energy, Flexible Electronics, and Medical Clusters

The state of Ohio is financially backing the development of clusters as a part of its economic development strategy. Under the Ohio Third Frontier program, the state is investing $2.3 billion to support applied research, commercialization, entrepreneurial assistance, early-stage capital, and worker training to create an 'innovation ecosystem' for a number of clusters.[39] Since its launch in 2002, Third Frontier is credited with creating 55,000 direct and indirect jobs, as of 2009; creating, capitalizing, or attracting more than 600 companies, and generating $6.6 billion in economic impact – nine times more than the state has invested (Camp et al., 2007). In 2010, Ohio taxpayers approved a $700 million funding boost so that Third Frontier can continue its activities through 2015. These and other initiatives have from 2004 to 2008 doubled early-stage investment in the state to $445.6 million (Camp et al., 2007).

Northern Ohio is especially active in its efforts to diversify an economy whose manufacturing base has been battered by the recession, offshore outsourcing, and imports. Economic development officials are developing road maps to nurture clusters in sectors such as energy storage, photo-voltaic cells, smart-grid technology, electric transportation, and conversion of biomass and waste into energy.

Concerted efforts are under way by regional development organizations so that the next round of innovations can translate into regional industries. Federal awards are now complementing and reinforcing many of their initiatives.

The Northeast Ohio Technology Coalition (NorTech), a nonprofit funded by business associations and foundations, is spearheading efforts to create a new cluster in flexible electronics in Northeast Ohio (Bagley, 2012). Funding from the federal government, including the US Small Business Administration's Innovative Economies initiative, is helping to support the growth of regional clusters in flexible electronics.

A group called Ohio Advanced Energy is seeking to advance the region's small but growing cluster in photovoltaic cells and modules. This effort is supported by the expansion of US Air Force funding to the University of Toledo from approximately $1 million to $3 million annually, as well as the award of a $1 million NASA grant to establish a photovoltaic test facility at the University of Toledo.[40] Another group, PolymerOhio, is working with the Manufacturing Extension Partnership to expand Ohio's strong bases in polymers and plastics, which includes

2,800 companies and research institutions employing 140,000 skilled workers.[41]

BioEnterprise, another state organization, is promoting the development of a biomedical cluster in Greater Cleveland, which is supported by significant funding by the National Institutes of Health. The cluster has so far drawn together more than 600 companies, including imaging giants such as Philips, General Electric, Siemens, Hitachi, and Toshiba.[42]

Kansas

Kansas has adopted a focused strategy that leverages existing capacities and strengths to develop industries deemed to have the highest potential for growth. KTEC, the state's economic development agency, conducted an assessment that found that Kansas had high capacity ratings in four areas: human biosciences, agriculture and agricultural biotechnology, information and communications technology, and aviation. In consultation with the state's four major universities, KTEC determined that the biotechnology and biosciences sectors were the strongest candidates for the development of innovation clusters, followed by the information and communications technology sector. Interestingly, while the state has a significant agricultural sector, it was not seen to have the potential for strong future growth (Bendis, 2011).

Likewise, based on long-term projections of industry data and the state of the Kansas economy, KTEC judged that the state's aviation sector did not offer sufficient growth potential.[43] KTEC also decided not to compete with emerging nanotechnology clusters like Albany, New York because the state did not have the means to build new, large-scale infrastructure. Instead, as Richard Bendis observed at a National Academy of Sciences symposium, 'we chose to build on existing capacity and strengths' (Bendis, 2011).

The Kansas Economic Growth Act of 2004 led to the creation of the Kansas Bioscience Authority (KBA), a statewide bioscience initiative that guides the state's investment in the biosciences. The act provided an innovative funding mechanism for the KBA based on the growth of state income-tax withholdings from employees of bioscience-related companies. State taxes that exceed the base-year measurement accrue to the authority for investment in additional bioscience growth.[44] The development of a human, animal and plant bio-sciences cluster in the state has been further strengthened by the launch of the $600 million National Bio and Agro Defense Facility at Kansas State University.[45]

THE CHALLENGE: SUSTAINING FEDERAL-STATE SYNERGIES FOR INNOVATION CLUSTERS

US regional economies face mounting global competitive challenges. No longer do US states and cities compete only among themselves for talent, investment, and entrepreneurs in technology-intensive industries. They also compete against national governments that are executing comprehensive strategies that seek to create regional innovation clusters in many of the same important, emerging industries being pursued in the United States. Nations around the world are backing up these strategies with heavy investment in state enterprises, new and renewed universities, public-private research collaborations, workforce training, early-stage capital funds, and modern science parks, all reinforced by strong policy attention from top leaders.

This new competitive landscape is prompting federal, state and regional authorities in the US to take creative and comprehensive approaches to developing innovation clusters. Federally funded research programs at universities and national laboratories are in some cases being oriented toward the activities of local industrial clusters. Government agencies such as the departments of Energy and Commerce are aligning a wide range of existing programs to accelerate the development of strategic technologies within regional clusters. In many instances, federal agencies are sharing best practices with regional agencies and are facilitating networking among researchers, investors, and support organizations across the US. There is much greater awareness of the potential benefits of clusters and a concerted effort to create synergies across multiple federal and state programs.

These initiatives, while promising, face a number of challenges. Perhaps foremost among them is a sharp decline in the availability of federal funds for these types of initiatives. Current budget limitations already run the risk of providing resources that are inadequate to meet the often expansive objectives of the federal and state agencies. Sustaining this momentum for greater state and federal cooperation in regional innovation cluster initiatives, however, is an important challenge. Political attitudes, as well as funding levels, can change swiftly. Moreover, the premise that close coordination of federal agencies and multiple state-based cluster initiatives will lead to greater synergies has encountered growing skepticism. While few question the principle, the practical efforts required for greater coordination are daunting and can often drain managerial energy at the federal, state, and operational levels. Shared information and broad alignment rather than close coordination may prove more promising going forward. The fundamental challenge faced by US regional innovation cluster initiatives is the lack of policy consensus regarding their benefits at the state and especially the federal level, with the attendant risk that the necessary continuity of policy and funding will not be maintained. This is particularly unfortunate in a world that has seen sustained efforts and great policy continuity by America's competitors.

NOTES

1. For an insightful review of the interface of the entrepreneur in regional growth dynamics, see Desai et al. (2011).
2. For example, substantial federal funding for Stanford University has played a key role in the development of Silicon Valley (Adams, 2011).
3. For an analysis of the military role in the origins of Silicon Valley and the high-tech industry in Boston, see Leslie (1993).
4. The Bayh–Dole Act of 1980 (PL 96-517, Patent and Trademark Act Amendments of 1980) permits the transfer of exclusive control over many government-funded inventions to universities and businesses operating with federal contracts for the purpose of further development and commercialization.
5. There are, of course, exceptions; for example, the Tennessee Valley Authority, which was created by an Act of Congress on 18 May 1933.
6. See, for example, Muro and Katz (2010).
7. The America COMPETES Act (P.L. 110-69), enacted on 9 August 2007, directed national laboratories owned by the Department of Energy to establish Discovery Science and Engineering Innovation Institutes to co-develop applications for technology with universities and industry. On 4 January 2011, President Obama signed the America COMPETES Reauthorization Act of 2010. However, as an 'authorization bill', 'COMPETES will only have an impact to the extent that the funding levels it lays out are actually appropriated over the next three years' (Reich, 2010).
8. For a review of current trends in the globalization of innovation and the nature of locational competition, see Jaruzelski and Dehoff (2008).
9. In their review of the genesis of clusters, Feldman and Braunerhjelm note that 'clusters are born and develop on the basis of specific combinations of capabilities, incentives, and opportunities.' The presence of *capabilities* – including the presence of localized knowledge, a skilled workforce, and the availability of capital – creates *opportunities* for entrepreneurship and collaboration, where these opportunities can be realized in the presence of appropriate *incentives*. See Braunerhjelm and Feldman (2006); see also Feldman and Francis (2004).
10. Robert Lucas has long argued that the clustering and density of talented people is a key driver of innovation and economic growth (Lucas, 1988). Richard Florida has popularized the characteristics and economic advantages of innovative clusters (for example, Florida, 2002).
11. See Mills et al. (2008).
12. See http://www.nouvelleuniversite.gouv.fr/.
13. Access at http://ec.europa.eu/invest-in-research/funding/funding03_en.htm.
14. Access at http://ec.europa.eu/regional_policy/cooperate/regions_for_economic_change/index_en.cfm.
15. As of April 2012, the United States has no legislatively authorized programs specifically dedicated to comprehensively supporting cluster initiatives. Many of the Department of Labor's WIRED (Workforce Innovation in Regional Economic Development) projects are cluster-focused, but WIRED is not solely a cluster initiative program. See the Department of Labor WIRED website at http://www.doleta.gov/wired/about/.

16. See Mills et al. (2008; see also Ed Paisley and Jonathan Sallet, 2009; Muro and Katz, 2010).
17. The report by the Brookings Institution, for example, called on the federal agencies to 'link, leverage, and align' their resources with regional innovation cluster initiatives (Mills et al., 2008).
18. See Energy Department Website: http://energy.gov/articles/energy-efficient-building-systems-regional-innovation-cluster
19. Access at http://www.knowyourregion.org/.
20. NIST, 2007, "NIST, SRC-NRI Enter Partnership to Drive Search for Next-Generation Computer Technology" September 13, 2007. See http://www.nist.gov/public_affairs/releases/src.cfm.
21. NIST-CNST At a Glance. Access at http://www.nist.gov/cnst/upload/CNST_2008_report.pdf.
22. For an empirical analysis of the significant positive impact of semiconductor based technologies on US productivity growth, see Jorgenson et al. (2005).
23. Congress established the SBA with the Small Business Act of 30 July 1953, to 'aid, counsel, assist and protect . . . the interests of small business concerns' and to ensure small businesses get a 'fair proportion' of government contracts. The SBA guarantees small-business loans. In 1982, the Small Business Innovation Research (SBIR) program was established to administer small grants by various federal agencies to boost commercialization of innovations derived from federal R&D, among other things.
24. The Michigan Automotive Robotics Cluster Initiative Workshop, 28 July 2009.
25. The SBA's Regional Innovation Clusters aim to provide business training, counseling and mentoring to help grow existing small businesses and start-ups. SBA's advanced defense technology clusters provide similar services to small businesses working in high-growth industries such as robotics, cyber-security and energy innovations.
26. The Federal Technology Transfer Act of 1986 (Public Law 99-502) amended the Stevenson-Wydler Technology Innovation Act (Public Law 96-480) and made technology transfer the responsibility of every federal laboratory scientist and engineer and mandated that technology transfer be considered part of employee performance evaluations.
27. Created by the Stevenson–Wydler Technology Innovation Act of 1980 and amended by the Federal Technology Transfer Act of 1986, a CRADA (Cooperative Research and Development Agreement) is a written agreement between a private company and a government agency to work together on a project.
28. Title X, Sections 1001, 1002, and 1003 of the Energy Policy Act of 2005 (PL 109-58) contained several provisions to promote technology transfer and commercialization by federal laboratories, including establishment of a technology transfer coordinator at the Department of Energy, a working group of laboratory directors, an energy commercialization fund, a technology infrastructure program, and a small-business assistance program.
29. National Research Council, 1999. The review provided an early validation of the park's concept, its rationale and current plans, as well as identifying potential operational and policy issues that helped to guide the growth of Sandia S&T Park.
30. For an empirical analysis of the Valley of Death phenomenon, see Branscomb and Auerswald (2003).
31. For information on North Carolina's small business program, see http://www.nccommerce.com/scitech/grant-programs/one-n.c.-small-business-program.
32. For information on Florida's Phase 0 program, see http://www.eflorida.com/Why_Florida.aspx?id=8804.
33. http://www.fraunhofer.de/en/.html.
34. Presentation by Roland Schindler, executive director of Fraunhofer, at National Academies Symposium, 1 November 2010, Washington, DC: Meeting Global Challenges: US–German Innovation Policy.
35. http://www.fraunhofer.de/en/.html.

36. Ibid.
37. Some studies have criticized the highly bureaucratic structure of the Fraunhofer-Gesellschaft as creating a rigidity that leads to a focus on sectors traditionally strong in the German economy to the possible detriment of emerging sectors. See, for example, Astrom and Arnold, Faugert & Co Utvardering AB, Technopolis, December 2008, 'International Comparison of Five Institute Systems' (Forsknings-og Innovationsstyrelsen).
38. Michigan's new Centers of Energy Excellence (COEE) program provides grants totaling $45 million over three years to for-profit companies that are commercializing innovative energy technologies with support from a university. See http://www.michiganadvantage.org/News/Centers-of-Energy-Excellence-Program/.
39. http://thirdfrontier.com/.
40. http://www.development.ohio.gov/ohiothirdfrontier/ToledoSolarHotspot.htm.
41. PolymerOne data. Access at http://www.polymer1.com/.
42. http://www.bioenterprise.com/.
43. Wichita, often called the 'Aircraft Capital of the World,' is the manufacturing base of Cessna, Hawker Beechcraft, Bombardier Learjet, Spirit AeroSystems, and Boeing Integrated Defense Systems. See http://www.wingsoverkansas.com/about/ Given that the Wichita aviation industry is dependent on small personal aircraft or corporate fleet sales, the performance of this sector has been cyclical, following macroeconomic cycles.
44. http://www.kansasbioauthority.org/about_the_kba/KEGA.aspx.
45. http://www.dhs.gov/files/labs/editorial_0762.shtm.

REFERENCES

Adams, Stephen B. (2011), 'Growing where you are planted: exogenous firms and the seeding of Silicon Valley', *Research Policy*, **40** (3), April, 368–79.

Bagley, Rebecca (2012), 'Cluster development in Ohio', in National Research Council, *Clustering for 21st Century Prosperity, Report of a Symposium*, C. Wessner (ed.), Washington, DC: National Academies Press.

Bendis, Richard (2011), 'Building and branding clusters: lessons from Kansas and Philadelphia', in National Research Council, *Growing Innovation Clusters for American Prosperity, Report of a Symposium*, C. Wessner (ed.), Washington, DC: National Academies Press.

Branscomb, Lewis, and Philip Auerswald (2003), 'Valleys of death and Darwinian seas: financing the invention to innovation transition in the United States', *The Journal of Technology Transfer*, **28** (3–4), August.

Braunerhjelm, Pontus, and Maryann Feldman (2006), *Cluster Genesis: Technology Based Industrial Development*, Oxford: Oxford University Press.

Camp, M., K. Parekh, and T. Grywalski (2007), *2007 Ohio Venture Capital Report*, Fisher College of Business, Ohio State University.

Desai, Sameeksha, Peter Nijkamp, and Roger R. Stough (eds) (2011), *New Directions in Regional Economic Development: The Role of Entrepreneurship Theory and Methods, Practice and Policy*, Cheltenham, UK and Northampton, MA, USA: Edward Elgar.

Duranton,Gilles, Philippe Martin, Thierry Mayer, and Florian Mayneris (2010), *The Economics of Clusters. Lessons from the French Experience*, Oxford: Oxford University Press.

Feldman, M.P. and Johanna L. Francis (2004), 'Homegrown solutions: fostering cluster formation', *Economic Development Quarterly*, **18** (2), May.

Fernandez, John (2012), 'Building out the infrastructure: expanding the EDA role', in National Research Council, *Clustering for 21st Century Prosperity*, C. Wessner (ed.), Washington, DC: National Academies Press.

Florida, Richard (2002), *The Rise of the Creative Class*, New York: Basic Books.

Haldar, Pradeep (2011), 'New York State's nano initiative,' in National Research Council, *Growing Innovation Clusters for American Prosperity, Report of a Symposium*, C. Wessner (ed.), Washington, DC: National Academies Press.

Jaruzelski, Barry and Kevin Dehoff (2008), 'Beyond borders: The Global Innovation 1000', *Strategy and Business*, **53**, Winter.

Jorgenson, Dale W., Mun S. Ho, and Kevin J. Stiroh (2005), *Productivity, Information Technology and the American Growth Resurgence*, Cambridge, MA: MIT Press.

Katz, Bruce, Jennifer Bradley, and Amy Liu (2010), 'Delivering the next economy: the States step up', Brookings-Rockefeller Project on State and Metropolitan Innovation, November.

Lerner, Joshua (1999), 'Public venture capital', in National Research Council, *The Small Business Innovation Research Program: Challenges and Opportunities*, C. Wessner (ed.), Washington, DC: National Academies Press.

Leslie, Stuart W. (1993), *The Cold War and American Science: The Military-Industrial-Academic Complex at MIT and Stanford*, New York: Columbia University Press.

Lew, Ginger (2012), 'The administration's cluster initiative', in National Research Council, *Clustering for 21st Century Prosperity*, C. Wessner (ed.), Washington, DC: National Academies Press.

Lucas, Robert (1988), 'On the mechanics of economic development', *Journal of Monetary Economics*, **22**, 38–9.

Mills, K. (2011), Luncheon Address in National Research Council, *Growing Innovation Clusters for American Prosperity, Report of a Symposium*, C. Wessner (ed.), Washington, DC: National Academies Press.

Mills, Karen G., Elisabeth B. Reynolds, and Andrew Reamer (2008), 'Clusters and competitiveness: a new federal role for stimulating regional economies', Brookings Institution, April.

Muller, Emmanuel, Andrea Zenker and Jean-Alain Héraud (2009), 'France: innovation system and innovation policy', Fraunhofer ISI Discussion Papers Innovation Systems and Policy Analysis, No. 18 ISSN 1612-1430, Karlsruhe, April.

Muro, Mark and Bruce Katz (2010), 'The new "cluster moment": how regional innovation clusters can foster the next economy', Brookings Institution, September.

National Academy of Sciences, National Academy of Engineering, Institute of Medicine (2007), *Rising Above the Gathering Storm, Energizing and Employing America for a Brighter Economic Future*, Washington, DC: National Academies Press.

National Research Council (1999), *A Review of the Sandia Science and Technology Park Initiative*, C. Wessner (ed.), Washington, DC: National Academies Press.

National Research Council (2008), *An Assessment of the SBIR Program*, Charles W. Wessner (ed.), Washington, DC: National Academies Press.

National Research Council (2009), *Understanding Research, Science and Technology Parks: Report of a Workshop*, Charles W. Wessner (ed.), Washington, DC: National Academies Press.

National Research Council (forthcoming), *Building the US Battery Industry for Electric-Drive Vehicles: Progress, Challenges, and Opportunities, Report of a Symposium*, C. Wessner (ed.), Washington, DC: National Academies Press.

National Research Council (2012), *Clustering for 21st Century Prosperity*, C. Wessner (ed.), Washington, DC: National Academies Press.

NIST (National Institute of Standards and Technology) (2007), *NIST, SRC-NRI Enter Partnership To Drive Search for Next-Generation Computer Technology*, 13 September, available at: http://www.nist.gov/public_affairs/releases/src.cfm.

Paisley, Ed and Jonathan Sallet (2009), 'The geography of innovation: the Federal Government and the growth of regional innovation clusters', Center for American Progress.

Pezzini, Mario (2003), 'Cultivating regional development: main trends and policy challenges in OECD regions', Paris: OECD.

Pezzini, Mario (2012), 'Best practice in cluster strategy: the OECD perspective', in National Research Council, *Clustering for 21st Century Prosperity*, C. Wessner (ed.), Washington, DC: National Academies Press.

Reich, Eugene (2010), 'US Congress passes strategic science bill', *Nature*, 22 December.

Rottler, J. Stephen (2012), 'Sandia national laboratories as a catalyst for regional growth', in National Research Council, *Clustering for 21st Century Prosperity*, C. Wessner (ed.), Washington, DC: National Academies Press.

Shapira, Philip (2001), 'US manufacturing extension partnerships: technology policy reinvented?', *Research Policy*, **30** (6), June.

Shapira, Philip, Jan Youtie, and Luciano Kay (2010), 'Building capabilities for innovation in SMEs: a cross-country comparison of technology extension policies and programmes', *International Journal of Innovation and Regional Development*, **3** (3–4).

Shreffler, Eric (forthcoming), 'Michigan investments in batteries and electric vehicles', in National Research Council, *Building the US Battery Industry for Electric-Drive Vehicles: Progress, Challenges, and Opportunities, Report of a Symposium*, C. Wessner (ed.), Washington, DC: National Academies Press.

Tan, Justin (2006), 'Growth of industry clusters and innovation: lessons from Beijing Zhongguancun Science Park', *Journal of Business Venturing*, **21** (6), November, 827–50.

Tzeng, Cheng-Hua (2010), 'Managing innovation for economic development in greater China: the origins of Hsinchu and Zhongguancun', *Technology in Society*, **32** (2), May, 110–21.

Zanardelli, Sonya (forthcoming), 'Department of Defense battery R&D programs and goals', in National Research Council, *Building the US Battery Industry for Electric-Drive Vehicles: Progress, Challenges, and Opportunities, Report of a Symposium*, C. Wessner (ed.), Washington, DC: National Academies Press.

8. Evolving technologies and emerging regions: governance for growth and prosperity

Thomas Andersson

1. INTRODUCTION

An extensive literature has examined the advance of globalization coupled with technical progress and the associated implications for growth and development. The focus has gradually shifted from the role of cross-border product and factor flows across the internationalization of firm-specific assets by transnational companies to the growing economic interdependency of countries and regions around the world (Dunning, 1977; Ohmae, 1995).

A separate track has examined the scope for national or regional policies to attract mobile resources and create synergies between complementary assets and capabilities in the local environment. Examples are the works on competence blocs (Dahmén, 1950), industrial districts (Brusco, 1982), clusters (Porter, 1990), innovation systems (Lundvall, 1992), the Triple Helix (Etzkowitz and Leydesdorff, 1997), and even the creative class (Florida, 2002).

In the case of developing countries, the early focus on gaining control of natural resource extraction and refining (Nurkse, 1953; Rostow, 1960) gave way to an emphasis on promoting industries capable of achieving competitiveness in world markets (Krueger, 1978). The importance of putting diverse local drivers for growth in place soon became evident for these countries as well. The so-called 'four pillars' proposed a comprehensive approach spanning regulatory and institutional reform, education, ICT, and innovation for developing countries to take advantage of the expanding global knowledge flows for development (World Bank, 1999/2000; Dahlman and Andersson, 2000).

Whereas commercial relations and transactions in the wake of European colonization long remained marked by uneven power relations and lop-sided access to capital and technology, the rise of information and communications technology (ICT) has created a more level playing field. Developing and emerging economies, including natural resource rich countries, are now outgrowing the advanced economies more or less across the board. Increasingly fierce competition across a wide spectrum of manufacturing and service industries, along with intensified innovation processes and shortening product cycles, are pushing for structural change. The advanced countries, however, suffer from weakening sentiments under conditions of bulging public debt, stifled growth and rising unemployment.

In the modern-day landscape taking shape, it is crucially important for any country or region to be interconnected and plugged in with the expanding international product and factor flows. At the same time, it will be the features and qualities of the local environment that determine its ability to attract and maintain productive and internationally mobile assets. The plethora of profligate recommendations has left many countries and regions scrambling to foster clusters, innovation systems, triple helix collaboration, and so forth. Despite a number of success stories, the continued struggle to get on top of the issues suggests that the prevailing frameworks for policy guidance somehow lack applicability and relevance on the ground when it comes to addressing the prime issues that signify our era.

In this chapter, following this introduction, Section 2 takes note of the most important drivers of growth, their interrelated nature and the varying fortunes of different regions. In Section 3, I review the so-called resource 'curse' and the issues surrounding the 'Arab Spring', highlighting some ongoing forces of change. On this basis, Section 4 synthesizes observations on the growing challenge of managing human capital and labor market outcomes. Consequently, in Section 5 I argue for adopting a *motivational* approach to the strategic management of places. Section 6 concludes.

2. DRIVERS OF GROWTH AND DEVELOPMENT

Explaining the origins of economic growth has always been difficult. One strand of literature has focused on international trade and investment, especially so-called foreign direct investment (FDI). Both trade and investment were recognized early on to be associated with static gains emanating from an improved division of labor, as well as dynamic gains emanating from deepening specialization and learning processes. In addition, FDI was viewed as positive for recipient countries not because of capital contributions, but because the transfer of firm-specific assets generates returns they cannot fully appropriate but which 'spill over' to other actors in the local environment (Dunning, 1977).

In practice, however, the empirical evidence is inconclusive. Impacts of 'globalization' and cross-border goods and factor flows 'depend on circumstances' (OECD, 1998). Where conditions are favorable, international trade and investment dynamics will be beneficial; where conditions are unfavorable, market forces will exploit the deficiencies and may well worsen outcomes, unless they are able to trigger correction of the sources of inefficiency. The extent to which FDI triggers spillovers and growth has been found contingent on other factors, such as the presence of R&D among local firms (Blomström and Kokko, 1998; Kathuria, 2000), infrastructure, or human capital (Yamin and Sinkovics, 2009).

Another tack has been the attempt to ascribe variation in growth to different production factors. Economists, including Prof. Robert Solow (1957), recognized long ago that natural resources, land, capital, and labor, explain little. Most variance is associated with total factor productivity, in essence the unexplained residual, largely recognized as associated with new technology or 'how' production factors are put to use. Further studies have nailed down the following important growth factors:

Research and Development   R&D has been found to exert a significant impact on productivity growth at firm and industry level. It is not merely how much is invested that matters, but the purpose and quality of R&D, and how different kinds of R&D (including basic, applied, etc.) relate (Guellec and van Pottelsberghe, 2001). External flows of technology and knowledge need to complement own R&D. Absorption requires exploiting synergies between own capacity and learning from others, centering on the exchange and transfer of knowledge, networks, movement of people, etc. (Table 8.1), rather than technology per se.

Information and Communications Technology (ICT)   Not its production but its use is a major determinant of productivity growth at firm, industry and country-wide levels. ICT has emerged as a generic-purpose technology to transform economic activities across the board (Stiroh, 1999). This applies to the most advanced societies as well as laggard economies that undertake effective reforms, where ICT works as a key vehicle for catch-up (UNCTAD, 2011). On the other hand, putting in place ICT capacity can be expensive and use of ICT can serve as a distraction and ultimately dilute rather than strengthen skills, again underlining the importance of taking quality aspects into account. With the rise of mobile technology, convergence, clouds, the Internet of things, etc., ICT use is likely to keep evolving as a fundamental differentiator.

Table 8.1   Evolution of innovation metrics

1st generation input indicators (1950s–60s)	2nd generation output indicators (1970s–80s)	3rd generation innovation indicators (1990s)	4th generation process indicators (2000s plus emerging focus)
• R&D expenditures • S&T personnel • Capital • Tech intensity	• Patents • Publications • Products • Quality change	• Innovation surveys • Indexing • Benchmarking innovation capacity	• Knowledge • Intangibles • Networks • Demand • Clusters • Management techniques • Risk/return • System dynamics

Source: Milbergs and Vonortas (2004).

Innovation   The effort through which new technologies or ideas are put to commercial use has been identified by multiple studies and surveys as greatly important for productivity growth and economic expansion. Different kinds of innovation (product versus process, incremental versus radical, technical versus social, etc.) play their roles. Innovations are dependent on various interrelated functions, typically progressing within so-called *systems of innovation* (Lundvall, 1992). As big organizations grow defensive and entrenched, ecosystems of nimble and fast-moving small and medium-sized companies (SMEs), along with start-ups and the risk-taking of entrepreneurs, gain in importance for innovation (Audretsch and Thurik, 2001). On measurement, we may conceptualize 'generations' of metrics, as illustrated in Table 8.1. The traditional, on the left, are relatively easy to measure, but are now recognized as insufficient. The search is on for indicators to measure intangibles, synergies, ways of handling risk and resistance to change, as displayed in the right-hand column.

Human capital   is hard to measure. More important than commonly used indicators such as literacy levels, the level of degrees, or the number of years in school, is the motivation for education, which skills are promoted, and how skills are put to use in labor markets. Various studies have verified the critical influence of human capital on other main growth factors, such as ICT, R&D, or innovation (OECD, 2001). There is huge variation in productivity between organizations and also between people, as the relevance of skills is constantly changing. With productivity rising for labor with certain skills and in certain operations, others become obsolete. Reskilling and restructuring take time and idle human resources experience rapidly deteriorating skills. Many countries now display rising levels of structural unemployment.

Social capital, organizational and leadership capacity, and management These have been identified as critical for performance at both aggregate and firm level, operating through the way that they influence the availability and use of tacit knowledge, the incentives for learning and putting skills to work, the synergy between complementary skills and the degree to which costly fragmentation or blocking of some useful skills can be overcome.

The above explanatory factors are interrelated. Without leadership abilities and organizational change to attract required talent and human capital, and a continuous upgrading of relevant work force skills, R&D investment and ICT may primarily inflict costs while providing few benefits. Also, outcomes depend critically on quality aspects that are hard to measure.

Meanwhile, the determinants of growth play out very differently across countries and regions. Indicators based on R&D, publications and patents demonstrate the presence of a distinct hierarchy in most innovative activities, with a strong tendency for spatial agglomeration to reproduce itself in new knowledge-intensive fields. In nanoscience, for instance, some 20 percent of total scientific production worldwide in 2005 took place within 12 districts, 40 percent within only 35 and more than 70 percent in 200 districts (www.nanotrendchart.com). Among the top 12, two are European (Paris, ranked 6th with 11,550 articles, Berlin, 12th with 7,662). The leading European areas invariably include major cities (London, Zurich, Madrid). The first medium-sized European municipality in this listing is Louvain (23rd with 5,782 articles), then Grenoble, Aachen and Delft. The four largest areas are in Asia (Tokyo, Beijing, Kyoto, Seoul). While this might at first sight appear remarkable, because nano-S&T, differently from biotech, has many scientific origins (e.g., matter physics, chemistry, electronics, biology, materials science) and could thus be expected to be based on a more diffused pattern, it is plausible that precisely because nanotechnology has to build on so many existing strengths, it links naturally to existing concentrations, particularly when local conditions are conducive to applying them in new fields.

There is no universally applicable answer to the question how different industries may deviate or escape from current concentration dynamics, providing opportunities for new countries and regions to enter the race, including in the infant stages when activities are particularly prone to fuelling new industries marked by high economic returns. However, although most new technologies continue to emanate from industrialized economies, whereas emerging and developing economies focus on uptake of already existing technologies, a distinct reconfiguration is now ongoing. This is particularly the case for China and India, which have used their huge domestic markets and partly the attraction of foreign R&D units as a springboard to establishing their own technological edge. The changes are more far-reaching than that though, as many developing countries are on track towards assuming a significant role in various technological areas (Castellaci and Archibugi, 2008).

At the aggregate level, we observe dramatic reversals in the fortune of different regions. Faced with the rising competitiveness on the part of non-OECD countries, stiffening international competition and the need of adjustment, many of the previously dominating western economies have been running out of steam. There is, however, a general need for nations and regions to counter conditions of stifling growth and, in many instances, worsening social and environmental issues. These aspects play out the most clearly at the local level, where people after all live their lives and engage in everyday activities that, at the end of the day, are crucial for economic and social outcomes. In that context, we have to come to grips with essential institutional and behavioral issues, which is not new to economic writings. To manage the current issues, however, we need to add new ingredients, to reflect the changing nature of the way that people engage with their surroundings and put their skills and efforts to use. This is further addressed in Sections 4 and 5.

3. THE FATE OF NATURAL RESOURCE-BASED ECONOMIES

On the shifting geopolitical scene, much attention has focused on the rise of the Asian Tigers followed more recently by China and India, along with the other 'BRIC' countries (Brazil and Russia being the other two). However, we are also witnessing the comeback of a broader set of countries, which for years have been viewed as laggards: the category of so-called natural resource rich countries. These developments are related to the changing roles and influences of the fundamental growth factors.

Much of the natural resource debate has been about macro-economic factors. The 'Dutch disease' syndrome holds that natural resource abundance boosts foreign exchange earnings, leading to an appreciation of the exchange rate and the subsequent crowding out of other activities in the open and tradable part of the economy, while benefitting public sector growth and non-tradables. High fixed costs in natural resource industry coupled with the volatility of most commodity prices was further argued to hurt long-term investment, e.g., in R&D. Several analysts went well beyond that, however, using empirical evidence to claim that wealth in natural resources has, de facto, served as a drag on development (Sachs and Warner, 1995; Gylfason, 2001) – the natural resource 'curse' (rather than a 'blessing').

The generality of the curse argument is contestable. Examining variation in growth between different countries, the impression of a curse may arise purely for statistical reasons. If natural resource earnings, as a share of Gross Domestic Product (GDP), are used as a proxy for natural resource assets, the group of countries that are defined as rich in natural resources will by definition include agriculture-dependent and undiversified economies. These would probably be better defined as 'innovation and human capital poor', and a high share of natural resources in the economy is then as much an outcome of slow growth, and a proven inability to diversify, as the opposite (Smith, 2007).

Others have questioned to what extent natural resource abundance really can be observed to act as a drawback for a given economy. Lederman and Maloney (2007) found Sachs and Warner's results not to hold given a different specification of the studied time period, although they did conclude that high export concentration exerts a robust negative effect on growth. Gylfason's result similarly appears to depend on a few outliers that achieved high growth without natural resources. Herb (2005) and Alexeev and Conrad (2009) evaluated a range of statistical studies and concluded against the presence of a curse, especially when it comes to oil and mineral wealth. Meanwhile, changes in external conditions may also serve to build a more benign case for the role of natural resource abundance in growth. As financial markets have deepened, for instance, they cushion the impact of price volatility (van der Ploeg and Poelhekke, 2010).

It appears, however, that the key factors shaping the validity of the curse argument operate at the micro-level and have to do with institutions and people (Sala-i-Martin and Subramanian, 2003). Natural resource generated revenues invariably boost the public sector and thus tend to inflate the status and rewards associated with public service. In the absence of taxes of the general public, there is also less accountability and pressure on government to make best use of public resources (Devarajan et al., 2010). A lure for rent-seeking may create a particularly strong incentive to gain privilege in order to earn a share of the riches through political clout rather than economic achievement, which has been seen to depress the rise of local capabilities (Djeflat, 2009).

On this basis, natural resource wealth is running the risk of translating into poor governance. A 'cozy life' takes hold, a kind of complacency that reduces pressure to pursue needed structural reforms, sheltering against competition and hurting economic efficiency. The same phenomenon serves to hold back the quest for improving education, lessening the presence of merit-based promotion and reducing work effort. There may also be less pressure for reforms to facilitate the establishment of new enterprises and the growth of existing ones (Amin and Djankov, 2009).

In recent years, however, there are signs that things are changing. Part of the picture is the rise of new industrial powers, notably in Asia, and the lift of billions of people from states of poverty into a situation where their demand for modern day products and commodities has picked up. In this situation there has been a general lift to the price of many commodities, further strengthening the returns to natural resource providers. Several resource-rich countries, including Malaysia and Indonesia in East Asia, South Africa and Botswana in Africa, and Colombia in Latin America, have clearly strengthened their growth record in recent years. In the presence of booming investment from China and other new customers, most African resource-producers have experienced an economic uptake. A special case is that of the oil and gas rich GCC countries.[1] While displaying a continued extreme dependence on limited natural revenue, their economic rise has now allowed several to join the ranks of the richest countries in the world, as measured by traditional income measures.

In order to cast light on how to judge the role of natural resource wealth, some indications can be obtained by comparing the performance of the GCC countries with that of their peers in the wider Arab region, including northern Africa (Andersson, 2011; Andersson and Djeflat, 2012). The high-income GCC countries have taken various initiatives to strengthen their growth and social development. Relative to their less affluent peers, they have invested a larger share of GDP in education while their ICT infrastructure and mobile penetration levels are approaching, and in some cases surpassing, those of advanced countries. Abu Dhabi, the Sultanate of Oman and Qatar have initiated institutional platforms to support research and innovation.

Despite these advances, as elsewhere in the Middle East and North Africa region, there is a heavy emphasis on family business, operating under informal governance practices and with very low risk profile. Investment remains concentrated in traditional assets and sectors, whereas there is a lack of mindset for research, innovation and potential high-impact start-ups. Education remains oriented to servicing the public sector, which maintains higher anticipated salaries and status than a business career. On this basis, it is far from clear to what degree the GCC countries have indeed made a lasting transition away from the resource curse or whether they have merely been able to transform their oil and gas revenue into wealth on a transient basis.

A new – and different – wave swept the region in 2011, the so-called 'Arab Spring'. Millions of ordinary, mainly young, people have, for the first time, made their voices heard through an intense and mostly peaceful movement of protest against the prevailing political and economic order. Unarmed and seemingly rudderless – although still organized – people, who were determined not to back down in the face of individual humiliation and death, through synchronized movement brought down four iron-fisted governments which had been entrenched for decades. Tunisia, Egypt, Libya, and Yemen fell within the first year of the Arab Spring. A number of other regimes were forced to toe the line, while others instituted political and economic reforms with an intensity never seen before, either in this region or in most other parts of the world. In the absence of democratic government and the means of an organized civil society, streets and squares became the arena for action. Crucially, mobile telephony and social networks such as Twitter and Facebook facilitated coordination.

Having flared up in the 'Arab Street' of the relatively poor and also extremely unequal societies of northern Africa, the movement has thus spread at formidable speed throughout the Arab world, affecting nearly every single country, leader, and policy framework in some way. It no doubt helped inspire the 'Occupy Wall Street' movement, triggered more vocal opposition from Moscow to Beijing, and caused repercussions that are felt widely across the developing world.

Widespread protest against the ruling order is of course nothing new. Nor does the Arab Spring represent the only source of such movement in our time. On the northern shores of the Mediterranean, a protest movement against austerity has been prompted by deteriorating public services and attacks on the privileges of previously protected vested interests in countries marked by unsustainable public debt and a rapidly ageing population. By contrast, the Arab Spring carries the voice of surging young generations who were never part of the welfare state but are becoming better informed and better educated in societies where both labor markets and conditions for enterprise development are basically dysfunctional.

The outcome of the Arab Spring is far from given. The Middle East and Northern Africa have been badly hit by the fallout. Capital outflows are up, tourism revenues are down, and private sector activity has suffered throughout the region. A horrific upscaling of violence and insecurity has taken place, notably in Syria, which has slid into civil war, but also in Egypt and Libya. Conservative counter-action is threatening a backlash e.g. against women in labor markets. The agendas of the regimes that have taken over thus far hardly reflect the desires of the young who were pressing for new social and economic openings, but rather reflect the preferences of a vast, partly uneducated majority that is concerned with the erosion of traditional values.

Furthermore, in the face of a weakened private sector performance, the Arab Spring has resulted in more expansionary macroeconomic policies along with more generous conditions for public sector work, such as new vacation days, increased pensions, extra salary payments, etc. This trend is most pronounced in the '*rentier* fixated' GCC countries which can afford them, and where there is a particularly 'tangible investment' fixated society. By boosting the public sector, political leaders have calmed the situation, but they have not embarked on reforms that provide lasting solutions, or address what is required to counter the natural resource curse. If anything, the measures taken have moved the region closer to ending up in the situation of the South European crisis-hit economies, perhaps another decade down the road from now.

New products, enterprises, industries and jobs must see the light of day – as must the conditions that can allow them to flourish – if there is to be a real response to the outstanding issues: one that is capable of meeting the aspirations of the many young people across emerging and developing economies. Natural resource abundance makes available the cash to provide temporary relief to cool off their demands, but unless there is lasting reform and investment in education, new assets, industries and skills, the problems will linger and the risk is they will pop up again to bite even harder than in the past. The risks indeed appear to be worsening in economies with a growing number of young people who attain education, cultivate dreams and opt for a meaningful professional life.

4. HUMAN CAPITAL, LABOR MARKETS AND ENTREPRENEURSHIP

Whereas the issues confronting the Middle East are partly specific, they also partly reflect broad-based general trends at work basically everywhere around the world. One year after the Arab Spring broke out, the unemployment issues, especially for youth, are even worse in the crisis struck economies of southern Europe, with Spain in the most extreme position: some 50 percent of youth are unemployed. The Mediterranean economies, marked by their excessive expansion of the public sector, red tape hindering private sector development and high public sector indebtedness, find themselves in a situation marked by recession, capital flight, despair and indignation on the part of the growing generations, and

Creating competitiveness

resistance to reform. As in the Middle East, to a varying extent there is a state of popular revolt on the streets of Athens, Barcelona, and Rome.

Young people are now increasingly wired, informed and capable of taking part in communication exchanges within an extended digital universe, including through the facets of social networks. The evolving applications of communications technology translate into an unprecedented potential for bottom-up initiatives among people for various purposes. Some may opt to react against oppression, others to resist reform they perceive as threatening, no matter how needed it may be for the aggregate economy and for sustained long-term macroeconomic balance and growth. Whatever their motivations, people devote more and more effort and attention to their societal interaction spanning also the wider digital sphere, which influences the direction of their inspiration.

A lot of work undertaken over the years has highlighted the factors leading to substandard labor market outcomes, spanning inefficiencies in education systems, labor market regulations, macroeconomic outcomes, product market regulations, and so forth (OECD, 1999). Today, however, at least six developments threaten to worsen outcomes: (i) weakening demand due to macroeconomic conditions and public sector indebtedness; (ii) the barriers to corporate strategies for investing more in people and intangible intellectual assets; (iii) a worsening mismatch in skills offered compared to those demanded in the work place; (iv) technical progress leading to higher shedding of labor in existing organizations and raising the bar in terms of reskilling as a prerequisite for new jobs; (v) rising barriers to entrepreneurship and growth of new firms; and (vi) the perception of growing income differences and social imbalances at the national level in most parts of the world.

While the macroeconomic outlook was already commented on above, investment in intangibles and intellectual capital clearly requires another sort of judgment and management skill than what applies in the case of tangible investment. Especially in economies with strong generation of returns from tangible assets such as natural resources and real estate, there will be a deceptive impression that things are OK and less pressure for developing the abilities required to manage investment in intangible assets. Again, the recent boon of natural resource rents may in fact worsen the willingness to adjust. Yet, in order to benefit from new technologies and create the basis for sustainable long-term growth, modern organizations must navigate investment, risk-taking and use in regard to the new knowledge assets.

Undoubtedly there is a common mismatch between the supply of skills accompanying graduates emanating from educational institutions relative to the demands of the modern and rapidly changing work place. The discrepancy appears to be widening both when it comes to substantive skills in the area of specialization, and in regard to general employability and critical soft skills that are needed for effective learning and team effort. This is related to the faster state of organizational change going on in the private sector, which is constantly subdued to the requirement of competition, compared to the government and the educational sector, which are less exposed to the new demands.

Accelerating technical progress creates ferocious productivity growth and economic expansion of some kinds of goods and services production, but also shedding of workers and jobs (Brynjolfsson and McAfee, 2011). Some new jobs arise because economic expansion may emanate from the multiplier effects that are associated with the need of new products and companies arising around a core of sharpening highly efficient production processes (OECD, 1998). However, the indications are that the job displacement effect is getting stronger whereas the upskilling, reskilling and restructuring processes required for redeployment of human capital are becoming more demanding.

The diffusion of technologies and skills transforms industries more quickly and bolsters the rise of fierce competitors. This is now happening not only in the manufacturing sector but increasingly in services as well. Even sophisticated jobs in both manufacturing and advanced services activities become routinized at high speed, making continuous innovation a prerequisite for staying ahead of the pack and allowing value-added to stay high. It is primarily where technologies are still new and the skills to exploit them not yet widely diffused, and also in activities that are able to enjoy a lucrative immediate interface with consumers, that it remains possible to reap significant rents. In the value-added chain, R&D and after-sales services thus commonly account for the bulk of revenues today.

As jobs in existing firms and industries are waning, there is an uptake in start-ups and entrepreneurship. As mentioned, this is also needed as an outlet for experimentation with new ideas and innovations, which would not find their way within the limited scope of established business with tightly defined core business. Worldwide entrepreneurial activity has reportedly surged with a rise of newly established companies since 2008 throughout the US, Europe, Asian economies, etc. On the other hand, the regulatory environment continues to be marked by red tape and practices that drive up transaction costs, in some cases discriminating against small firms outright, in others hurting them because burdens get disproportionately heavy for firms at small scale. Meanwhile, the general economic situation in most parts of the world over the last years means that seed and venture funding for start-ups and expansion has dried up (GEM, 2011).

Finally, while large numbers of people have been lifted out of poverty, income differences are on the rise within most societies, and they are also becoming more visible with increased transparency and media coverage. Part of this emanates from the rise in unemployment and weakening of public sector services that follow enhanced indebtedness. The handling of the financial crisis, which meant that taxpayers had to bail out the financial sector juggernauts only to then see the latter soon return to the same practices and privileges that brought the world economy to its knees, has contributed to undermining faith in the mainstream economic system in the eyes of the general public.

At the core of the modern-day economy and policy agenda stands the challenge of guarding and strengthening public goods that are crucial to societal stability and development. This task includes securing a high quality education sector, basic research, fundamental health services and a secure and environmentally sustainable society. In addition, there is the task of shaping the conditions that can allow for generating synergies and enhanced value-added through constructive interfaces between complementary institutions and competencies around the development and use of knowledge. A pertinent issue is that of strengthening labor market outcomes, bridging the gap between the demand for and supply of different skills, coupled with the need of generating opportunities for spinoffs and entrepreneurship so as to enable the rise of new industries, and jobs. The vastly increased potential of people to put their learning and communications skills to use, to make a difference, to have their voice heard, should be mobilized in that context. If channels are lacking for orderly economic and social engagement, it will find different directions and outlets.

5.   TOWARDS A MOTIVATIONAL APPROACH

The forefathers of economics, such as Adam Smith or Thomas Hobbes, paid considerable attention to human values and behaviors, as expounded by McCloskey (2006) in work on the origins of the industrial revolution. In the modern era, the opportunities of new technology and diffusion through ICT, along with accompanying social change, bring, as indicated above, a new kind of urgency to people-centric reforms.

At the core of the challenge stands the need to pave the way for a more strategic management of places. Although ICT has brought the wired and partly borderless communications of the modern era, people continue to live their lives in a *place*; this is where they relate to others in everyday life and where their ambitions or frustrations will play out, although the implications and consequences will fuse with those of others, who live in other locations, and multiply over large distances. Also, in regard to policymaking it is at the local level that actors have first-hand information in regard to a range of relevant circumstances that apply there specifically. The implication is the necessity of a shift in the kind of strategic capabilities that are needed for decision makers locally, along with new kinds of autonomy and accountability.

A particular challenge in this context is the strong tendency towards herd behavior in human action and also policymaking. The word is spreading about particular new industries in the making and which new technologies bring great potential for improvement. National governments invariably mainstream and standardize multiple institutional functions of great importance to the scope for location specialization, including the organization of universities, the direction and content of higher education, the availability of research funding in various domains, and so forth. In some cases governments dictate a differentiated pattern of specialization between different sub-national regions, possibly at the municipality level. Again however, the key to genuine valued-added in the knowledge economy is the ability to attain a unique edge, to run ahead of others in a particular slice or combination of activities.

Notwithstanding the advance of internationalization, increased mobility for some production factors co-exists with relative immobility for others, and with some factors inherently fixed geographically. Factors that are immobile (or, at least, more deeply rooted) can, if they stand out from what is offered elsewhere, give rise to rents that serve as 'glue' capable of drawing in and committing what would otherwise be footloose.

Most countries, as well as many regions and individual municipalities, pursue more or less targeted policies aimed at attracting foreign investors and facilitating operations and expansion in their territories, e.g. by removing bureaucratic procedures regarding visas, renting or acquiring land, setting up production or research facilities, and so forth. Most prioritize the provision of excellent physical infrastructure, including offering amenable housing. Some present offers to attract individual business people, scientists and experts. Some spot successful diaspora, e.g. through the alumni networks of prime universities, and entice them to return back in order to capitalize on their international networks and acquired skills.

Such efforts matter and depending on circumstances one avenue or another has proven decisive for particular regions. This includes India's drive to bring back home large numbers of its highly successful IT specialists and entrepreneurs who had established themselves abroad, to build and boost its software industry out of growth poles such as those in Bangalore and Hyderabad, on the way forging the country's most successful export and job creation machine of the 21st century. Countries and regions that strangle knowledge and expertise, or lose access to competencies (such as the United States of recent years with reference to security concerns, or countries in the Middle East reallocating expatriate positions to untrained locals), will conversely suffer setbacks.

More than any other single factor, the availability of human qualities and skills forms a decisive attraction for high-performing internationally mobile units. This is because people do not operate in isolation. They interact, compete and collaborate with others, in their immediate vicinity, as well as over vast distances. In stages of intensive knowledge creation involving multiple competencies, however, critical elements of the human interface, such as those related to risk-taking and trust-building between diverse actors, are inevitably tacit rather than codified. This implies that geographical proximity and face-to-face contact matter critically (Utterback, 1974; Saxenian, 1988). Creative exchange processes often have at their center a special environment, a 'meeting place'. Depending on the local situation, chambers of commerce, libraries, university campuses, sport arenas, logistical hubs, lunch restaurants, bars, cafés, festivals, churches, beaches, etc. exemplify the kinds of sites in which more or less unplanned exchanges can take place and allow for unexpected synergies between different kinds of competencies.

In addition, however, there is a need of the 'structured' innovation and entrepreneurship ecosystem that can allow for a consistent multifaceted effort to keep sharpening a particular and unique portfolio of human resources and assets. Success will surely hinge on the nature of interface between actors contributing from different directions, including the sphere of knowledge creation, financial intermediaries, IP competences, marketing and those that master channels for accessing customers. To the extent that these are interdependent, the weakest link in the chain will determine to what extent a genuine edge is achieved compared to what exists elsewhere. A 'critical mass' of resources, within a particular scientific discipline or emanating from another kind of knowledge domain, may serve as a decisive asset. Generally, it will be essential to move beyond this, to form a pool of competences that, whatever the source (large companies, high quality public research, networks of SMEs, etc.), will entice others – who stand to gain from that proximity – to co-locate in the same place. Exactly 'how much' is required to achieve 'critical mass' cannot be given a meaningful answer. The strengths of combinations will matter more, as will the degree to which local units in one place can connect with and thrive on exchanges with complementary ones elsewhere.

While agglomeration processes may be cumulative with, for instance, enlarged numbers of skilled people getting together in bigger cities (Glaeser and Resseger, 2009), scale is not necessarily an advantage. For one thing, large conglomerations may bring devastating congestion. Equally important, the flipside of success is complacency – establishing a market position and carving out a niche brings with it defense mechanisms and the preparedness to shun ideas that threaten what has been put in place. Any advance or source of strength carries with it the seeds of routinization and stagnation.

The importance of 'culture', in societies as well as in markets and in organizations, cannot be overstressed. Favorable conditions for reliability, security and trust obviously reduce transaction costs and provide an edge particularly for delicate affairs and sensitive business. The ability of a location to enable constructive synergy, support positive externalities and favor inclusion rather than turf, isolation and obstruction, will matter anywhere. And outcomes are not a given. Those who find themselves 'in the wrong company' risk suffering the consequences.

There are inherent contradictions to human behavior, however, which cannot be avoided but must be managed. The scope for innovation is fuelled by forces of curiosity and persistence in trying out what is new, but cooled by skepticism and resistance to what threatens the ruling order. The latter tends to become inherently pervasive in large and well-established institutions, both public and private, with huge 'sunk' costs. The adoption and realization of breakthrough radical innovations must thus generally have access to that alternative route offered by options of spin-offs or take-up by relatively smaller and younger ventures.[2]

To withstand such sentiments, it is essential to foster an environment capable of reconciling the driving forces for success and achievement with those that are required for learning and renewal. The room for individuals to experiment, assume risk, and challenge the limits of what can be achieved through what has yet been untested, requires 'free zones' for human creativity and ingenuity. Whether in the regulated and protected context of the advanced economies that have grown used to technological superiority, in natural resource-based economies where governments are awash with cash, or whether in the embrace of established corporate juggernauts or the most prestigious academic institutions, a conscientious effort is required to open up for such alternative avenues.

This goal cannot be achieved through precise directions issued centrally or through one-dimensional efforts. Nor can it be achieved by trying out the same avenues as everybody else. The decisive element is that of finding a formula for enticing the societal partners in participatory and constructive processes, embracing bottom-up initiatives while allowing for structure in cherishing unique local specialties and combinations. A traditionalist university, for instance, cannot and should not be bent on reorienting itself for the purpose of becoming a powerhouse of commercialization.

But there are tools that enable a broadening of its scope, for example by providing the incentives that allow universities to embrace multiple career or graduation paths for faculty and students respectively. Policymakers cannot achieve much by walking out to companies and asking them to train their staff or liaise with a university, but they can work with industry to identify champions within the business sector that believe in the merits of mentoring students and engaging in university research projects, or entering the doors of academia to pursue dialogue on what skills graduates should display in order to increase their employability. In all societies, there are pools of development-oriented practitioners who crave for better access to channels and outlets for their ideas, but who often have to walk in the desert. Instituting and providing a bit more than the minimal support for so-called 'inventors' associations' can make a difference. Still, few places attempt such routes.

6.   CONCLUDING REMARKS

In conclusion, the strategic management of places is about adopting a *people-centric* development approach that is tailored to value creation by leveraging specific local opportunities. It is not about public authority determining directions; it is about crafting a motivational agenda. If anything, the task is one of 'smart coaching' – of engaging stakeholders in a sort of collaboration that counters herd behavior, intimidation and turf, and opens up for uniqueness, bottom-up inspiration and inclusion.

The strategic management of places is not a zero-sum game. With qualified human resources on the move, internationalization brings the potential for win-win through dynamic exchange processes involving specialization and division of labor between complementary knowledge domains and locations, making the concern with 'brain drain' or 'brain gain' less critical than that of 'brain circulation'.

NOTES

1. The members of the Gulf Cooperation Council (GCC) are the Kingdom of Saudi Arabia, the Kingdom of Bahrain, Kuwait, the State of Qatar, the Sultanate of Oman, and the United Arab Emirates (UAE).
2. A parallel can be drawn with the processes leading to scientific breakthroughs, i.e. the overthrow of frameworks of established dogmas by the rise of a radically different line of thought more capable of explaining outstanding anomalies, often advanced by individuals who were relatively young and came from outside the prevailing communities, often even from another discipline (Kuhn, 1962).

REFERENCES

Alexeev, M. and R. Conrad (2009), 'The elusive curse of oil', *Review of Economics and Statistics*, **3** (91), 586–98.

Amin, M. and S. Djankov (2009), *Natural Resources and Reforms*, Washington: The World Bank.

Andersson, T. (2011), 'Natural resource dependency and innovation in the GCC countries', in F.S. Nobre, D.S. Walker and R.J. Harris (eds), *Technological, Managerial and Organizational Core Competencies: Dynamic Innovation and Sustainable Advantage*, IGI Global.

Andersson, T. and A. Djeflat (2012), *Addressing the Real Issues of the Middle East: Conditions for Research, Innovation and Entrepreneurship*, Springer.

Audretsch, D. and R. Thurik (2001), 'Linking entrepreneurship to growth', *OECD Growth Working Paper*, 27, Paris.

Blomström, M. and A. Kokko (1998), 'Multinational corporations and spillovers', *Journal of Economic Surveys*, **12**, 247–77.

Brusco, S. (1982), 'The Emilian model: productive decentralisation and social integration', *Cambridge Journal of Economics*, **6**, 167–84.

Brynjolfsson, E. and A. McAfee (2011), *Race Against the Machine: How the Digital Revolution Is Accelerating Innovating, Driving Productivity, and Irreversibly Transforming Employment and the Economy*, Lexington, MA: Digital Frontier Press.

Castelacci, F. and D. Archibugi (2008), 'The technology clubs: the distribution of knowledge across nations', *Research Policy*, **37** (10), 1659–73.

Dahlman, C. and T. Andersson (2000), *Korea and the Knowledge-Based Economy: Making the Transition*, Paris: OECD and the World Bank Institute.

Dahmén, E. (1950), *Entrepreneurial Activity and the Development of Swedish Industry 1919–1939*, Homewood, IL: American Economic Association Translation Series.

Devarajan, S., T. Minh Le and G. Raballand (2010), 'Increasing public expenditure efficiency in oil-rich economies: a proposal', Policy Research Working Paper 5287, World Bank, Africa Region, Chief Economist Office, Washington, DC.

Djeflat, A. (2009), 'Universities and scientific research in the Maghreb states: power politics and innovation systems', *International Journal of Technology Management*, **45** (1/2), 102–13.

Dunning, J.H. (1977), 'Trade, location, of economic activity and the MNE: a search for an eclectic approach', in B. Ohlin, P.O. Hasselborn and P.M. Wijkman (eds), *The International Allocation of Economic Activity: Proceedings of a Nobel Symposium Held at Stockholm*, London: Macmillan, pp. 395–418.

Etzkowitz, H. and L. Leydesdorff (eds) (1997), *Universities in the Global Knowledge Economy: A Triple Helix of University-Industry-Government Relations*, London: Cassell.

Florida, R. (2002), *The Rise of the Creative Class: And How It's Transforming Work, Leisure, Community and Everyday Life*, New York: Basic Books.

Glaeser, E.L. and M. Resseger (2009), 'The complementarity between cities and skills', National Bureau of Economic Research Working Paper 15103.

Global Entrepreneurship Monitor (GEM) Global Report (2011), San Francisco.

Guellec, D. and B. van Pottelsberghe (2001), 'R&D and productivity growth:

a panel data analysis for 16 OECD Countries', *OECD Economic Studies*, 29, Paris.

Gylfason, T. (2001), 'Natural resources, education and economic development', *European Economic Review*, **4/6** (45), 847–59.

Herb, M. (2005), 'No representation without taxation? Rents, development and democracy', *Comparative Politics*, **3** (37), 297–317.

Kathuria, V. (2000), 'Productivity spillovers from technology transfer to Indian manufacturing firms', *Journal of International Development*, **12** (2), 343–69.

Krueger, A.O. (1978), *Foreign Trade Regimes and Economic Development: Liberalisation Attempts and Consequences*, New York: National Bureau of Economic Research.

Kuhn, T. (1962), *The Structure of Scientific Revolutions*, Chicago: The University of Chicago Press.

Lederman, D. and W. Maloney (2007), 'Neither curse nor destiny: introduction to natural resources and development', in D. Lederman and W. Maloney (eds), *Natural Resources, Neither Curse nor Destiny*, Palo Alto, CA and Washington, DC: Stanford University Press and World Bank, Latin American Development Forum Series.

Lundvall, B.-Å. (ed.) (1992), *National Innovation Systems: Towards a Theory of Innovation and Interactive Learning*, London: Pinter.

McCloskey, D.N. (2006), *The Bourgeois Virtues*, Chicago: University of Chicago Press.

Milbergs, E. and N. Vonortas (2004), *Innovation Metrics: Measurement to Insight*, Center for Accelerating Innovation and George Washington University, National Innovation Initiative 21st Century Working Group, 22 September.

Nurkse, R. (1953), *Problems of Capital-Formation in Underdeveloped Countries*, Oxford: Oxford University Press.

OECD (1998), *Policy Coherence Matters*, Paris: OECD.

OECD (1999), *Assessing Performance and Policy, Implementing the OECD Jobs Study*, Paris: OECD.

OECD (2001), *The New Economy: Beyond the Hype*, Paris: OECD.

Ohmae, K. (1995), *The End of the Nation State: The Rise of Regional Economies*, London: Harper Collins.

Ploeg, F. van der and S. Poelhekke (2010), 'The pungent smell of red herrings: subsoil assets, rents, volatility and the resource curse', *Journal of Environmental Economics and Management*, **1** (60), 44–55.

Porter, M.E. (1990), *The Competitive Advantage Of Nations*, New York: The Free Press.

Prebisch, R. (1950), *The Economic Development of Latin America and its Principal Problems*, New York: United Nations Economic Commission of Latin America.

Rostow, W.W. (1960), *The Stages of Economic Growth: A Non-Communist Manifesto*, Cambridge: Cambridge University Press.

Sachs, J. and A.M. Warner (1995), 'Natural resource abundance and economic growth', in G. Meier and J. Rauch (eds), *Leading Issues in Economic Development*, New York: Oxford University Press.

Sala-i-Martin, X. and A. Subramanian (2003), 'Addressing the natural resource curse: an illustration from Nigeria', *IMF Working Paper*, **3** (139).

Saxenian, A. (1988), 'The Cheshire cat's grin: innovation and regional development in England', *Technology Review*, February/March, 67–75.

Smith, K. (2007), 'Innovation and growth in resource-based economies', Hobart: Australian Innovation Research Centre, University of Tasmania.

Solow, R. (1957), 'Technical progress and the aggregate production function', *Review of Economics and Statistics*, **99**, 312–21.

Stiroh, K. (1999), 'Is there a new economy?', *Challenge*, **42** (4), 82–101.

UNCTAD (2011), *Global Information Economy Report*, Geneva: UNCTAD.

Utterback, J. (1974), 'Innovation in industry and the diffusion of technology', *Science*, 183, 658–62.

World Bank (1999/2000), *Knowledge for Development*, World Development Report, Washington, DC.

Yamin, M. and R. Sinkovics (2009), 'Infrastructure or foreign direct investment? An examination of the implications of MNE strategy for economic development', *Journal of World Business*, **44**, 144–57.

9. Collective entrepreneurship: the strategic management of Research Triangle Park

Dennis P. Leyden and Albert N. Link

INTRODUCTION

The entrepreneur and the actions of the entrepreneur, entrepreneurship, have over time been characterized in many ways, and those characterizations are as varied as the scholars who have proffered them. As Hébert and Link (1989, p.41) wrote, 'the entrepreneur has worn many faces and played many roles.' But Hébert and Link (2009) go further, synthesizing extant thought by suggesting that an entrepreneur is one who perceives opportunity and has the ability to act on that perception.

Perception and action describe the entrepreneur as a dynamic, not static, figure in economic activity. It follows then that entrepreneurship entails a process that begins with perception and is completed with action. This action may or may not be successful over time. Regardless of how the market reacts to the entrepreneurial undertaking,[1] boldness and risk taking have nevertheless been demonstrated.

When it comes to places – meaning physical localities – rarely is it the case that the perception of opportunity and the ability to act on that perception are embodied in a single individual. This is not to say that one individual is not capable of such behavior. Machlup (1980, p.179) noted that an entrepreneur is 'alert and quick-minded, [one who perceives] what normal people of lesser alertness and perceptiveness would fail to notice.'

When it comes to places, however, timing is not in the sole control of the entrepreneur. He/she is often shackled with ownership and regulation issues as well as competing personalities. These constraints often dampen a single person's ability to move a place in a new direction.

When it comes to the strategic use of places, history will show that several entrepreneurs have had critical roles to play.[2] Closely related to the use of places is how those places have been strategically managed.

This chapter illustrates the strategic management of one place in particular, Research Triangle Park in central North Carolina. This history of Research Triangle Park suggests that the early perception for the park, and the action to see it from 'seed to harvest' (Link 2002), were the result of many individuals each exhibiting their own entrepreneurial ability along the way.[3] Thus, we introduce in this chapter the notion of collective entrepreneurship, and we suggest that it might be a critical ingredient to a recipe for the successful strategic management of places.

THE PLACE: RESEARCH TRIANGLE PARK

Research Triangle Park is an actual tract of land of approximately 6,800 acres (approximately 2,750 hectares) located in the center of a scalene triangle formed by (alphabetically) Duke University, North Carolina State University,[4] and the University of North Carolina at Chapel Hill, as shown in Figure 9.1.

At present, there are about 170 global companies in the Park employing nearly 39,000 individuals and contractors.

THE PERCEPTION OF A PARK

Brandon P. Hodges, elected North Carolina State Treasurer in November 1948, sought to bring new types of industry, in particular technology-based industries, into the state. At that time, the North Carolina economy was centered on the traditional industries of furniture, textiles, and tobacco. In 1950, according to the US Department of Commerce, there were only five states in the nation that had a per capita income level lower than North Carolina's. By 1952, only two states did – Arkansas and Mississippi. There was justifiable concern that the economy needed to diversify in order to grow, and some thought that the state's university structure could possibly be used as a key element in an economic development plan.

Romeo Guest, a Greensboro North Carolina contractor, is generally credited with the Research Triangle concept.[5] His idea was simple. For many years, North Carolina, and the South in general, lagged in scientific research and in the application of research to industry. So, perhaps the triangle universities could act as a magnet to attract research companies into the area, and this in turn would lead to the development of new technology-based industries throughout the state.

Guest was able to sell his idea to Brandon Hodges, and in early December 1954 Brandon Hodges took the Research Triangle idea to

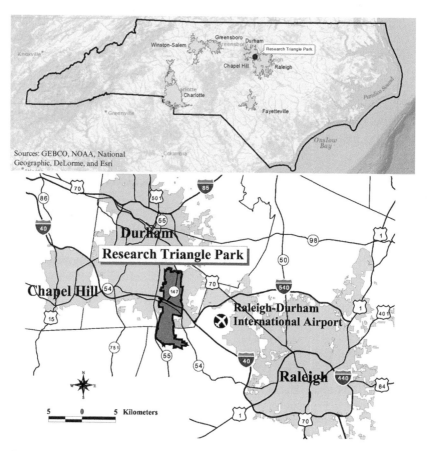

Source: Top map courtesy of the Indiana University Libraries, drawn on publicly available data sources; bottom map courtesy of the North Carolina Department of Commerce.

Figure 9.1   The Research Triangle area and the Park

Governor Luther Hodges (no relationship). But, the Governor was at that time only lukewarm to the concept.

It has been argued (Link 1995) that the Governor, because of his textiles background, did not fully understand the nature of research and development (R&D), much less its role in economic development. After the unsuccessful December meeting with the Governor, William Newell, director of the North Carolina Textile Research Center and one intimately familiar with the importance of R&D, prepared, at the urging of Brandon Hodges and others, a report entitled 'A Proposal for the Development of an Industrial Research Center in North Carolina.' The report was sent to the Governor in late January 1955. Records from the ensuing meeting with the Governor show that the meeting went well; archival communications suggest that thereafter the Research Triangle idea became known simply as 'the Governor's Research Triangle' (Link 1995).

MANAGEMENT OF THE PERCEPTION

Guest took it upon himself to meet with the relevant leadership at the three triangle universities. These meetings were not simply an altruistic gesture. Rather, Guest saw a specific role for himself in the Research Triangle project. He hoped to become the contractor for all of the companies that would eventually locate in the Park, so university commitment to the park idea was critical.

Throughout early 1955 there were numerous meetings about how to implement the Governor's Research Triangle idea, including the creation of several committees and working groups. For example, in May of that year the Research Triangle Development Committee was established, and a formal statement of the relationship between the park and the three universities was articulated:[6]

> The basic concept of the Research Triangle is that North Carolina possesses a unique combination of educational and research resources and communication facilities eminently suitable to the fostering of industrial research. It is not anticipated that the three universities in the Triangle shall engage directly in the conduct of industrial research, except under carefully designated and administered policies. Rather, the principal functions of the Universities are to stimulate industrial research by the research atmosphere their very existence creates, and to supplement industrial-research talents and facilities by providing a wellspring of knowledge and talents for the stimulation and guidance of research by individual firms. (quoted in Link 1995, pp. 28–9)

In March 1956, William Friday became acting president (and later president) of the University of North Carolina system. He, along with Governor Hodges, was instrumental in forming the Research Triangle Committee, Inc. This was a non-stock, non-profit, benevolent, charitable, and educational corporation for the purpose of encouraging and promoting the establishing of industrial research laboratories in North Carolina primarily in the triangle area. This organization became the motivation for North Carolina representatives from the public sector and the university communities to publicize the Research Triangle concept and to attempt to recruit companies into the area. But, a place was needed to demonstrate to research companies that the triangle concept was viable and was coming to fruition.

The Research Triangle Committee, Inc. attempted to identify investors in land that would eventually become the park. Simply, it was believed that companies that were interested in the concept would want to visit North Carolina and see something tangible. One investor, Karl Robbins of New York, was found. Robbins had in his earlier years been involved in North Carolina's textile industry so he knew people in the state as well as its citizenry. He initially invested $275,000, and those funds were used by Guest and others to option parcels of land under the name of Pinelands Company. By the end of 1957, just over 3,500 acres had been optioned with another 440 acres pending; the final purchase price would be $700,000.00. However, Robbins became reluctant to meet his promised $1 million investment. The reason for his waning interest in the project was the visible lack of North Carolina investors. Robbins would not send any additional moneys unless matched by investments by North Carolinians. But, such moneys were not to be forthcoming at that time.

ACTION ON THE PERCEPTION

The for-profit Pinelands Company vehicle for obtaining land for the Park did not seem to be working. While Guest's perception of the role of a research park as a driver for North Carolina's future economic development was widely accepted as sound, neither Guest nor the Governor's office had the ability to act on that perception in a way that would bring the idea to fruition.

Robert Hanes, President of Wachovia Bank and Trust Company, who was a supporter of the triangle idea, and Governor Hodges realized that it was time for a change in course. They approached Archie Davis, chairman of Wachovia Bank and Trust Company, to sell stock in Pinelands Company.

Davis, who knew nothing about Research Triangle or Pineland Company before his meeting with Hanes and Hodges in August 1958, realized immediately on hearing about what had transpired that Guest's perception of the role of a research park for the state was sound, but that the management of the park idea to date was flawed. As Davis noted (Link 1995, p. 68):

> To me, I just felt without knowing anything about it, [the park idea] just didn't make sense. If this [park] indeed was designed for public service, then it would be much easier to raise money from corporations and institutions and the like, who were interested in serving the State of North Carolina, by making a contribution.

At an October 1958 meeting of the Research Triangle Committee, Inc., Davis pointed out that the idea of a research park has a public character and should be a non-profit undertaking. It was agreed that Davis would raise $1 million for the Committee plus $250,000 for a main building. Within a 30-day period Davis traveled the state, at his own expense, speaking one-on-one with people about supporting a research park for the good of North Carolina, and by the end of December he had exceeded his fundraising goal.

What Davis did, Guest could never have done. While Guest was entrepreneurial in his perception of the idea of a research park, it took Davis's ability to act on that perception to raise sufficient funds to launch the Park.

THE STRATEGIC MANAGEMENT OF THE PARK

One of the most significant events in the history of North Carolina took place on 9 January 1959, in Raleigh. Governor Hodges announced that Davis had raised $1.425 million. These funds were to be used for three purposes:

1. To establish the Research Triangle Institute to do contract research for business, industry, and government;
2. To construct a new building to house the Institute in the park; and
3. To acquire the land that was assembled by Robbins and to pass control of Pinelands Company to the non-profit Research Triangle Foundation.

Soon thereafter Guest resigned from his role in Pinelands Company and watched, as an outsider, what was to happen.

In early October 1959, Chemstrand Corporation purchased 100 acres and broke ground on a research facility later that month. However, it was not until April 1965 that the park idea was validated. IBM announced that it would locate a 600,000 square foot research facility on 400 acres in the Park. That event foreshadowed future events.

Research Triangle Park is arguably the most successful research park in the United States (Link 2002), and, perhaps, this is due to a unique management strategy. It was written into the certificate of incorporation of the Research Triangle Committee, Inc. in 1956:

> It is the intent and purpose of the corporation to promote the use of the research facilities of the [Duke University, North Carolina State, and University of

> North Carolina at Chapel Hill] ... through cooperation [among] the three
> institutions and cooperation [among] the institutions and industrial research
> agencies .... . The corporation is a non-profit, benevolent, charitable, and
> educational corporation and has no capital stock. Upon the dissolution of the
> corporation, all assets of the corporation shall be divided equally among [the
> institutions] for the purpose for which [the] institutions were founded. (Link
> 2002, p. 63)

In 1974, Davis, in his role as president of the Research Triangle Foundation,
realized that the universities needed a presence or home in the Park noting
(Link 2002, p. 64): 'It would be a shame ... for the principal beneficiaries
of the Park – the universities – not to have some land in the Park for their
own use.' In 1975, the Triangle Universities Center for Advanced Studies,
Inc. (TUCASI), a non-profit corporation, was established on 120 acres in
the center of the Park.

According to news reports at that time:

> A unique undertaking, TUCASI, represents the nation's first three-university
> corporation designed to plan and develop joint research and educational activi-
> ties in a major research park ... The major purpose of [TUCASI is] to assist
> in and facilitate the planning and execution of non-profit research and educa-
> tional programs that utilize and enhance the productivity of the intellectual and
> physical resources of [three world-class universities]. (Link 2002, pp. 72–3)

In a sense, TUCASI is the universities' home within Research Triangle
Park. TUCASI is an ever-present symbol that the universities are at
the heart of the Park's mission and therefore at the heart of its success.
TUCASI is like a park within a park.

TOWARD A THEORY OF COLLECTIVE ENTREPRENEURSHIP

Figure 9.2 presents a simple representation of the development process.
Measured on the axes are the allocation of time and effort to public interest and to self-interest that characterized Research Triangle Park.[7] For
Guest, the ideal mix of effort to public and private interest is represented
by point G. This point represents the result of a complex calculus of both
Guest's preferences for the characteristics of the park and the likelihood
that a park could be developed with such a mix, that is, it represents for
Guest the mix of public and private interest with the highest expected
utility. As represented in Figure 9.2, this mix is consistent with Guest's best
estimate, I_G, of the isoquant that would produce the park.[8] In his attempt
to put together a workable plan for the park, Guest would presumably

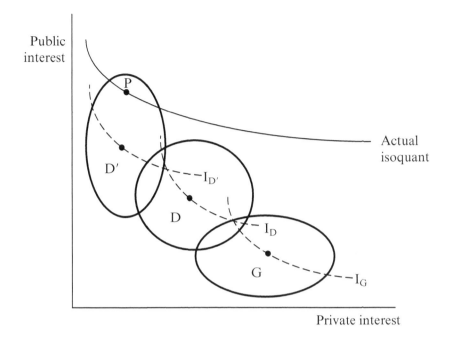

Figure 9.2   Sequential learning with competing utility functions and perceptions

have been flexible and willing to explore a variety of public/private combinations different from point G, but sufficiently close so that the net utility after subtracting the additional cost of exploring such alternatives was still positive. The ellipse surrounding G represents the boundaries of his area of exploration with the horizontal orientation of the ellipse indicating that given Guest's experience, contacts, and interests, he had greater flexibility in exploring a range of private interest levels than public interest levels. Guest, as we know, was unsuccessful in furthering the park concept, that is, in bringing it to a reality. Thus, the actual isoquant lies outside of Guest's area of exploration and remained unknown after his efforts.

A similar process occurred with Davis with the addition of the fact that Davis could learn from Guest's (failed) efforts. We suppose that initially, that is, before Guest's efforts, Davis had a relatively balanced ideal mix of public and private interest at point D. And, associated with that initial ideal, Davis would have had a region over which he would have been willing to explore, as noted by the circle around point D, and a best estimate I_D of where the isoquant for the park lay. However, having observed Guest's unsuccessful efforts, Davis revised his estimates of the I_D to $I_{D'}$.

With that change, his ideal moved to the point D′, and the area of exploration to the ellipse surrounding the point D′. The vertical orientation represents the apparent fact that Davis's ability to search over a range of possible level of public interest was now greater than it was over ranges of private interest. As we know, Davis was successful, and hence the actual isoquant, while not perhaps equal to his hypothesized $I_{D'}$, lay within the area he explored. He thus identified a combination such as point P of public and private interest that worked, and the park was created in a manner that would facilitate growth.

To the extent that the above description approximates the strategic management of the development of Research Triangle Park, then one might hypothesize that the strategic management of places is functionally related to the collective positive entrepreneurial effort of individuals, each exercising his/her perception and action at different time based on their personal preferences, expertise, and estimation of the best steps forward. Collectively, they engage in what might be called a process of social sequential learning that moves a place forward for the common weal.

NOTES

1. Link and Link (2009) argue that the public sector, absent a market mechanism, can exhibit entrepreneurial behavior.
2. See, for example, this discussion by Safford (2009) about the strategic management of Youngstown, Ohio, and Allentown, Pennsylvania.
3. The remainder of this chapter draws directly from Link (1995, 2002).
4. North Carolina State College of Agriculture and Engineering of the University of North Carolina at Raleigh became North Carolina State University in 1965.
5. Although, as the history of the Park shows, many individuals took credit for the Park idea especially after it became successful (Link 1995).
6. This is an important statement, and one that at the time was often overlooked and misunderstood by non-academicians. The universities saw themselves as magnets to attract research companies to the area, not as participants in those companies' research efforts.
7. One could alternatively view this as a tradeoff between proposed levels of public capital and private capital.
8. It is possible for Guest's ideal G to not be on his best estimate I_G of the isoquant for producing the park if his preferences differ from his subjective judgment of the likelihood of how the park can be developed.

REFERENCES

Hébert, Robert F. and Albert N. Link (1989), 'In search of the meaning of entrepreneurship', *Small Business Economics*, 1, 39–49.
Hébert, Robert F. and Albert N. Link (2009), *A History of Entrepreneurship*, New York: Oxford University Press.

Link, Albert N. (1995), *A Generosity of Spirit: The Early History of the Research Triangle Park*, Research Triangle Park, NC: Research Triangle Foundation of North Carolina.

Link, Albert N. (2002), *From Seed to Harvest: The Growth of the Research Triangle Park*, Research Triangle Park, NC: Research Triangle Foundation of North Carolina.

Link, Albert N. and Jamie R. Link (2009), *Government as Entrepreneur*, New York: Oxford University Press.

Machlup, Fritz (1980), *Knowledge and Knowledge Production*, Princeton, NJ: Princeton University Press.

Safford, Sean (2009), *Why the Garden Club Couldn't Save Youngstown: The Transformation of the Rust Belt*, Cambridge, MA: Harvard University Press.

10. The invention of San Diego's innovation economy*

Mary Lindenstein Walshok and Abraham J. Shragge

INTRODUCTION

Second tier cities such as San Diego, Seattle and Phoenix often have distinguishing features that allow them to be more nimble and adaptable than first tier cities such as New York, Chicago or Miami. Many metropolitan areas whose citizens decry their lack of Fortune 500 companies, large employers, established multigenerational leadership and family wealth have developed out of necessity, high risk, innovative, entrepreneurial, and frequently collaborative approaches to economic growth, which today are the envy of many first tier cities. New York, Stockholm and Bogota have all launched CONNECT programs, originally created in San Diego. Chicago, Detroit and Atlanta have launched technology venture funds based on a model originally created in Austin, Texas. It could even be argued that in the absence of large scale established companies and powerful centers of civic leadership, second tier cities often, out of necessity, develop experimentation and risk taking that can end up paying off in a big way for an innovation economy. That has certainly been the case in San Diego since the turn of the last century.

It is also the case that cities in the American Southeast and West developed unique industrial capabilities at different times than other American cities, which affected how their economies evolved over time. There is a growing body of literature focused on how regions diversify their economies over time that suggests that new industries are often technologically related to pre-existing industries. A rich empirical study in the *Journal of Economic Geography* argues that the 'rise and fall of industries is strongly conditioned by industrial relatedness at the regional level' (Neffke et al. 2011: 238). There is a paucity of research on these regional transformations over time, in part because the nuanced, qualitative dimensions of economic transformation are difficult to capture. Neffke et al. offer a new framework that enables a more systemic analysis based on the idea of 'technological readiness,' which (1) describes how 'technological readiness' gives rise to pronounced path dependencies in the diversification process of regional economies; (2) empirically tests how this branching process occurred within 70 Swedish regions from 1969 to 2000 using a new indicator of inter-industry relatedness; and (3) utilizes case studies to enrich the more quantitative analysis of technological cohesion over time (Neffke et al. 2011: 238–9).

The story of San Diego's transformation over time reflects the sorts of technological relatedness and path dependencies so well described by Neffke et al. (2011). In this chapter we introduce an historical overview of the evolution of San Diego's economy pointing out the distinctive forms of technological relatedness and social dynamics that enabled its transformation from a military metropolis 1890–1950, to a cold war R&D mecca 1950–90, to a collection of dynamic globally competitive technology based clusters since the 1990s. The San Diego story suggests that, important as the technology trajectories that developed over time are, the highly opportunistic civic culture of the region may be equally important. This civic culture includes an ability to recognize not only existing assets but how they can be transformed or repurposed as economic conditions change. Many communities with substantial technical assets have not had the kind of adaptive civic culture that has allowed them to achieve similar economic transformations. San Diego's civic culture was such that it has moved through a series of reinventions over the last 100 years.

A careful analysis of San Diego's history reveals the early development of a civic culture that enabled a succession of opportunistic and adaptive responses to the changing geo-political realities of the twentieth century. This specific culture was one that was animated by a desire to build a prosperous economy and a thriving city while preserving the natural amenities of the region: its beautiful landscape, its semi-arid climate and its distinctive flora and fauna. To this end, the expansion of US Military forces in the Pacific represented, for many, a clean, orderly and noble industry that fit San Diego's civic aspirations. It contrasted vividly with the grimy, smoke-stack industries and unruly laborers of the booming Northeast and Midwest from which many of San Diego's early settlers had migrated. Many of the early families who came to San Diego, confirmed by letters and archival documents (McClain 2010), were seeking regeneration and renewal during a time of growing anti-modernism in the United States. This anti-modernism spirit was pointedly described in T.J. Jackson Lears's book *Anti-modernism and the Transformation of American Culture 1820–1920* (Lears 1994).

By leveraging its land and assets for military purposes, San Diegans found a way to attract investments (the federal government), expand in-migration (military professionals, technocrats, entrepreneurial small business people and land developers) and eventually industrialization. This industrialization, however, as early as the 1920s, was one decidedly focused on aviation, ship-building, communications and, eventually, munitions. It was a type of industry that, because it served national security interests, was continuously advancing technologically, primarily through federally funded research and development. Thus, San Diego's core economic strategies for more than a century have been tied to tight relations with the federal government and its evolving needs.

The region built, over time, civic institutions, public policies and development strategies that reinforced the importance of defense related technology industries to regional prosperity. Throughout World Wars I and II, the Korean War and, especially, the Cold War, San Diego's civic culture facilitated the evolution of a high-tech economy built upon the technological achievements of preceding epochs. Since the mid-1980s, this economy has elaborated into a very different kind of city from that which existed 100 years ago. It is a city with a diverse array of globally competitive technology clusters, as well as one of the largest life-sciences research/business clusters in the world. This modern transition was significantly enabled by a catalytic civic initiative known as CONNECT, which since 1985 has helped to leverage the abundance of research and development that grew out of the region's long history of military technology development. A brief overview of this history is important for elucidating the character of San Diego's contemporary achievements.

THE RISE OF THE MARTIAL METROPOLIS

Despite the best efforts of an energetic and enterprising business community to generate sustained development over the 50-year period between 1852 and 1902, San Diego experienced only spasms of growth followed by dramatic contractions that kept it struggling, deep in the shadow of San Francisco and Los Angeles. This was largely due to a landlocked harbor that, in its undeveloped state, was difficult and dangerous to navigate. Further, the city's ecology, without wood or water, in combination with a rugged mesa and canyon topography, was inhospitable to large-scale agriculture. San Diego's growth opportunities began to shift largely as a result of events occurring across the Pacific, principally the US acquisition of Hawaii through annexation, and victory in the Spanish American War, which eventually brought the former Spanish colonies of Guam and the Philippine Islands under American control. In 1906 President Teddy Roosevelt oversaw the reorganization of the Navy's battleships in anticipation of expanded commercial and political engagements in the far Western Pacific (Shragge 1998: 104–5). Over the next five years San Diegans organized multiple events and presentations to convince the US Navy of the strategic advantage of San Diego for military installations including: (1) planning in earnest as of 1909 for a major exposition to honor the opening of the Panama Canal; and (2) securing funds to dredge its main harbor to accommodate larger ships. In less than two decades San Diegans were able to attract a number of critical naval institutions through aggressive courtship of military and congressional leaders in Washington, DC, all of which was accelerated by the spectacular success of the Panama/California Exposition of 1915.

The opening of the Panama Canal provided San Diegans with a tremendous opportunity to turn a corner in their quest for growth, an idea that had incubated in the minds of the city's leaders for years before the event occurred. Having decided to celebrate the 'joining of the old Atlantic with the virile Pacific' in the grandest possible fashion, the business community, taxpayers, voters and most ordinary citizens prepared to show the city to the world. Although the Exposition itself barely generated an operating profit, as its boosters promised it would, it spun off myriad long-lasting benefits to the struggling city. Of greatest significance was the way San Diegans used the fair to showcase the city and its harbor to influential outsiders, top military decision-makers in particular, and thus seduce them with the potential of the place (Lotchin 1992; Shragge 1998).

Almost as soon as the Exposition closed for good – 1 January 1917 – the Chamber of Commerce, at Kettner's urging, convinced the city council to lease the Balboa Park grounds to the Navy to use as a wartime training complex and hospital, at a rent of one dollar per year. In the meantime, both the Army and Navy ramped up their aviation activities on John D. Spreckels' North Island. For the next two decades San Diegans lobbied in Washington, DC, made land deals and aggressively integrated the military into the social fabric of the community; all in an effort to build a city around the 'clean' naval and aviation industries. The citizens succeeded, building a true 'metropolitan-military complex' or 'martial metropolis,' to invoke expressions coined by historian Roger Lotchin (Shragge 1998). According to Lotchin, a number of cities across the country sought to overcome perceived economic and especially industrial 'backwardness' by offering the military services various inducements to locate there, thus contributing in some significant way to the local economy. San Diego was becoming a true navy town. By the 1930s San Diego added navy flyer training; with 11 auxiliary airfields around the county, San Diego had become the self-proclaimed 'air capital of the west' (Lindbergh Field, San Diego, 1935).

With the momentum established by the 1930s, San Diego also began to attract defense manufacturing, most particularly Rueben H. Fleet's Consolidated Aircraft Corporation of Buffalo, New York, signaling the city's further movement into aviation. It also obtained New Deal funding for the dredging of the harbor to accommodate 200 warships. San Diego was directly dependent on federal dollars, not only from large military payrolls but also through a growing cluster of private entities that served the military by providing the R&D, equipment and services needed by the expanding US forces.

Then came Roosevelt's War Emergency Act of 1939. The War Emergency Act and the subsequent mobilization of military resources required huge leaps of infrastructure development – housing, sewerage, roads, schools – leading to the designation of major centers, such as San Diego, as 'federal cities' eligible for new forms of federal investments in core city infrastructure that supported the expansion of the war effort. For San Diego, these investments included, for example, $1 million to complete the sewer system, $10 million for an aqueduct from the Colorado River, $1.5 million for city roads as well as other investments in housing and schools. Approximately 4,000 people worked in manufacturing in the late 1930s, and by 1943 there were 70,000. By 1947 the Navy's active duty and civilian employees represented 41 per cent of the city's labor force. San Diego was firmly established as a Martial Metropolis (Shragge 1998: 539–40).

In sum, during the final decades of the 19th century while cities like Chicago, Detroit, St. Louis and even Los Angeles and San Francisco were booming, San Diego experienced practically no growth, a matter of great disappointment and frustration to those who firmly believed in a brilliant future for the city as well as their own investments there. While the city-builders tried to harness the limited resources available to them, in particular the bay and the climate, they found themselves thwarted at every turn by forces beyond their control. National and international events at century's end, however, enabled San Diegans to create and exploit a connection with the federal government, turning the government into a pivotal partner in subsequent processes of urban development which carried the city through the first fifty years of the twentieth century.

THE COLD WAR R&D EXPANSION

As the end of World War II approached, San Diegans realized the need to re-engineer their vision in order to cope with a rapidly changing world and keep their city on an upward growth trajectory. While a significant portion of their revised outlook incorporated lessons well-learned during the past, they also embraced innovation in ways that, within a decade or two, led to a virtual reinvention of the city. What San Diegans did not – and, very likely, could not – anticipate was the impact the atomic bomb, the dawning of the nuclear age, and the Cold War would have on San Diego's economy. The national security and national defense appetites for R&D and advanced weaponry in the late 1940s and early '50s post-war era presented San Diego with new opportunities to leverage the civic culture, technological readiness and economic capabilities embedded in its long love affair with the military.

Once again, local boosters and entrepreneurial outsiders identified new opportunities to secure expanded forms of federal largesse; these efforts converged into a concerted strategy to aggressively grow and attract new federal R&D investments and defense contracting to the region. This resulted in a series of land use decisions and lobbying activity in Washington that enabled the Martial Metropolis to re-invent itself as a Cold War economy built on R&D and innovation in diverse technologies needed for national security purposes. There is much to suggest that San Diego's *invention* as a martial metropolis in the early twentieth century represents the base from which all its subsequent economic *re-inventions* have been possible.

By the 1950s a core civic culture and approach to problem solving emerged that characterized how economic challenges were subsequently met – and still are, even today. This civic culture included such things as (1) seeing the federal government as a primary customer/investor in the local economy (in 2010 still close to 50 per cent of GDP); (2) focusing on 'clean' technologies as growth enterprises in order to protect the pristine environment, thus attracting and keeping both the military and R&D; (3) leveraging land and real estate development schemes to attract and retain promising not-for-profit and for-profit enterprises; (4) social dynamics that welcome outsiders with connections or distinctive talents; and (5) a business culture that supports entrepreneurship, collaboration when needed, and shifting centers of leadership. In addition, the technologies that were developed in the region throughout the 1950s and '60s 'mapped' well with technological capabilities honed through the military focused 1930s and '40s.

Civic leaders, in the aftermath of World War II, capitalized immediately on the city's diverse wartime activities, transforming them into what soon became mainstays of the evolving economy: high-tech research and development, in combination with manufacturing geared toward the emerging peacetime/Cold War environment (Day and Zimmerman 1945: 28). In this regard, one of the most important wartime developments was the partnership between the Scripps Institution of Oceanography (SIO), then a part of the University of California's Division of War Research (UCDWR), and the National Defense Research Committee (NDRC) and its successor, the Office of Scientific Research and Development (OSRD). The OSRD came out of the 1938 establishment of UCDWR at Point Loma, which administered a new laboratory on the grounds of, and in coordination with the existing naval Radio and Sound Laboratory there. Much credit for this goes to Scripps scientist Roger Revelle, who, serving as 'principal liaison officer' between the Navy and certain divisions of NDRC, engineered trans-institutional collaborations that not only made huge contributions to the Allied victory, but firmly established the foundations for San Diego's high-tech future (Morgan and Morgan, 1996).

THE POST-WAR CONSOLIDATION OF RESEARCH ACTIVITIES

Naval Research

Within a few months of the end of the war, the Navy combined its two San Diego research labs into the single Navy Electronics Laboratory (NEL), a sure sign of the Navy's 'emphatic commitment for peacetime R&D, even as it demobilized its big wartime fleet' (NOSC 1990: 9). UC scientists continued their collaborations with naval research on Point Loma at the new Marine Physical Laboratory, commissioned in 1946 to continue the pure scientific research endeavors that had begun during the war. In fact, the research programs and the required infrastructure grew rapidly, with new labs, test beds, docks, and forests of experimental antennae taking over some of the Navy's earliest San Diego installations, including what had once been San Diego's first naval radio station. Among NEL's most important projects during the late 1940s were precision radar navigation systems and electronic recognition systems whose utility soon migrated from the military to the civilian sector, with important applications in commercial shipping and civil aviation (Walshok and Shragge, forthcoming 2013). By the early 1950s, with the endorsement of the Eisenhower administration's 'Second Hoover Commission,' this growing partnership between the university, military research institutions, defense contractors and civilian industry became the central feature of San Diego's post-war reinvention, a pattern that persisted until 1966, at which time the navy reorganized its entire research establishment. UC research programs at SIO throughout the 1950s included involvement in atomic and thermo-nuclear weapons as well as new initiatives in marine life research and, increasingly, climate research. By 1964 SIO had a budget of $12 million (Anderson 1993: 37). SIO's relationship with the Navy's research establishment grew in such a way as to give the Institution the scope and leverage to press for the creation of a new general campus of the University of California, an idea that San Diego boosters had advocated since the 1920s.

Atomic Energy

On the heels of the Navy's remobilization efforts, especially in R&D related to communications, came an expanded focus on nuclear energy. In 1955, John Jay Hopkins of General Dynamics activated the General Atomic Nuclear research division, choosing to locate it in San Diego rather than Monterey or Boston because of San Diego's salubrious environment and the promise of 300 acres of land on the Torrey Pines Mesa, a promise that 80 per cent of San Diego's voters approved in a public vote (Mitton 1987). He directed his senior vice president, Gordon Dean, the onetime head of the Atomic Energy Commission, to find a man to run it. Dean hired Vienna born, Harvard educated physicist Frederic de Hoffman. He was a charismatic, visionary philosopher-scientist. He attracted a dozen other prominent scientists, including Edward Teller to his board of advisors. He hired Ed Creutz as director of research. Creutz was a physicist turned metallurgist, with a brilliant professional track record extending back through the Atomic Energy Commission, Carnegie Tech, Los Alamos and Oak Ridge.

The atmosphere at General Atomics was particularly inviting. The firm encouraged its scientists to delve into uncharted fields of basic research in a stimulating environment, free of the pressure of producing immediate profits. It was a time, too, when all the other divisions of General Dynamics appeared to be doing very well, reporting substantial profits and growth. Thus, Hopkins was able to earmark $25 million for the San Diego laboratory, a very large sum of money for basic research in the 1950s. More would follow, as the other divisions' prosperity financed this newest developing division. The far-reaching impact of this division was anticipated in de Hoffman's remarks at the ground breaking ceremony at the Torrey Pines Mesa in 1956. Looking out over the Pacific, he predicted how their work would 'free hydrogen from the ocean water to provide energy at low cost, for even the most impoverished nations.' Their start was impressive. Dr de Hoffman grew a talented staff dominated by PhDs. He took pride in the fact that many of his researchers were comfortable in a number of scientific disciplines – philosophers as well as scientists (Mitton 1987: 3–4). During this time there was also a proliferation of small entrepreneurial defense-related technology supplier companies developing across the region.

By the 1980s, when wireless communications giant Qualcomm was founded and Hybritech, San Diego's first bio-tech company, was sold to Lilly, there were already more than 60 spin-off companies originating from General Atomic. Especially notable among these were SAIC (today a Fortune 500 company), founded by Robert J. Beyster, and Titan Industries, a major defense contracting company founded by Gene Ray.

The subsequent and dramatic growth of a diverse range of not-for-profit research institutions such as GA in San Diego throughout the 1960s and '70s parallels the history of the development of the military installations in the region earlier in the century. It includes the growth of Scripps Institution of Oceanography, the founding of General Atomic, the establishment, and subsequent rapid growth of the Scripps Metabolic Clinic in 1924, later The Scripps Research Institute, as well as the founding of the Salk Institute in 1960 by polio vaccine discoverer Jonas Salk. All of these institutions benefited from zoning decisions made by the city council throughout the 1950s, '60s and '70s, which fostered the creation of a collection of contiguous not-for-profit research institutions on the Torrey Pines Mesa.

The Consolidation of Life-Science R&D capabilities

Many of the biographies of San Diego's early leaders underscore the extent to which the health-giving features of its natural environment – its arid climate, the warm sunshine, the invigorating waters of the Pacific, as well as year round availability of fresh fruits and vegetables – attracted them to the region. The anti-modernism sweeping Europe and America at that time led many of the early settlers to have highly idealistic, almost utopian views of how to develop San Diego as a city. Thus, from the early days onward, there were individuals promoting and investing in initiatives tied to the natural environment and the health-giving qualities of the region. San Diego truly offered newcomers a chance to build a different kind of city and many early families figured prominently in the definition of what the character of that city should be. This was especially true of the Scripps family, who migrated to the region in the 1890s. Well into the 1930s, the family contributed to the establishment of many of San Diego's key institutions, which today drive its outstanding achievements in the medical, biological and environmental sciences.

In 1907, E.W. Scripps, for example, donated his yacht to the newly formed Marine Biological Institute in La Jolla for ocean research at sea. The institute, which eventually grew into the formidable Scripps Institution of Oceanography, today is globally respected for its research. In the 1920s Ellen Browning Scripps, E.W.'s half-sister, made a sizeable contribution to establish a 44 bed hospital in La Jolla. And, she contributed an additional $50,000 to create a specialized research facility, the Scripps Metabolic Clinic, as part of the hospital. Its purpose was to diagnose, treat and investigate diabetes and other metabolic disorders. Insulin had just been discovered and she became excited about the promise of metabolic research. The clinic conducted modest research from the 1930s onward and benefited from gifts from Miss Scripps. By the 1950s the then-named Scripps Clinic and Research Foundation began a major expansion effort that ultimately, in 1959, resulted in a seven-year grant from NIH to support basic science. On the heels of this achievement, thanks to a biochemist recently hired from Harvard University, Scripps added substantially to its talent pool, recruiting major scientists from around the country, each, in turn, attracting major grants to the region. Today, The Scripps Research Institute (TSRI), as it is known, conducts more than $300,000,000 annually in basic research.

At the same time that TSRI was expanding its activities in the late 1950s and early '60s, Jonas Salk, the developer of the polio vaccine, was looking for a location for his new interdisciplinary Institute for Biological Studies. The University of Pittsburgh did not wish to be home to the Institute and, after a national search, Salk settled on La Jolla, in large part because of the availability of spectacular ocean-front land at no cost. The mayor of San Diego had been a polio victim and worked with Salk to achieve his vision, which included an iconic design for a new research facility developed by the architect Louis Kahn. In June of 1960, in a special referendum, the citizens of San Diego overwhelmingly voted to give land on the Torrey Pines Mesa to the Salk Institute. Salk, like his peers at TSRI and in the new medical school being formed at UC San Diego, began an aggressive campaign to attract world-class scientists to the region. He was able to attract Nobel laureates and other internationally respected scientists in areas such as genetics, molecular biology, neurosciences and plant biology. Today, the Salk Institute employs 60 scientific investigators, plus a staff of 850, including visiting scientists, post-docs and graduate students from around the world.

The Rapid Rise of UC San Diego

In 1955, thanks to a civic initiative led by local citizens Jeffrey Archer, Pat Hyndman and Phil Anewalt, and backed by the power and influence of both General Atomic and the Scripps Institution of Oceanography, San Diegans, in yet another referendum, approved approximately 1,000 acres of its pueblo lands, plus 545 acres from the former Camp Mathews, for a new campus of the University of California established in La Jolla (Anderson 1993: 21) and called the University of California San Diego (UCSD). UCSD formally opened its doors in 1960.

The champion of the UCSD project, SIO director Roger Revelle, framed his vision for UCSD, from the start, in grand terms. The new university should be 'like a cathedral, the center to which all men turn to find the meaning of their lives and from which emanates a wondrous light, the light of understanding' (Anderson 1993: 22). Moreover, any delay in its establishment 'would be tragic, and might affect to a significant degree the very survival of the United States.' Revelle harbored no thought whatsoever of creating a conventional university campus (Anderson 1993: 23). The city's business leaders pressed for a university that would turn out physicists and engineers to man nuclear-oriented defense industries; Revelle accepted this view, at the same time seeking to cool the political heat and anger emanating from San Diego State College by leaving undergraduate instruction to that venerable institution. Thus the vision that coalesced between Revelle/ SIO, John Jay Hopkins/GA and the Chamber of Commerce became the first full iteration of the plan for UCSD: a graduate school composed of an 'Institute of Pure and Applied Physics' and an 'Institute of Mechanics.'

Once the Regents gave their go-ahead for the new campus, Revelle began his faculty recruitment program 'from the top down,' beginning with Nobel laureate chemist Harold Urey, whose august presence provided the new school with 'instant legitimacy' and 'a guarantee of seriousness' that soon attracted other leading academicians – a 'dream campus,' as Revelle's biographers put it (Anderson 1993; Morgan and Morgan 1996). Early recruits comprised a prestigious roster of highly qualified, restless, ambitious leaders in their fields who collectively aspired to be the 'best research faculty in the world,' even before the bulldozers broke ground to build the new campus. As early as 1961, UCSD's graduate program in physics 'was second to none in the country'; biology, chemistry and experimental psychology were not far behind. As of 1963, the faculty numbered 80, mostly scientists, including two Nobel laureates and thirteen National Academy of Sciences members.

By the late 1960s, UCSD had become a renowned center for classified research, 'founded on the fortunes [provided by] outside funding and already . . . one of the principal recipients of federal research grants in the nation' (Anderson 1993: 48). Quite a bit of the 40 million dollars' worth of outside funding (spread across 135 contracts) was indeed classified as 'mission-oriented' work and was thus a subject of concern to university administrators, students, and the general public during the politically turbulent period precipitated by the Vietnam War. In January 1971 the Academic Senate expressed strong opposition to research related to defense – a far cry from the institution's critically important research and development activities that were conducted by SIO during and after World War II. It was clear, as Nancy Anderson (1993) has pointed out, that UCSD had, after just over a decade, 'outgrown its beginnings as a creature of the national and local military industrial complex. It would continue to progress as a stellar scientific research institution supported by vast sums of outside funding, but UCSD had become independent' (Anderson 1993: 37).

All these science and technology research institutions grew rapidly throughout the 1960s and '70s thanks to the increasing research budgets in federal agencies, which were in large part fueled by the Cold War. Talent was drawn by the promise of environments in which new, interdisciplinary and game-changing science was carried out. This unparalleled and unrelenting effort to bring the best and brightest, at whatever cost, to the region worked. By the 1980s the world was taking notice of the scientific arsenal on the Torrey Pines Mesa. However, at this same moment in time, global events precipitated San Diego's next reinvention.

CONNECTING SCIENCE AND BUSINESS: 1985–2010

Throughout the 1960s and '70s, the not-for-profit research enterprises on the Torrey Pines Mesa grew at phenomenal rates. This was aided by the expansion of federal research funding in the health and life sciences, as well as through the National Science Foundation (NSF) and the Department of Defense. President Richard Nixon's declaration of a War on Cancer in 1971 fueled much of the life sciences growth in the already strong cluster consisting of the Salk Institute, The Scripps Research Institution and UCSD School of Medicine. The expansion of California's higher education system enabled similar rapid growth on the relatively young UCSD campus. In 1984, Richard C. Atkinson became the fourth Chancellor of the UCSD campus, coming to La Jolla after six years as director of the NSF.

While at the NSF he had been instrumental in passing the 1980 Bayh–Dole Act, which freed research institutions to actively commercialize federally funded research outcomes with commercial potential. He also set up NSF's university/industry research partnership program, SBIR, the Small Business Innovation Research program. When approached by civic leaders to find a way to 'grow more San Diego Companies' from the wealth of research on the Torrey Pines Mesa, he dispatched his new Extension Dean, a sociologist well connected to local industry, to interview the community in order to identify what approaches would be best to help increase the number of locally based high growth science and technology companies. Out of this process came the founding of the UCSD CONNECT in the fall of 1985. Bill Otterson was hired as its CEO in the spring of 1986. This

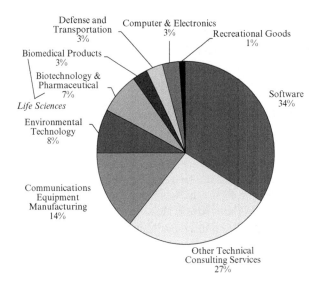

Source: National University System Institute for Policy Research; California Employment Development Department (EDD) Q1 2011 data; commissioned by CONNECT.

Figure 10.1 *San Diego innovation economy companies, by sector*
(n = 5,978)

ushered in the next reinvention of San Diego's economy, moving it from a primarily defense related R&D company town to a community of diverse science based clusters of companies succeeding in the global market for IT and wireless, software, medical devices and pharmaceuticals.

Once again, the community leveraged critical regional resources – technological readiness, land use and superb federal relations. It also re-engaged the embedded social dynamics that included a willingness to embrace outsiders and new leaders, both necessitated in part by an absence of old companies or families. A business culture of 'we can do' and 'we'll show you' had developed in the region. Throughout the 1980s and '90s, CONNECT was able to catalyze tremendous growth, building on the successes and relationships established by early science and technology enterprises such as GA, Linkabit, Hybritech, SAIC, SpinPhysics and Mycogen.

And the rest is history, as they say. Over the last 25 years, the San Diego region has supported the emergence of six distinctive, robust, high-tech clusters, while continuing to incubate new clusters. Where few or no high-tech companies existed in the 1980s, by 2010 thousands of companies, representing tens of thousands of jobs, now flourish, most on or near the Torrey Pines Mesa. The data speak for themselves (Figures 10.1–10.4).

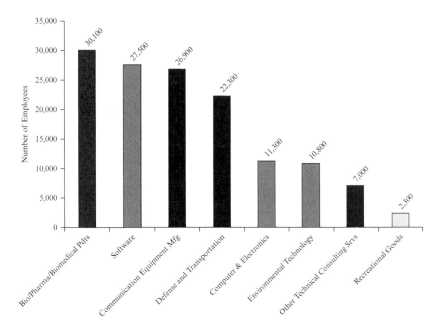

Source: National University System Institute for Policy Research; California Employment Development Department (EDD); commissioned by CONNECT.

Figure 10.2   San Diego county: estimated innovation economy employment by industry cluster (Q4, 2011)

The importance of the civic initiative UCSD CONNECT, launched in 1985, to the success cannot be overstated.

THE ROLE OF UCSD CONNECT

Even before the reduction in defense spending in the 1990s, San Diego faced a series of serious economic disruptions, culminating in the US Savings and Loan crisis of the late 1980s. These crises led to a rethinking of economic development strategies in the region. It had become clear that traditional business development strategies were not working and regional leaders realized that they needed to re-imagine San Diego's future. San Diego then attempted to attract two major national corporate research consortia, the Microelectronics and Computer Technology Corporation (MCC) and SEMATECH, losing both in the final rounds. It was in

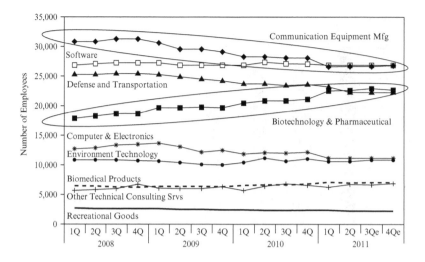

Source: National University System Institute for Policy Research; California Employment Development Department (EDD); commissioned by CONNECT.

Figure 10.3   San Diego tech sector employment trends, 2008–11

reaction to this time of turmoil that the San Diego community began looking for new ways to 'grow' the regional economy.

Starting in 1985, civic leaders increasingly focused on extracting economic value from the consolidation of the not-for-profit enterprises on the Torrey Pines Mesa, looking to the maturing UC San Diego campus for help in doing this. In the early 1980s the city began incentivizing private developers to build industrial parks and lab space to accommodate hoped for science and technology enterprises on the Torrey Pines Mesa. The Economic Development Corporation also began shifting its recruitment strategies to industries that were aligned with the types of R&D going on in the region. The private research institutions like Salk and TSRI had firmly established research partnerships with global pharma companies such as Lilly, Novartis and Johnson & Johnson. Additionally, the Scripps Institution of Oceanography had added to its tight linkages with federal agencies such as ONR and DARPA, as well as its close ties to global petroleum companies such as Shell. In 1983 UCSD created the first of many industry/university collaborative initiatives, the Center for Magnetic Recording, in order to advance the state-of-the-art in information storage technology and to develop professionals for the data storage community. Companies such as 3M and Spin-Physics were founding partners of the center, which included a research library of timely books and

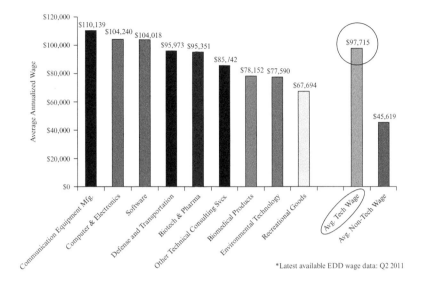

Note: Latest available EDD wage date: Q2 2011.

Source: National University System Institute for Policy Research; California Employment Development Department (EDD); commissioned by CONNECT.

Figure 10.4 San Diego average tech sector wages, by industry

relevant journals as well as an ongoing program of translating research reported in Japanese journals and trade publications relevant to the data storage industry.

Nonetheless, links to industry across the Mesa were still weak, in part due to the basic science focus of not just the institutes, but also UCSD departments. At UC San Diego, for example, the computer science and engineering departments focused primarily on PhD students, with few awarding Master's degrees, which is what industry valued. Similarly, most medical school graduates at this time gravitated in large numbers to research careers and not to clinical medicine. Other than medicine, UCSD had no professional schools such as Business or Management, Public Policy or Education. And, at that time the campus had no technology transfer office, relying on the Office of the President for the entire University of California system, to assist with technology transfer in the pre-Bayh–Dole era. In other words, in the early 1980s it was unclear to the new Chancellor, Richard C. Atkinson, how to actively help grow local science and technology based start-ups in the short term.

In response to overtures from the director of the San Diego Economic Development Corporation, UCSD leaders worked with a small group of entrepreneurial community leaders to create a program that would accelerate innovation and entrepreneurship in the region. What they quickly learned was that San Diego faced two major challenges. The first (just described) was a research culture on the Mesa that was rich in both its quantity and quality of basic research but with few pockets of interest in applied problems or technology transfer and commercialization. The second was a business culture and capabilities tied primarily to defense contracting, real estate development, tourism and the hospitality industry. And, San Diego had no venture capital funds, equity bankers or major financial institutions given its long history of government contracting and an economy dominated by the defense industry. San Diego's local networks were less focused on for-profit business development than they were on government relations and procurement well into the 1980s.

Private capital had not fueled General Dynamics, General Atomics, Rohr or National Steel and Shipbuilding – these enterprises were based on federal government contracts. Consequently, for early non-defense high-tech entrepreneurs in San Diego, accessing capital and other resources was a problem. In the 1970s, San Diego had no major banks or local venture capital firms. Nor did it have many professional and business services that supported science-based, commercially focused innovation. Early technology entrepreneurs had to rely on personal contacts to obtain introductions to the resources they needed. Often this required going outside the region for help. At the same time, local business service providers had few contacts in the wider venture capital and management consulting community and they knew little about high-tech start-ups and how to service the needs of these clients.

Starting a company in the 1970s and early '80s was a hit-or-miss process. For example, Hybritech's founders, Ivor Royston and Howard Birndorf, received venture funding from Kleiner, Perkins, Caufield & Byers, one of Silicon Valley's top venture firms, through personal contacts. Kleiner Perkins approved the proposal that the company stay in San Diego, because Royston's research at UCSD provided the underlying technology and because of a very favorable arrangement for facilities offered by an entrepreneurial local developer. The venture firm not only provided financing; it also helped Hybritech to hire the experienced technical managers that it needed from large pharmaceutical firms outside San Diego. Had Royston not had these personal contacts in Silicon Valley, it is unclear whether his new firm would have ever received the funding and other help that it needed.

Local service providers in San Diego were not aware of Hybritech or its needs. One leading service provider in San Diego said in an interview

(Porter 2001) that he first learned about Hybritech while he was working for his firm on assignment in Brussels. On returning to San Diego, this individual realized that young entrepreneurial companies needed assistance to break into European markets and that servicing the San Diego start-ups might become a major growth area for his firm. He then devoted time and energy to learning more about these new companies, as did a few other pioneering business service providers in San Diego. However, there was no formal mechanism for facilitating this process in a deliberate and high-impact way across the entire region.

With the focus on global competitiveness that emerged in the mid-1980s, San Diegans understood the need to leverage the R&D assets that had been unwittingly incubating in isolation from the rest of the local economy since the mid-1960s. San Diego business and education leaders founded CONNECT in 1985 in a deliberate attempt to jump-start the process for developing contacts, social networks, and business services of the type that had not been readily available to early entrepreneurs. Its origins – and the strong commitment people made to it – derived from the economic turmoil San Diego experienced in the early and mid-1980s.

The key purpose of UCSD CONNECT was to link academic researchers with entrepreneurs, and then to link both of these parties to venture capitalists and business service providers who could help grow new companies that would create high-wage jobs and regional prosperity at a time when a number of regional economic 'drivers,' such as real estate, banking and defense contracting, were in disarray. CONNECT was truly a bottom-up collaborative which developed after extensive consultation with university researchers, private-sector executives and professional business service providers (Walshok et al. 2002).

The transition to a more entrepreneurial culture and social dynamics enabling of innovation capitalized by CONNECT resulted in new regional capabilities. The journey from a promising idea or finding into a useful technology that solves a real problem in a manner that is scalable, affordable, and marketable is what technology commercialization is about. It goes beyond issues of patenting and knowledge transfer and focuses squarely on testing, demonstrating, validating, and ultimately translating a promising idea into a useful and marketable product. It is a journey that Duane Roth, the current CEO of CONNECT, describes as involving 'four D's': *discovery* research; *defining* a potential application; *developing* and validating the application; and, finally, *delivering* the solution to a market (Roth and Cuatrecasas 2010). For this to occur, a number of conditions are necessary and a variety of competencies are essential, all of which were captured by the CONNECT model developed through trial and error at UCSD in the 1980s. This pro-active focus on technology commercialization is widely acknowledged as having enabled the rapid growth of robust science-based company clusters, such as those established in IT, life science, and software, in San Diego between 1985 and 2000 (Porter 2001: 62–4). In fact, in 2010 *Time Magazine* described CONNECT's role in the region as follows:

> In 1985 CONNECT sprang up to link the scientists and inventors at top research institutions . . . with investors, advisors and support services so their new ideas could become new products and companies . . . . The inventive brew that CONNECT fermented has made San Diego home to a cluster of life sciences and technology companies such as Qualcomm, Biogen Idec, Life Technologies and Gen-Probe.

CONNECT, from day one, drew on knowledge of the social dynamics in Silicon Valley and interviews with key potential supporters in San Diego. A brief report for the chancellor and early stakeholders was prepared describing what the community needed to build on the successes of early start-up companies such as Linkabit and Hybritech, in order to grow robust clusters of science and technology companies similar to those in Silicon Valley. It was at this time that a core and distinctive approach to building an ecosystem emerged. When the scientists and engineers that started successful companies were interviewed, their primary emphasis was on the need for a more responsive, nimble, and technology-savvy business community. Of particular note was the need for service providers with some understanding of technology, intellectual property, and the risk cycles involved with start-ups, as well as a knowledge of global regulatory and marketing challenges – competencies not resident in a community whose economy heretofore had been characterized by tourism, agriculture, and defense contracting.

In contrast, when local business leaders were asked about what they felt would be needed to grow robust science-based clusters, predictably they emphasized the need for scientists and engineers to become more sophisticated about the real costs of producing particular technology solutions, the importance of developing a clearer sense of the market for their technologies, and the need for increased willingness to work with more professional managers in realizing the potential of their technology, particularly through a profitable business. In other words, they needed business skills. These two contrasting views of pressing needs actually became two interlocking themes in all of the developments within UCSD CONNECT over the next 20 years.

Today, 25 years later, everybody recognizes that innovations in science and technology are supported by an 'ecosystem' of complementary competencies and resources. What was distinctive about the CONNECT program in the 1980s was that, in mirroring the success of Silicon Valley, it set out to become the hub or connective link within that ecosystem of innovation for the San Diego region: an ecosystem that was about a wide range of business competencies as well as diverse technologies. In its mission and goals, represented in a one-page statement, its early programs reflected these two themes: the need to develop more science and technology product development sophistication among the business community in combination with increased financial, marketing and management intelligence among the scientific community. Throughout its early years programs focused on themes such as 'Meet the Researcher' for businesspeople and 'Global Strategies for Financing High-Tech Companies' for scientists and engineers. In this manner the CONNECT program was able to build the cross-professional knowledge networks so essential to innovation.

The evolution of CONNECT from 1985 through 2010, vis-à-vis its expansion of programs and seeding of related regional initiatives to further support the growth of globally competitive, high-tech clusters was presented in a chart created by the CONNECT organization on the occasion of its 25th anniversary. Highlights from that chart are presented in Figure 10.5.

CONCLUSION

San Diego's technological evolution is chock full of stories about the links between the pre-war capabilities of the region, the Cold War R&D expansion of the region and the commercial cluster growth that occurred in the late 1980s and continues today. The largest radio tower in America, built by the Navy in 1920, links to the war era research in remote signal processing, which in turn connects to the many Navy contracts that Linkabit won, which enabled further development of the CDMA platform, which is the foundation of a San Diego Fortune 500 company, Qualcomm. The founding of the Marine Biological Station in 1906 and its subsequent evolution into SIO, a university anchored center of Naval research, produced a critical partner in both WWII and the Cold War technology developments. SIO gave rise to IMED and IVAC – two medical device companies that brought Lilly to San Diego. Since the 1980s, scores of energy related companies have been started and now are the center of San Diego's renewable energy cluster, all of them rooted in the Marine Biological Station. The decision in 1924 by La Jolla based Scripps Hospital to create a clinical research unit, the Metabolic Research Institute, which morphed in the post-war era into a major clinical research institute led by Edward Keeney, resulted in today's TSRI, with an annual research budget approaching

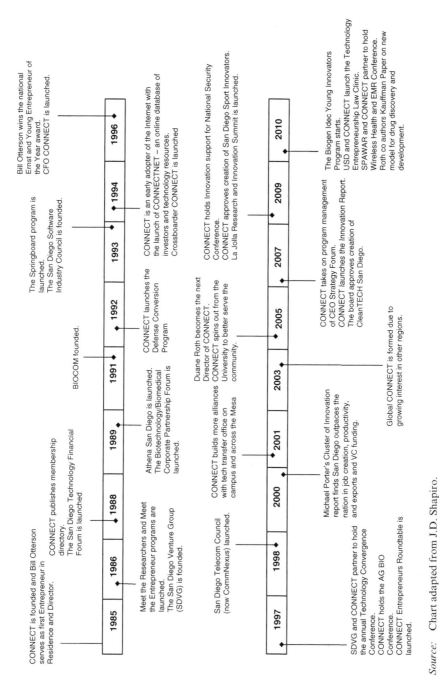

Source: Chart adapted from J.D. Shapiro.

Figure 10.5 CONNECT: 25 years of innovation highlights

$400 million and a multitude of spin-off pharmaceutical companies in the region. Consolidated Aircraft moved to San Diego in 1935, in order to serve the aviation needs of the military, evolved into the General Dynamics Company, and in the post-war era founded GA (1955), which subsequently spawned more than 60 spin-offs, notably SAIC and Titan. General Dynamics remains a major defense contractor responsible for the design and manufacture of unmanned aerial vehicles such as the Predator. Even the burgeoning sports innovation cluster of golf clubs, surfboards, skate boards, clothing, helmets and cycling equipment is integrally connected to the developments in the composite materials R&D community, which, in turn, has its roots in developments by the aerospace industry (Stealth Bomber) and the Navy (rust resistant ships) and more recently investments in earthquake resistant materials for bridges and roads.

San Diego, at the end of 100 years of invention and reinvention, finds itself at another crossroads as a regional economy. The question is will San Diego sustain its hard earned innovation economy going into its next 50 years? Civic leaders, thanks to a collaborative, opportunistic culture, are determined that it continues to innovate and leverage its technological assets in new and converging ways. Promising new developments in the region abound. Many reflect the accumulated assets and civic capabilities of the previous one hundred years, such as:

1. Early experiences with telecommunications, electronics, and materials science as well as a long history of developing new solutions in the health and life sciences, the technology relatedness analyzed by Neffke (Neffke et al. 2011).
2. Linking basic and applied research early and in an iterative manner thanks to intermediary institutions.
3. An understanding that addressing big 'hairy' questions, such as how the brain processes information, renewable energy, regenerative medicine or Alzheimer's, requires multi-disciplinary concepts and research tools that can eventually lead to economic returns thanks to a more than 50-year history of interdisciplinary work.
4. A history of linking invention, innovation and production, building on its military roots.
5. An ability to move from vertically integrated organizations to networked organizations, operating wirelessly and using cloud computing to create things and deliver value thanks to a long romance with advanced technology.
6. A civic culture focused on the ever shifting technology needs of the American economy and of San Diego's most important customer today, as it was in 1915: the federal government.

The next 50 years of San Diego's economic evolution will likely be an era of convergence: converging disciplines and technologies, converging invention and production assets. New institutions, which are enabling the region to continue to innovate and be competitive, are continuing to be created and championed by an opportunistic civic culture, and shifting centers of leadership. The multiple applications on our wireless phones, the medical monitoring devices we will carry with us, the diversifying waste management and recycling tools at our disposal, the commitment to rebuilding our manufacturing and supplier resources to support emerging technology companies, the renewed interest among charter schools and community colleges in technical and skilled trades training all represent examples of how these convergences are being engaged by the region. All are possible in the region's future because of firmly established technology platforms and opportunistic civic culture.

NOTE

*   The historical citations, contemporary data and interpretations provided in this chapter are drawn from a forthcoming Stanford University Press book, *Invention and Reinvention: The Evolution of San Diego's Innovation Economy*, 2013, by Mary L. Walshok and Abraham J. Shragge.

REFERENCES

Anderson, Nancy Scott (1993), *An Improbable Venture: A History of the University of California, San Diego*, 1st edn, San Diego: UCSD Press.

Day and Zimmerman Incorporated (1945), *Report No. 4072: Industrial and Commercial Survey*, City of San Diego County.

Lears, T.J. (1994), *No Place of Grace: Anti-modernism and the Transformation of American Culture, 1880–1920*, Chicago: University of Chicago Press.

Lindbergh Field, San Diego (1935), Pamphlet published by Harbor Department, City of San Diego.

Lotchin, R. (1992), *Fortress California, 1910–1961: From Warfare to Welfare*, New York: Oxford University Press.

McClain, M. (2010), 'The Scripps family's San Diego experiment', *The Journal of San Diego History*, **56** (1–2).

Mitton, D. (1987), 'The Blue Brothers – an act to watch: the magic of transforming a pattern of venturing by defecting scientists into fruitful corporate sponsored ventures', presented at the Babson College Entrepreneurship Research Conference, Pepperdine University, 1 May.

Morgan, N. and J. Morgan (1996), *Roger: A Biography of Roger Revelle*, Scripps Institution of Oceanography, University of California, San Diego.

Naval Ocean Systems Center (NOSC) (1990), 'Fifty years of research and development on Point Loma: 1940–1990', available at: http://www.spawar.navy.mil/sti/publications/pubs/td/1940/index.html.

Neffke F., M. Henning and R. Boschma (2011), 'How do regions diversify over time? Industry relatedness and the development of new growth paths in regions', *Economic Geography*, **87** (3), 237–65.

Porter, M. (2001), 'Clusters of innovation initiative: San Diego', Washington, DC: Council on Competitiveness.

Roth, D. and P. Cuatrecasas (2010), *The Distributed Partnering Model for Drug Discovery and Development*, San Diego, CA: Ewing Marion Kauffman Foundation.

Shragge, A. (1998), 'Boosters and bluejackets: the civic culture of militarism in San Diego, California 1900–1945', unpublished dissertation, UC San Diego.

Walshok, M. and A. Shragge (forthcoming 2013), *Invention and Reinvention: The Evolution of San Diego's Innovation Economy*, Stanford, CA: Stanford University Press.

Walshok, M., E. Furtek, C.W.B. Lee and P.H. Windham (2002), 'Building regional innovation capacity: the San Diego experience', *Industry and Higher Education*, **16** (1), 27–42.

Index

Index